Net Ready

*Strategies for Success
in the E-conomy*

Net Ready

*Strategies for Success
in the E-conomy*

Amir Hartman
and
John Sifonis
with
John Kador

McGraw-Hill

New York   San Francisco   Washington, D.C.   Auckland   Bogotá
Caracas   Lisbon   London   Madrid   Mexico City   Milan
Montreal   New Delhi   San Juan   Singapore
Sydney   Tokyo   Toronto

McGraw-Hill

*A Division of The **McGraw·Hill** Companies*

0 DOC/DOC 0 9 8 7 6 5 4 3 2 1 0

ISBN 0-07-135242-2

It was set in ITC Garamond and Poppl-Laudatio Bold Condensed by Impressions Book and
Journal Services, Inc.

Printed and bound by R.R. Donnelley & Sons Company.

McGraw-Hill books are available at special quantity discounts to use as premiums and sales
promotions, or for use in corporate training programs. For more information, please write to
the Director of Special Sales, McGraw-Hill, Professional Publishing, Two Penn Plaza,
New York, NY 10121-2298. Or contact your local bookstore.

 This book is printed on recycled, acid-free paper containing a minimum of 50%
recycled de-inked fiber.

To Jennifer and our wonderful new journey. A.H.

To Diana for her patience, encouragement, and insights. J.S.

For Daniel and Rachel, who are Net Ready in a way
their father can never hope to be. J.K.

Of all things in the world, ask not that events should happen as you will, but let your will be that events should happen as they do, and you shall have peace.

—Epictetus, Roman Stoic philosopher

Contents

Part I Strategies for Success in the E-conomy

1. The Four Pillars of Net Readiness

Net Readiness is a combination—unique to each organization—of four drivers that enables enterprises to deploy high-impact Web-enabled business processes that are focused, accountable, and measurable.

2. Net Readiness Trends Enabled by the E-conomy

This chapter explores eleven trends of Net Readiness. As these eleven drivers of the new economy converge, they redefine the very foundations of business behavior. The E-conomy makes the old rules of orderly processes, static measures of supply and demand, segmented pricing, and mass production null and void.

3. Identifying Strategic Options   75

The E-Business Value Matrix is an assessment tool useful for evaluating E-business initiatives. This chapter describes how organizations can map themselves against the background of Internet initiatives from a cross section of industries and how the assessment can suggest subsequent strategies.

4. Extended E-conomy Business Models   101

Opportunities abound for Net Ready organizations willing to focus on one or more of the five business models the E-conomy offers.

Part II Techniques for Creating Sustainable E-conomy Value

5. Product and Market Transformation   149

If you don't like the constraints of the business environment in which you operate, create new constraints and make your competitors abide by them. There is nothing sacred about the constraints you inherit. Transform them and you may reveal an opportunity. Product and market transformation is the first critical dimension of creating E-conomy value.

6. Business Process Transformation   181

Enterprise focus is the second critical dimension of creating E-conomy value. Deconstructing the infrastructure enabling the business reveals new opportunities for business process transformation.

7. Industry Transformation   207

Industry focus is the third critical dimension of creating E-conomy value. Sometimes the best strategy is to redefine the industry in which you operate or, better yet, start a new industry.

Part III Net Readiness Realities

8. Net Readiness at Cisco Systems   237

Cisco's success in the E-conomy derives from its Net Readiness, exhibited by seizing control of the Net's infrastructure, setting the rules, and then executing ruthlessly.

9. Finding Order in Chaos   271

The Net may well become the primary space in which we all do business, but it is still a hostile environment for organizations unprepared for the uncertainties and risks. Luckily, Net success has been shown to be a function of Net Readiness. Is your organization prepared?

Foreword

The Internet is driving an Internet economy that is creating unprecedented opportunities for countries, companies, and individuals around the world. In just five years, since the introduction of the World Wide Web, the Internet economy—what the authors of *Net Ready* term the *E-conomy*—already rivals the size of century-old sectors such as energy, transportation, and telecommunications.

The impact of the Internet economy is global, reaching both business and government. Business leaders worldwide recognize the strategic role that the Internet plays in their company's ability to survive and compete in the future. To be competitive in this new economy, companies need to harness the power of the Internet.

Through Internet solutions, Cisco has maintained its agility and competitive advantage. All our business operations—from supply chain management to employee communications—are Internet-based. Today, 80 percent of our orders and more than 80 percent of our customer inquiries are transacted over the Web.

As a result, we are growing faster than all our key competitors, have been rewarded with one of the top ten market capitalizations in the world, and are recognized as the fastest growing, most profitable company in the history of the computer industry.

Many of the business practices we have employed to become the leading example of an Internet economy company are readily identified in *Net Ready,* an important book that analyzes the practices that will move businesses along the road to success in the Internet Economy. *Net Ready* helps build a road map that can guide companies to take advantage of six key areas that I believe are fundamental in building an Internet-based business:

Customers. Customers in the Internet economy are well informed, and their expectations continue to increase. Therefore, the ability to respond rapidly to customer demands and deliver value is imperative.

Globalization. The Internet economy is leveling the playing field for big and small companies. This leveling goes hand in hand with globalization.

Being able to deliver consistent value irrespective of geographic proximity is necessary to be successful in today's constantly changing competitive landscape.

Partnerships. The rise of the Internet economy can be tied to an emerging "Internet E-cosystem," a new business model for Internet-connected businesses to serve Internet-connected customers. The open nature of the Internet encourages complementary business alliances that create a unique set of interwoven dependencies and relationships.

Employees. A key change being driven by the Internet is how companies share information with their employees. In an Internet economy company, employees are empowered to make the decisions that are in the best interest of the customers. Only when employees have access to information are they truly empowered.

Culture. The ability to turn change into competitive advantage for your company and for your customers is critical for success in the Internet economy. Of course, at the center of any successful company's culture is also dedication to customer satisfaction.

Access. In the past, information and internal systems have been viewed as strategic assets to be selectively shared. Today, companies must balance the need for both security and open access to information.

The Internet economy is creating tremendous opportunities, and we are seeing individuals, businesses, and countries use Internet technology to reeducate and reinvent themselves. The overwhelming acceptance of the Internet is one of the biggest stories of the 1990s, as this book so compellingly documents. *Net Ready* outlines the lessons and the steps that many companies have experienced in their quest to attain the elusive quality of Net Readiness.

My challenge to you is, "Are you ready?"

John Chambers
President and Chief Executive Officer
Cisco Systems

Introduction: Net Readiness and How This Book Will Help You Be More Net Ready

Look carefully, as we did, and you can see the E-conomy enterprise taking shape. The components that make up Net Readiness are well developed at a handful of companies, in their infancy at a few more, practically nonexistent in most. Net Readiness® never comes easy or without a cost. To be sure, it comes easier to some organizations than to others. Born-on-the-Web companies such as eBay or Yahoo! more easily achieve Net Readiness. By virtue of being created in the image of the Net, these companies avoid much of the industrial-age baggage with which their more-established counterparts must contend. Born-on-the-Web companies don't have to worry about existing channels, sales staffs, and brick and mortar facilities. Even so, the demands of the E-conomy are such that most born-on-the-Web companies fail.

Many of the executives we have worked with over the last five years have struggled with how to compete and win in this new economy. Everyone is looking to score in E-business. We have encountered countless managers who want to make their fortunes doing E-business. They want to pursue the newest chapter in the American dream: find a niche, launch an E-business start-up, file for an initial placement offering (IPO), lose money for a couple of years, and build a large market capitalization. We characterize most of these people, including ourselves, as "Web wannabees" because they have their eyes on the prize of making it on the Net. Unfortunately, E-business is not that simple. Most managers lack an understanding of the hard work and discipline that is required for success in E-business. That hard work and preparation is the stuff of Net Readiness.

The realities of success in the E-conomy are very different from the assumptions that have guided companies to date. Despite appearances, Net

Readiness is not easy. It recognizes that the very basis of doing business has shifted (see table 1). The drivers of success are elusive, while the drivers of failure are as familiar as existing management practices. Companies with roots in the traditional economy have a much more difficult experience making the transition to the E-conomy. The promise of the E-conomy frequently eludes these companies because they have trouble articulating a clear value proposition, mostly because such propositions are difficult to translate in this new space. These companies' economies of scale tend to focus on mass markets instead of the one-to-one relationships that the E-conomy favors. Hierarchies in organization and compensation within these companies tend to limit their ability to motivate people in new and creative ways.

Companies must fundamentally change the way they approach planning and executing. Conventional thinking has these companies assuming that variables are stable in their marketplace, that boundaries (industry, geographical, etc.) are clearly articulated, that the endgame is known or predictable. Moreover, the inertia in these companies makes it difficult for them to execute ruthlessly.

By *ruthless execution,* we mean the ability to define a course of action swiftly and to implement it competently. Based on our analyses of what sets successful companies apart in the E-conomy, ruthless execution is definitely one of the key drivers. But as just a phrase, *ruthless execution* doesn't drive anything except lip service. *Ruthless execution* and other pieces of jargon such as *learning organization* don't mean anything if they are not attached to meaningful, measurable activities. In our examination of Net Ready organizations, we have identified common attributes that contribute to either success or failure. In addition, the realities of the E-conomy require the adjustment of long-held business values and assumptions.

What makes some E-business initiatives succeed while others become virtual toast? And what about the tens of thousands of existing organizations desperately trying to extend themselves into the new E-conomy? These organizations do not have the privilege of starting from scratch. Moreover, although most of the fuss about the E-conomy focuses on consumer activity such as Amazon.com, eBay, and E*Trade, the-less-sexy-but-nonetheless-high impact is and will continue to be in business-to-business interactions online by well-established organizations who have successfully made the transition to Net Readiness.

This book offers help to both camps: companies born-on-the-Web and companies moving to the Web. The goal of this book is to explain what

Table 1. Business Drivers in the Traditional and Net Economies

Net Ready enterprises must attend to the differences in the traditional and Net economies and respond with appropriate strategies.

Traditional Economy	E-conomy
Stable, predictable franchise	Free-for-all
Economies of scale	One-to-one relationships
Stasis; reliance on geography, capital	Movement
Positioning	Value migration
Long-range planning	Real-time execution (agility)
Protect products, markets, channels	Cannibalize products, markets, channels
Predict future	Shape or adapt to future
Encourage repetition	Encourage experimentation
Detailed action plans	Managing options
Structured formal alliances	Webs of informal alliances
Aversion to failure	Failure is expected
Weak links between reward and outcomes	Direct links between risk and reward

the Net Ready organization of the twenty-first century will look like, how it will operate, and how it will relate to other Net Ready organizations. The book will introduce the concept of Net Readiness and define its attributes. *Net Ready* will also identify some things you can do today to prepare for that new order. We also want to be clear about what *Net Ready* will not offer you. If you are looking for advice on the following subjects, please look elsewhere. This book will not help you with

- Cool Web site design
- Selling stuff on the Web
- Management by buzzword
- Quick fixes
- Cookbook processes
- "Me, too" solutions

Net Ready, however, can move your agenda forward if you are looking for deeper perspectives on the following strategies:

- Organizing your company for success in the E-conomy
- Planning for E-business initiatives
- Aligning governance models for optimum leverage of the Net
- Promoting E-business leadership
- Linking Net and business strategies
- Helping identify opportunities for competitive advantage
- Identifying best practices

How Net Ready is your organization? Are you asking the same questions that the companies we talk to regularly ask us? (See "The Most Common Questions Asked by Our Clients.")

The Most Common Questions Asked by Our Clients

- Which particular E-business opportunities should we pursue?
- What's the best way to integrate new E-business initiatives with existing processes?
- How do we measure Return on Investment?
- How do we define an E-business for our industry?
- How do we organize structurally to do E-business?
- What skills and capabilities do we need to develop? Do we grow what we need, or do we acquire or rent it?
- How will E-business impact our existing channels?
- How does our long-term vision of the evolution of the E-conomy impact our business strategy?
- How do we protect our value chain from competition?
- How do we react to the inevitable cannibalization of our core businesses?
- How can we avoid ceding essential parts of our value proposition to new entrants?

Success in E-business is possible. Popular hype about such success—think of the relentless press coverage of Amazon, America Online (AOL), Dell, or Cisco—makes it look easy. Nothing is further from the truth. Media coverage, which looks at the facts in hindsight, inevitably makes success look easy and orderly. The recipe is remarkably similar: Start with a visionary leader, preferably young and a college dropout; season with a brash idea; add a dash of venture capital; cook at high pressure for a couple of years; garnish with an IPO and serve.

What these entertaining stories ignore—and what this book is about—is the more difficult question of what really are the attributes of success in E-business. Put another way, what happens at the majority of Web-in-the-eyes organizations that seem to follow the recipe but nevertheless fail to meet any of their objectives? As we carefully studied the engagements that led to success, and those that failed, and all the rest that were in between, we started to see some commonalties. We began to compile our observations about the drivers that predicted success in the E-conomy, and we soon gathered these together into a list of indicators.

Let's Define Our E-Terms

Before we go any further, let's define our terms. Although we will describe them operationally in more detail, here are a few of the terms we use and how we distinguish them:

- *E-conomy:* the virtual arena in which business actually is conducted, value is created and exchanged, transactions occur, and one-to-one relationships mature. These processes may be related to, but are nevertheless independent of, similar activities occurring in the conventional marketplace; sometimes called the digital economy or the cyber economy.

- *E-commerce:* a particular type of E-business initiative that is focused around individual business transactions that use the Net as medium of exchange, including business-to-business as well as business-to-consumer.

- *E-business:* any Internet initiative—tactical or strategic—that transforms business relationships, whether those relationships be business-to-consumer, business-to-business, intra-business, or even consumer-to-consumer. Any executive who thinks E-business is merely about selling products on the Web is missing the big picture. E-business is really a new way to drive efficiencies, speed, innovation, and new value creation in an organization.

Understanding the terms we use is less important than is a visceral understanding that today's business world deals with a radically different set of processes. Whether we talk in terms of E-conomy, Internet commerce, the real-time economy, cyberspace value chains, or the digital economy, our central point is that you can't afford to avoid asking difficult questions about the impact of these processes on your business.

We'd like to offer more precise definitions, but the E-conomy resists being pinned down. That's the first lesson of the E-conomy: it features unprecedented thresholds of uncertainty and discontinuous change. By the time we agree on a definition, new developments will have rendered it obsolete.

With its relentlessly real-time attributes, the E-conomy demands a new lexicon to describe it as well as a new mind-set to embrace it. As the E-conomy imposes a new order to every economic and structural dimension, the terminology that informs the industrial view of the world is wholly inadequate to the task of understanding and anticipating the opportunities created by the E-conomy. Nor is your big struggle to master the new definitions. No, your most difficult struggle is to forget definitions and practices that you have already learned. The hardest thing in the world is to give up practices that have made you rich. Yet this is exactly what success in the E-conomy demands.

In our work, we have seen a natural evolution that companies follow in their E-business efforts. The majority of companies we have studied go through a series of predictable phases (see figure 1). Let's look at the phases.

- *Brochureware.* At the beginning of the Net Readiness era, organizations use the Internet as a bulletin board for brochures, employee telephone directories, and over time, for more critical documents such as catalogs and price lists. For these companies, the Net is a one-way publishing mechanism. Brochureware is certainly progress, but it does not begin to exploit the next phase: interactivity.

- *Customer interactivity.* In the next phase, companies create a dialog with customers (empowering the customer to come in, ask, demand, dictate the kind of value that needs to be delivered). The term *customer* here could be consumer, end-customer, employee, and so on.

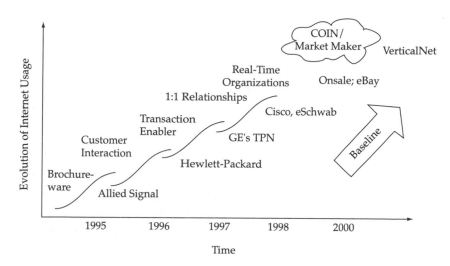

Figure 1. Evolution of E-business initiatives. Internet initiatives have gradually increased in levels of virtual interactivity and of support for one-to-one relationships. At the same time, the baseline that represents minimal competencies is gradually getting higher. Expectations are being set higher every day. The implication: continual innovation is critical.

- *Transaction enabler.* Companies begin using the Net to expand transaction-oriented processes (selling product, procuring supplies, enabling internal processes such as human resources activities, etc.).

- *One-to-one relationships.* The Internet is used to create customized silos of interactivity. Because Web technology allows companies to deal with customers on a one-to-one basis, product pricing becomes fluid, dictated by individual customers, often in an auction process.

- *Real-time organizations.* Zero latency organizations are able to plan, execute, and aggregate buyers and sellers in a virtual arena. These companies understand needs and deliver value in real time.

- *COINs (Communities of Interests).* The Internet helps companies create communities of interests (content, community, and commerce) that closely link various partners in a value chain.

Note in figure 1 that as the sophistication of E-business usage goes up, the baseline is continually rising. This trend should raise some red flags for executives because it means that the hurdles are getting steeper all the time. In other words, the minimum competencies required to simply enter a particular corner of the E-conomy are becoming more challenging every day. E-business is not like a light switch. You don't turn it on or off at will. Net Readiness needs to evolve over time. If you are not honing your Net Readiness, you will have a very difficult time migrating from one phase to the next.

Net Readiness is impossible without seamless interactivity informing every process in the organization. The most difficult leap for many companies is the change in leadership mind-set and organizational governance required to implement interactivity. As organizations came to see the Net as a robust, bisynchronous channel, offering real-time communications in both directions, from the company to the customers and the customers to the company, the most time-honored assumptions crumbled. Power shifted from companies to customers. Interactivity gave customers perfect information. Net Ready companies quickly learned that perfectly informed customers couldn't be trifled with.

Interactivity first created new communities, such as the Motley Fool investment community on AOL. By 1997, interactivity led inexorably to the use of the Net as a transaction enabler. The E-conomy was truly born when the average consumer could easily and securely conduct online transactions such as buying and selling stock, ordering books and CDs, and selecting and paying for airline tickets. These truly Net Ready companies had no analogue in the physical world.

Companies soon saw that the Net catalyzed a change from the one-to-many relationships that corporations knew to a new world of one-to-one customer management. It suddenly became possible for companies such as Cisco and Schwab to manage unique relationships with each of its customers. That possibility, in turn, changed many transactional relationships into transformational relationships, characterized by an aligning of interests that would have been thought impossible a few years earlier. Enterprises such as Onsale and eBay are representative of firms exploiting one-to-one transformative relationships.

The E-conomy redefines every assumption about dealing with customers. Consider the strategy of customer relationship management (CRM). The E-conomy throws this well-intentioned but unworkable management discipline on its ears. Because Net Ready customers have so many options to choose from in any product or service category, it is most certainly not the customer who's being managed. That system is way too passive. In the E-conomy, as this book shows you, the customer gets to manage the relationship. Net Readiness requires organizations to let go of the arrogance that customers and clients can be manipulated. In the E-conomy, customers can only be served, listened to, and valued. Then, if the company does everything right, the customer may agree to be served.

In the last year or so, the intensity of Net usage has led to a new class of enterprises that use the Net as a collaborative platform in exciting new ways to create value. COINs such as VerticalNet and market makers such as Buy.com (see "Explode Price/Performance Ratio," page 202) currently represent the epitome of a curve that has no limit. Net Readiness, in this sense, measures the ability of enterprises to blaze this path in an effort to carve out new possibilities.

What does it take to succeed in this digital, Web-centered world of electronic commerce, this perpetually shifting landscape that we call the E-conomy? When you look past all the hype and a handful of well-publicized success stories, you see that most organizations have racked up abysmal records of creating high-impact benefits through E-business initiatives. We're not saying that companies have not seen any E-business success. A number of our customers have indeed driven projects that have seen a return. Many companies, unfortunately, have not seen truly transformative impacts on competitiveness and new value creation. Instead, the unvarnished truth reveals that most organizations

- Have deployed E-business initiatives on an ad hoc, somewhat opportunistic basis insufficiently supported by the structural requirements to execute competently.

- Have sunk unmeasured resources into E-business initiatives without seeing results anywhere near the returns they expected.

- Have little or no clue about the total costs of ownership of their Web initiatives nor about how they would measure any positive return on investment.

Based on our research, we have reached a key conclusion. The companies with the most demonstrated ability to execute in the E-conomy have optimized the four most important properties of success in E-business—leadership, governance, competencies, and technology—which together create the critical quality we call Net Readiness. These pillars of Net Readiness are the subject of chapter 1.

Without Net Readiness, even the most inspired strategic initiative is doomed to flounder. Although big ideas are important in the E-conomy, they don't guarantee success. Compelling vision is indispensable in the E-conomy, but vision doesn't amount to much until it leverages something else. That is, vision only creates value when it can be put in the service of an activity that has some economic impact and can be executed ruthlessly. Fleeting attention and even a modicum of success may come to companies with technological savvy, but technology is easy to duplicate in the E-conomy. If you want that success to persist, look somewhere else. Look to Net Readiness.

We have seen that one of the biggest obstacles to progress is the oversupply of opportunities. We call it the curse of abundance. Companies have so many avenues to explore, so many initiatives to deploy, so many partnerships to form. This abundance is a problem because the crush of opportunities makes organizations stupid. They fail to discriminate high-impact opportunities from marginal efforts. As a result, a "me, too" mentality runs amok. Fresh thinking stumbles in the marketplace, and copycat opportunism becomes the order of the day.

Some analysts may claim that opportunities are so abundant in the E-conomy that even organizations that are less than Net Ready can find a profitable niche among the jewels just waiting to be picked up. We respond that the plethora of opportunities is actually a curse to companies that have not been intentional in maturing themselves along the four dimensions of Net Readiness. Plenitude obscures a company's ability to focus, to discriminate, to set priorities. Without the discipline of Net Readiness, it's easy to become paralyzed or to move along a path of marginal productivity. Finally, even if by pure fortune a company happens on a considerable opportunity, its lack of Net Readiness will almost certainly prevent it from fully extracting all the value possible.

Together, the Net Ready attributes describe a constellation of skills, attitudes, and values that the most successful companies—the Dells, Amazons, Ciscos, Schwabs, Onsales—display on a day-to-day basis. These companies are Net Ready companies. If you aspire to the same level of success and reward, you need to be Net Ready, too. This book lays out the lessons that will prepare you for the challenges of the E-conomy and what you have to take on—and, almost as critical, what you have to let go—to be Net Ready.

Core Attributes That Predict Vulnerability

A revolving door in a crowded office building at lunch time. That's exactly the experience you will have while conducting business in the E-conomy. The velocity of the rotary motion is not under your control; the occupants are not of your choosing and are grasping for any advantage; and the way out becomes rapidly confused with the way in, so that eventually you feel you are just along for the ride.

Welcome to the E-conomy, an environment that differs from the traditional economy precisely because of that dizzying, uncontrollable pace. It's a different world. The E-conomy's imperative for action negates many of the payoffs that the traditional economy assigned to such strategies as early mover advantage, durability, and linear product development cycles designed to protect existing lines. In the digitally lubricated E-conomy, early mover advantage can be instantly replicated. Netscape successfully transformed its lead in the browser war into a dominant market position but found that position quickly eroded by Microsoft's offering.

Product cycles in the E-conomy are relentless and parallel. It doesn't make sense to think of the beginning, the middle, and the end of product lines as clearly delineated functions of traditional operations. Activities such as research, design, manufacturing, distribution, and marketing continue, but more as concurrent processes in an endless feedback loop focused on the customer. This year's product has been replaced by constant innovation that drives a continuous stream of versions, upgrades, and improvements. Nothing is built to last anymore because change is prized over constancy.

The half-life of competitive knowledge is shrinking so quickly that it's often better to share it while it still has value than to hoard it and watch its value decrease. In the E-conomy, storefronts pay big bucks for advantages that are measured in weeks. When Yahoo! acquired Viaweb for $49 million in June 1998, chief operations officer Jeff Mallett noted that "60 days is the biggest lead a storefront can have in the online space, and that's what Yahoo will get for its investment."

The lesson here is that E-business initiatives are never done, never complacent, always beginning. Your latest offering is always an approximation of reality. The E-conomy loathes maturity the way nature abhors a vacuum. The traditional economy had a four-step product life cycle: gestation, growth, maturity, and decline. The E-conomy has only the first two. Get used to a product life cycle that not only never reaches maturity but doesn't even aspire to it. When your offering has achieved some success, you should already be launching the next new thing that is piggybacking off the last new thing.

In the last five years of our work with Net Ready companies, we have seen many characteristics that revealed how vulnerable companies were to new entrants poised to compete directly or to seize smaller pieces of the value chain. Here are a few of our most common observations.

Competitive advantage. In the E-conomy, competitive advantage is more difficult to attain and even more difficult to sustain.

- The E-conomy requires companies to continuously identify and execute new opportunities rather than try and sustain old ones. Those companies that have the competency to make these changes rapidly will have a distinct advantage.
- A focus of Internet initiatives on critical business practices is necessary but not sufficient, because E-business initiatives are often easily replicable.
- The E-business bar is rising and is going to continue to rise. Initiatives and the business processes they impact need to be questioned constantly and revisited continuously.

Never being satisfied. Complacency is incompatible with Net Readiness. Internet initiatives, the business procedures they impact, and the products and services they enable need to be in constant question.

- Changes and introduction of new technologies and business solutions should cycle every six to nine months.
- Your initiatives must be continuously questioned, improved, and explained to the customer.
- Your products, processes, and other key value drivers need to stay in revision and version mode.
- You are never done; you must never be complacent; you should always be beginning.

E-conomy deliverables. The value proposition you offer must be compelling and immediately conspicuous to the customer. Before you implement it, have its replacement ready, because if you don't obsolete your deliverable, your competitor will.

- You must be able to transform key business processes via Internet technologies.
- Internet technologies and applications are, for the most part, easier to develop, easier to use, and easier to replicate, rendering any advantage less sustainable.
- Your Internet strategies must be ruthlessly implemented.

Intellectual underpinnings. The expanded E-conomy requires a shift from hierarchical, linear thinking to a more holistic approach characterized by multidisciplinary rigor and dynamic planning.

- Traditional approaches to planning that assume long-range predictability cannot be sustained.

- A proactive attitude must replace the reactive stance.

- Discontinuous change, not incremental progress, informs the value propositions of the most successful Net Ready companies.

- E-conomy realities require simultaneous execution and nimbleness to permit real-time shifts in resources and direction.

Need for partnerships. No one can do it alone. The expanded E-conomy requires enterprises to form relationships to compete.

- The E-conomy will punish arrogant companies that think they have all the competencies.

- You must be able to shore up competencies and act quickly on an opportunity.

- Your ability to quickly select partners and create virtual organizations, and then dissolve those partnerships just as quickly is essential for success in the E-conomy.

Early mover advantages. Early movers accrue advantages when they develop new products/services or create new business models.

- Early movers get the first shot at the best talent. Who will lead your company tomorrow?

- Being first in a space provides access to the strongest partners.

- Early movers get a capitalization premium, both in terms of favorable access to venture capital as well as subsequent Wall Street capital.

- Early movers get access to higher-margin customers.

How vulnerable is your enterprise? Table 2 offers a worksheet to estimate the extent of your vulnerability. Are there information asymmetries operating in your business that can be appropriated by others? Can high-value processes of your value chain be digitized or made into commodities? If so, what's to stop an agile competitor from stepping in? Can any of the processes critical to your value chain be fragmented? Or can form be separated from function? If so, you are vulnerable and may not know it. Competitors are waiting to exploit such vulnerability. Don't wait for them. Exploit those weaknesses yourself. Doing so may create havoc with established channels and existing partners. Don't let that stop you. Shoot yourself in the foot, if you have to, before someone shoots you in the head.

Table 2. Vulnerability Grid

Estimate the risk for each of these exposures to indicate your overall vulnerability. The more high risks you check, the more vulnerable your operation is or, stated conversely, the more opportunities you have. If you see risks, you are operating as a Rule Taker; if you see opportunities, you are thinking like a Rule Breaker. This exercise indicates how much opportunity there can be in your market. Certain attributes drive the E-conomy: digitizability; fragmentation; customizability; asymmetries of information between buyers and sellers; velocity of the market.

	Your Risk		
Exposure	Low	Medium	High
Efficiency How efficient is the relationship between buyer and seller?	☐	☐	☐
Digitizability How digitizable is the product or service?	☐	☐	☐
Customizability How customizable is the product or service?	☐	☐	☐
Asymmetries of Information What is the balance of power in the buyer-seller equation?	☐	☐	☐
Commodity How commodity-like is the product or service?	☐	☐	☐
Fragmentation How fragmented is the market in which you operate?	☐	☐	☐
Attitudinal Readiness How ready are customers to accept new ways?	☐	☐	☐
Velocity How critical is the need for speed in the delivery of the product or service?	☐	☐	☐

Drivers of Success and Barriers to Success

In the work we've done, it's become clear to us that successful Net Ready organizations exhibit one set of characteristics while organizations that are less successful or that have failed exhibit a different set of characteristics. Let's consider these two sets of principles. We call them barriers to Net Ready success and drivers of Net Ready success. These two sets are flip sides of a coin that is surprisingly common to many of the organizations that we have observed. We have seen these principles play out in various permutations in almost all the clients we have studied.

Drivers of Success

- *Ruthless execution.* A company must have the ability to identify and execute quickly on opportunities. It must develop innovative business models, new practices, and perhaps governance models, and it must fundamentally reshape its new value creation process.

- *Metrics driven.* Emphasis on activities that can be measured and evaluated. Employees are given incentives to reach the established metrics.

- *Being focused on immediacy.* If the process can't be done in, say, three to six months, the company should move on to something that can.

- *A "versioning" philosophy.* Successful companies recognize the need for ongoing and continuous E-business development and modification.

- *Being customer focused and technology enabled.* Companies have to have a clear and customer-driven value proposition and must be focused on a customer value creation proposition.

- *Scalable and standardized architecture (application/network).* Organizations need to create a foundation by which they can lay in value-creating applications without worrying about disparate systems, data formats, and scalability issues.

- *Being driven by vision.* Companies must develop a portfolio of E-business solutions that support and communicate an articulated vision, usually in a twelve-to-eighteen-month road map.

Barriers to Success

- *"Field of Dreams" syndrome.* The illusion that if they build it, customers will come.

- *Inadequate architecture (application/network).* Companies fail to lay down a foundation, or plumbing, or a scalable infrastructure. Oftentimes they later have to come in with a forklift to rip out their previous work and install a larger infrastructure. They have committed the error of not planning for success.

- *Putting lipstick on a bulldog.* Companies "Webify" old business practices/models by sticking on a Web front end without regard to underlying process issues. They end up with a broken and inefficient process that has a pretty user interface (a good-looking bulldog).

- *Islands of Webification.* Companies engage in the creation of discontinuous and nonsynergistic applications, or pockets of E-business, that are oftentimes redundant, without driving toward an overall direction. This characteristic is endemic to most companies of any reasonable size.

- *"Me too" strategies.* Copying or following the moves of the competition keeps a company in reaction mode. This strategy is a losing proposition because merely replicating what the competitors are doing ensures a company of second-class status. Although benchmarking provides insights and allows a company to catch up, "me too strategies" are often a fast path to mediocrity.

- *One-time-effort mentality.* Under the old IT paradigm, IT got a project, went away, came back with something two years later, and said, "What's next?" This model will no longer do. E-business projects cannot be developed in isolation. Intimate, ongoing participation with end users is required. Projects must be completed in three months or less. Most important, the project can never be seen as done. E-business initiatives are always in a state of redevelopment.

- *Thinking too small.* Companies must not become overdependent on incremental progress. A company cannot increment its way to success. It must take big steps.

Welcome to the E-conomy. It's time for us to become active participants.

Acknowledgments

The quality of Net Readiness applies just as much to authors as it applies to organizations. Neither the concepts described in this book nor the book itself would have been possible without the manifold contributions of a number of individuals to our conceptualization and understanding of Net Readiness.

Many people at Cisco Systems contributed their experience and insights to sharpen the focus of *Net Ready*. We are especially thankful to John Chambers for encouraging us with this book and providing our readers with a timely foreword. We also express our gratitude to Pete Solvik and Sue Bostrom for their insights and ideas to support our work on *Net Ready* beyond the book.

We would also like to extend our thanks to all of our colleagues within the Internet Business Solutions Group at Cisco for their ideas and kind words of encouragement. A special thanks must go to Craig LeGrande, Lynne Eslick, Amy Horn, and Donna Sanekoff for their hard work in helping finish the book.

John Sifonis especially acknowledges Phil Osborne for his insights and thoughtful leadership over the past two decades. He has been a friend and a major contributor to many of the concepts put forth in this book. The authors thank Doug Aldrich for his insights and encouragement over the years. Our personal thanks also go to Gunnar Eriksen for his comments during the editing of our book.

We are indebted to numerous busy people throughout the Internet Industry whose views have informed this book. We are particularly grateful to the following individuals without whose generous assistance *Net Ready* would be impoverished, indeed: Leilani Allen, Marc Andreesen, Deborah Coughlin, Mark DuBois, Nat Goldhaber, Seth Godin, Robert Gordon, Robert Kadar, Robert Levy, Kevin O'Connor, Ken Seiff, Marc Sokol, Bruce Todesco, and Charles B. Wang.

For organizing our thoughts in a palatable way and helping construct *Net Ready,* we are grateful to John Kador, a superb writer, editor, and colleague. Our admiration goes to John for holding us accountable through-out the process and for his discipline. John Kador, in turn, appreciates a number of people who have made the writing of this book go just a little bit easier: Rita Hoover, George Moskoff, Anna Beth Payne, Stephanie Simmons Ray, Steve Vasilion, and Mary Wang.

Net Ready

*Strategies for Success
in the E-conomy*

Strategies for Success in the E-Conomy

The E-conomy is very much like Oklahoma just after the land rush. The land closest to the border has been grubstaked, and many of the most convenient and conspicuously valuable lots have been fenced to keep interlopers out. But much of the territory is still unmapped, and there remain enormous opportunities for Net Ready organizations willing to gamble. The successful E-business organizations will take on a variety of roles in furthering their fortunes.

Worldwide Internet commerce will top $1 trillion by 2003, according to a report by International Data Corp. The Framingham, Mass.–based research firm estimates that most of that growth is accounted for by more consumers buying online, by larger dollar amounts per transaction, and by increased business-to-business purchases on the Web. But perhaps the most startling change to shake up the status quo is reflected in this next estimate: by 2003, U.S.-based users should account for less than half of all Internet commerce, compared with 74 percent in 1999, the company said.

The question becomes, as competition in Internet space becomes truly global, how do you join the bandwagon, or better yet, get out in front so the world follows your lead? What do you have to do first to start a journey that leads to initiatives that can tap into the power of this curve? In Part I of *Net Ready,* we develop a framework to which emerging network-based businesses can map themselves. This framework helps companies determine to what extent their leadership, governance models, competencies, and tolerance for risk are aligned with their vision. After conducting a detailed examination of hundreds of experiments in the E-conomy, we have distilled a number of principles, dos and don'ts, and operating models. Almost all the most celebrated names in the E-conomy can map themselves to these designations.

A successful foray into Net Readiness requires you to forget most of what you learned about business and managing. This task will become harder as Net Ready companies extract more value from the traditional economy. When the practices that used to work are no longer working, the temptation among many of you will be to redouble your efforts. The following bit of Internet humor underscores the folly of this approach.

What Do You Do with a Dead Horse?

The lessons of Net Readiness hold that when you discover you are riding a dead horse, the best strategy is to get off and quickly find a new mount. In business, however, it's often difficult to let go of our investments in dead horses, which leads us to try other strategies to breathe life into hopeless investments, including the following:

- Change riders.
- Buy a stronger whip.
- Harness several dead horses together for increased speed.
- Emulate the best practices of companies riding dead horses.
- Outsource the ridership of the horse.
- Affirm that "This is the way we have always ridden this horse."
- Change the requirements, declaring that "This horse is not dead."
- Perform a cost analysis to see if contractors can ride it cheaper.
- Promote the dead horse to a management position.
- Have the lawyers bring suit against the horse manufacturer.
- Put out a news release that, in the unlikely event the horse is dead, it was dead before it ever came to the company.

1

The Four Pillars
of Net Readiness

Net Readiness is a combination—unique to each organization—of four drivers that enables enterprises to deploy high-impact Web-enabled business processes that are focused, accountable, and measurable.

Our development of the concept of Net Readiness follows a rigorous investigation of just what makes Web-enabled companies successful. Stated another way, we wanted to know if there are any commonly encountered barriers to success in the E-conomy. Based on our experience in the past five years, it turns out that there is, indeed, a set of attributes that seems to drive E-business success. At the same time, our research identified a number of attributes associated with barriers to success or with outright failure in E-business. We saw a remarkable consistency in both lists.

We have identified four key drivers that predict an enterprise's ability to succeed in the E-conomy by deploying high impact E-business initiatives. Those four drivers are

- Leadership
- Governance
- Competencies
- Technology

Taken together, these four dimensions underpin the concept we call *Net Readiness*. When an organization demonstrates the ability to consistently execute in these four dimensions, we say it is *Net Ready*.

Net Readiness is a measure of a company's preparedness to exploit the enormous opportunities in the E-conomy landscape. The four attributes combined in an infinite variety of permutations are consistently displayed by the most successful players in the E-conomy. Separately, these four attributes represent prerequisites, or barriers, to E-conomy success. It is unlikely that durable E-conomy success will come to any company conspicuously short in any of these four areas. In the following sections, we take a closer look at each of these dimensions and at what organizations have to do to execute each dimension well. We show how the E-conomy prospects of Cisco Systems—the company with which we are most familiar—are furthered by attention to these dimensions.

Leadership

Think about the outstanding Net Ready companies. Does it surprise you that most of them are so uncannily associated with their leaders? Michael Dell. Jeff Bezos. John Chambers. Bill Gates. As we surveyed the most successful companies in the E-conomy, it became clear to us that, without exception, they all had the benefit of a particular kind of leadership. What are the essential qualities of leadership in support of a Net Ready organization? Is your organization's leadership Net Ready? Ask yourself the following questions and see how often you can answer in the affirmative:

- Do we solve business process problems first?
- Is senior management attuned to the opportunities/threats enabled by the E-conomy?
- Is generating competitive advantage via E-business a top priority of senior management?
- Are our E-business initiatives integrated with our business strategy?
- Is senior management involved in, buying into, and participating in E-business efforts?
- Do we have an E-business vision or road map in the twelve-to-eighteen-month time frame, and is it communicated up and down the organization?
- Do we have an E-culture (Web-enabled business mind-set) up and down the organization?
- Do we have a culture of information sharing?

Net Ready leadership starts by empowering every corner of the organization—from the CEO to the custodian—to think and act in E-conomy terms, to use E-business tools, and to hold themselves accountable in measurable ways. The overriding leadership message must be: This organization is a Web culture from top to bottom, and everyone in this business is empowered to do E-conomy. The leader's job is to promote this vision by personal example.

Library shelves are groaning with the weight of books about leadership, so we propose to restrict our discussion here to the essential attributes of leadership that promote Net Readiness in its myriad manifestations. Although leadership in the E-conomy features some new wrinkles, its first goal, like the first goal of leadership in the traditional economy, is to define a workable balance between the visionary and managerial components. Leadership—when spread across functions, hierarchies, and structures—combines strategic thinking (that is, setting the vision, mission, and goals of the organization) and operational leadership (that is, ensuring that all the tasks involved in meeting performance measures are successfully accomplished). We have heard the adage, "A leader is one who does the right things, a manager is one who does things right." In the E-conomy, leadership evolves to a new reconciliation of this polarity. It's not enough to do the right things flawlessly; Net Ready CEOs must do it with a conspicuous display of vision and character. As General H. Norman Schwarzkopf says, "Leadership is a potent combination of strategy and character. But if you must be without one, be without the strategy."

The E-conomy needs leaders who evangelize rather than encourage, empower rather than delegate (see Table 1-1). More volatile business conditions and advances in technology mean that we have to move decision making and problem solving out of the corner office and distribute them throughout the organization.

The stewards of Net Ready companies constantly face the challenge of being barraged with too many ideas, proposals, partnerships, business opportunities, and barrels of cash. It takes a highly focused CEO and management team to navigate these treacherous waves. Cultivating the ability to say "no" is perhaps more important than getting people to say yes. "We get a thousand opportunities a day," says Kevin O'Connor, CEO of the Internet advertising company DoubleClick (see our profile of this company on page 224 in chapter 7). "Strategy is half deciding what to do and half what not to do." The E-conomy demands CEOs who can think paradoxi-

Table 1-1. Qualities of Net Ready Leadership

Net Ready leaders need qualities that enable them to thrive in an environment in which the sheer number of opportunities can overwhelm any strategy and in which the stakes and fast-moving pace of business leave no margin for error.

Traditional CEO	Net Ready CEO
"Do as I say"	"Do as I do"
"Get out of my way"	"Get on my team"
Focused on strategy	Focused on execution
Constrained by money	Constrained by time
Encouraging	Evangelizing
Cautious	Paranoid
Gets to "yes"	Is able to say "no"
Concerned with the long term	Concerned with the short run
Has a preference for comfort	Insists on truth
Market driven	Customer driven
Intolerant of ambiguity	Welcomes ambiguity
Sequential	Multitasking
Focused on retention	Focused on recruitment

cally. The following sections elaborate on tasks that E-conomy leaders must accomplish if they are to succeed.

Solve Business Process Problems First

Begin by solving the business process problems. Your fundamental goal is to define how to better address customer requirements. This goal takes precedence over everything else, including the development of information technology (IT) projects explicitly designed to support these business process improvements. There's good news when you attack process issues first. For example, many traditional order entry functions go away. Most customer service reps take on larger, more challenging customer management roles. In the self-help model enabled by Net Ready process changes, customers and partners willingly take on responsibilities formerly handled by the organization.

Have a High Tolerance for Ambiguity and Chaos

Gone are the days when business was so stable and predictable that long-range strategic plans actually made sense. Today, the game belongs to those who can think and act nimbly. When the relationships between the major storefronts in any given industry can completely shift in a matter of weeks, when even the definition of an industry is open for grabs, there is little profit in insisting on maps that refer to past behavior. E-conomy leadership means understanding that the competitive business environment is chaotic, and good leadership (at every level) means being comfortable dealing with the ambiguity caused by chaotic behavior.

At one point in our economy, past behavior offered reliable guidance for the future. Not in the E-conomy. Net Ready leaders acknowledge that the strategic landscape can be neither predictably known nor systematically addressed. Formalized strategic thinking—of the kind Michael Porter recommended in *Competitive Advantage* as recently as 1985—is doomed to failure in an ever-changing and technologically driven business environment. These facts may be inconvenient, but they apply equally to every storefront in the E-conomy. Advantage, then, accrues to the storefront that can adapt most quickly to the reality that the E-conomy is about change and movement. Net Ready leaders can learn from Epictetus—the first-century Roman philosopher who would have been very comfortable in the E-conomy and who provided the epigraph for this book.

Model E-Business from Top to Bottom

Net Ready companies have leaders who embrace the Web and extend it to every corner of the organization. Cisco's John Chambers believes that everything pertaining to Cisco belongs on the Web. If something's not on the Web, there has to be a good reason. These leaders not only embrace new technologies and new applications that are enabled by the Internet, they push its use within every level of the organization. In one company we worked with, for example, the CEO led the movement toward electronic communication on the company's recently implemented intranet. Although not an expert by any means in the use of E-mail or electronic calendaring, this CEO set the tone and expectation level for the rest of the organization by communicating electronically and refusing to accept written communications for most situations.

Even Cisco experienced a transition in going from a paper-based expense reporting system to their Intranet application, Metro. After the application was operational for several months, the paper-based expense system was eliminated, and it was no longer possible to submit an expense report unless it was done electronically. Such transitions force an E-culture up, down, and throughout your organization.

Avoid Incrementalism

E-conomy leaders realize that they cannot inch their way to Net Readiness. Doing something—customer service, TQM, benchmarking—incrementally better than the competition is useful, but is not a sufficient condition for competitive advantage. Operational excellence, as Michael Porter observes, means that you're running the same race faster. But Net Readiness involves, in addition to operational excellence, choosing to run a different race because it's the one you've set yourself up to win. He points to the dominant storefronts in the E-conomy as classic exemplars of successful strategic thinking. "The average technology company is not all that gifted in terms of strategy. But the most successful companies—the Dells, the Intels, the Ciscos—don't think about strategy as incremental or impossible. They have a clear sense of what they're trying to do and how to do it." Different may not be necessarily better, but better is always different.

Be Early

Net Ready leaders tend to be risk takers; they take on a set of behaviors we call Rule Breaking (see chapter 9 for a fuller discussion of Rule Breakers, Shakers, Makers, and Takers). Not all Rule Breakers are successful (witness Edwin Lands's instant movie flop, Polavision, or Federal Express's ZAP Mail). Federal Express spent millions of dollars on the infrastructure to enable ZAP Mail, a point-to-point facsimile service. Unfortunately, ZAP Mail arrived at the same time as the adoption of the personal fax machine and could never put a dent in the trend for every company to have a fax machine. To its credit, however, the leadership of Federal Express didn't let the failure of ZAP Mail get in the way of trying new rule-breaker concepts such as Internet tracking and shipping.

Engage in Counterintuitive Thinking

The E-conomy makes mincemeat of many sacred business values. Net Readiness teaches you that thinking small and acting small is the path to getting big. Net Readiness suggests that success is not something that you aim for. The more you aim at it and make it a target, the more elusive it is. Success, like happiness, cannot be pursued; it must ensue, and it does so only as the almost unintended side effect of focusing on customers and partners and serving them meticulously. In the E-conomy, Net Ready leaders let success happen by not caring about it.

Communicate Well

Effective leaders in the E-conomy are wired and thrive on E-mail. They promote the power of the network. Good leaders in the traditional economy communicated well with subordinates. Net Ready leaders help team members communicate with each other.

Cultivate a Culture of Information Sharing

Cisco's leadership model includes a piece of corporate culture that was considered very risky—almost radical—at the time, but has since proved to be visionary. From the beginning, Cisco has cultivated a culture of information sharing. From its first days, the company posted a list of all known bugs in its products on its Web site. At a time when the prevailing tradition in America was to hide mistakes and acknowledge them only in a very controlled way, Cisco's departure from tradition brought the company a lot of positive attention. Today, that culture of information sharing contributes to an effective record of knowledge management that, in turn, supports a stupendous level of product achievement.

Cisco is an excellent example of a Net Ready company. E-mail, for example, is an indispensable part of the culture of the organization, permeating every business process from top to bottom. One of the basic governing principles of Cisco is scaling—the capability to leverage through the use of Internet technology and Internet-enabled applications. The field sales offices of Cisco are primarily virtual offices. Account managers rarely come to a physical location; almost all communication and customer order tracking as well as the myriad of sales activities are conducted through E-mail or through Web applications. Cisco has learned that paper doesn't scale effectively—it is slow, insecure, and cumbersome. Any information or transaction that an account manager requires can be accomplished either through E-mail or through the Web. In almost all instances, the likelihood of getting a response to any query is higher via E-mail than via voice mail or fax or "snail mail."

Another Cisco principle is its focus on the customer—not merely satisfying the customer, but exceeding the customer's expectations. Customer satisfaction is absolutely critical to Cisco's success. Cisco's approach has always been to solve "customer-facing problems," that is, those problems that impact its customers and that, if not solved, would lead to a drop in customer satisfaction. For example, Cisco's success in Internet commerce wasn't the result of a well-planned and executed strategy. Rather, success came through a series of activities, each of which solved a customer problem. When it was most successful, Cisco streamlined processes that customers didn't even identify as problems. Aggregating these activities resulted in end-to-end solutions that allow Cisco to serve its customers more proactively.

Here's how Cisco's success came about. As recently as five years ago, obtaining the status of a Cisco order was a significant customer-facing problem. After studying the situation, the company realized that more than 70 percent of the customer calls were requesting the same information. This situation was a classic Pareto problem in that 70 percent of the customers requested the same 30 percent of the information. Instead of adding more customer service representatives, Cisco developed an application to handle the majority of the calls. Customers who couldn't find their answers on the Cisco Web site would be connected to a support person. By developing a Web-based application (basically, a self-serve model), Cisco increased its customer satisfaction ratings significantly. In fact, the self-serve model received higher satisfaction ratings than did the humans who previously answered routine customer queries. The original objective was to solve a customer-facing problem, raise customer satisfaction, and leverage scarce expertise—it was not to sell the most stuff on the Web. Cisco's success is a by-product of many initiatives to solve customer-facing problems and raise customer satisfaction one customer at a time. The lesson? One-to-one is how a Net Ready company measures success.

Exhibit Principles of Leadership

Even if three of the four pillars of Net Readiness—governance, competencies, and technology—were in place, without leadership, Net Readiness is out of reach. You would have a disciplined, competent, technologically adept organization going nowhere. For that reason, we say that if you had to choose only one dimension of Net Readiness to perfect, choose leadership. Everything else can be acquired, developed, or purchased. Only leadership, among the four attributes, seems to be innate.

Let's look at some of the points that were made in the questionnaire at the beginning of the leadership section. To make your organization Net Ready, follow these guidelines.

- *Solve business process problems first.* It's tempting to start with the technical issues. Resist the temptation. Investment in technology will be wasted unless the business issues are integrated with the technology.

Play the following game: list the top three factors that make it difficult to do business with me if I'm (an employee, a customer, a supplier, a partner, etc.). Then prioritize E-business around these issues.

- *Drive an E-business vision in a twelve-to-eighteen-month time frame.* Planning past an eighteen-month horizon is fruitless because events change too quickly in the E-conomy. Developing and driving an E-business road map with key deliverables over a twelve-to-eighteen-month span is critical (rapid execution in three-month components is fundamental to such a road map).

- *Communicate that vision up and down the organization.* Become an evangelist. Use every opportunity—especially Net-based channels—to spread the news.

- *Stay finely attuned to the opportunities/threats enabled by the E-conomy.* As Intel's Andy Grove says, "Only the paranoid survive."

- *Accept that generating competitive advantage via E-business technologies is a top priority.* You can't wait for the perfect moment at which the Dow does this and Microsoft does that. You have to act now.

- *Take personal responsibility for participating in E-business efforts.* Leadership is personal. If you don't do it, no one will. It is critical that senior management be conspicuously involved in driving E-business efforts. Build a mandate and stay involved.

- *Pay more than lip service to the education and empowerment of employees to drive E-business.* Put hard dollars into play to cement your vision of highly trained and empowered employees.

- *Model an E-culture of information sharing by sharing information.* People are going to look to you for clues about how to use information. If they see you hoarding information, they will hoard. If they see you sharing, they will share. Achieve information democracy by using the network as an enabler and by changing business processes where required.

- *Offer new incentives.* Old-world incentives have very weak links between organizational outcomes and individual rewards. Net Ready incentives create better alignment between risk and reward.

Governance

How do you organize around doing E-business? This central question sums up what governance is all about. Governance is the operating model—the glue—that defines the very nature of the organization. Governance is truly one of the most problematic issues that most organizations struggle with today. Should you spin off a separate organization ("pureplay")? Should you integrate these efforts into your existing structure? Answers to these questions are driven by a number of variables: the scope of E-business change, for example, and the impact on the business (see chapter 3 for more detail on specific organizational forms).

In addition to the central question, governance provides answers to some of the toughest questions organizations have to face:

- What are the E-business roles and responsibilities of each member of the organization?
- Is it clear who has decision-making authority on E-business initiatives?
- Are the limits of accountability clearly defined?
- How are E-business initiatives funded?
- Have we allocated sufficient funding for ongoing E-business maintenance?
- Do we have an established method for assessing and selecting Internet initiatives and for allocating resources?
- How do we incent E-business activities?
- Do we have established metrics for measuring the impact of our Internet initiatives?
- What drives our Internet initiatives (IT, marketing, customers, competitors, etc.)?

Governance determines the nature of relationships within the organization as well as relationships among the constituencies outside the formal organization. The issues concerned with governance go far beyond the rules and regulations that give an organization standing as a legal entity. Governance involves control, accountability, responsibility, and authority. The dynamics of these relationships determine how well an organization can maintain integrity in the face of changing values while shifting directions in response to external events.

Net Ready organizations have an operational framework that defines how attributes such as control, accountability, responsibility, and authority interrelate and how conflicts between them are rationalized. The type of structurally rigid frameworks that typified many organizations in the traditional economy tend not to be very successful in the E-conomy.

Organizational structure informs Net Readiness. Without a well-considered and even more well-articulated governance model, organizations have a very hard time exploiting creative energy. Without a satisfactory governance model, the creativity is dissipated in a whirlwind of initiatives that have little synergy to each other and cannot be distinguished as to their relative potential contributions to the bottom line. It's one thing to define and pursue a strategy; it's another thing to be able to change directions in midstream. In the E-conomy, a networked operating environment plays a vital role in facilitating the organization's flexibility to diverge from the defined strategy. While strategy may determine organizational structure, the right structure will determine the organization's ability to pursue the right E-business strategy.

A modern enterprise consists of multiple business units and, in many instances, overlapping business functions: administrative, manufacturing, marketing, support, and so on. To successfully drive E-business, an organization must have a mechanism that enables it to cut across all these functions, taking responsibility for business initiatives spanning different operating units.

In larger organizations governance is critical and often requires the creation of a formal body, often called a governance council. Such bodies used to be chaired by a high-level manager and called IT steering committees. E-business governance councils fulfill similar objectives but are empowered to take a much more comprehensive scope than merely aligning IT objectives with the broader aims of the business.

Governance and Operations Framework

Governance defines the organization's structures, roles, responsibilities, and accountabilities as well as the authority that supports the decision making in an organization. Primary areas of coverage include overall standards, vision and functionality, funding models, and financial management. Governance defines the structure and the tools; it does not have much, if anything, to say about processes.

Our intention here is not to add bureaucracy to the organization. We all know that one problem of corporations is too much hierarchy. But it is critical that organizations drive E-business processes in a rational manner. Non-born-on-the-Web companies trying to move to Net Readiness frequently need these high-level governance committees. Companies that are born on the Web tend to do these things much more naturally. After all,

E-business is their business. That said, there are numerous ways for companies to organize around E-business (see chapter 3 for a broader discussion on the different organizational forms). However, companies trying to integrate E-business into their traditional business activities need to consider these issues in order to scale their success.

The governance and operations framework consists of four core sets of disciplines: the governance model, decision processes, policies and standards, and goals and metrics.

Governance Model

The first area of the governance and operations framework, the governance model, defines the purpose and structure of the body that manages and partitions responsibilities for E-business as an organizational priority across the different organizational entities—corporate, groups, and divisions. Within each dimension is a range of possibilities that helps define the current and potential future governance structure of the organization. A governance body's charter should include the following responsibilities:

- Fostering improved coordination
- Ensuring consistency of decision making throughout an organization
- Responsibility for achieving specific and measurable objectives
- Granting authority to accomplish activities
- Accountability for actions taken

Organizational structure can consist of executive ownership, or it can resemble a representative assembly/federation with participation being either full-time or part-time. The governing body sets the rules and policies of execution but does not itself execute the rules and policies. The business units are responsible for implementation. This model is akin to the role of a board of directors, which sets policies and entrusts the CEO to carry them out.

Decision Processes

Decision processes define the decision-making and funding mechanisms for ongoing planning and management. These processes are further broken down into decision mechanisms, funding models, and escalation/appeals processes.

- Decision mechanisms—can vary from consensus building to employing a majority rule voting style (simple or weighted) to dictatorial.
- Funding—can refer to corporate allocation, specific project funding, or a combination of the two.
- Escalation/appeals processes —can either be explicitly sanctioned by general management or informal in nature.

Policies and Standards

Policies and standards involve guidelines for implementation of recommendations and performance monitoring, that is, definition of service levels. By standards, we mean ethical guidelines or principals, not standards in a technical sense. Policies and standards consist of standardization and enforcement.

- Standardization—Standardization can occur at the business-unit level with little corporate-wide standardization, or standards can be driven by a central body with strong guidance to the businesses.
- Enforcement—Adherence to policies and standards can be encouraged or strictly enforced.

Goals and Metrics

Goals and metrics define the business performance objectives and measures to guide E-conomy administration policies and investment decisions. The main areas of goals and metrics are scope and responsibility.

- Scope of metrics—Each governing body must determine to what extent it will guide the governance of metrics. Some governing bodies specify which metrics it wants and how they are to be measured. But we believe that for maximum agility, governing bodies should articulate a clear position on the imperative of metrics and leave the details to the business units.
- Responsibility—Responsibility can reside either with the business unit or with a governance body.

Metrics: Know What You Are Measuring

Net Ready companies measure ruthlessly, make corrections, and then measure again. Companies must have serious and accountable metrics and clear agreements about using them across the organization. It is in the appropriateness and completeness of the metrics selected that the most robust and ruthless Net Ready companies shine. In the E-conomy, the choice of metrics and the rigor with which processes are measured take on new importance. If you want to do serious E-conomy, you need serious metrics.

How do you put your arms around E-business initiatives? How do you measure a target that by its very nature refuses to be pinned down? What metrics make sense, and how do you apply them? Web site hits? Forget it. Web site hits were never a useful metric because no one knew what they measured. They had no context, business or otherwise. If you want reasonable evaluations of how much specific value each initiative is adding to your enterprise, use metrics such as those displayed in Table 1-2.

Table 1-2. Metrics for Net Ready Enterprises

Use the information in this table to raise awareness throughout your company of its transition to a Net Ready company and its execution of Net Ready objectives.

Cost Reduction
- Number of support calls; cost of call/revenue
- Total marketing/communications expenditures as a percentage of revenue
- Cost per order dollar
- Total dollars spent on Net Ready initiatives

E-conomy Growth
- Online sales dollars
- Number of transactions completed online
- Online support sales dollars
- Number of sales support transactions completed online
- Number of E-selling pages viewed online

Customer Satisfaction and Reach
- Online customer satisfaction survey score
- Numbers/percentages of return visitors
- Site reach (number of new site visitors, new registrants, etc.)

Operations
- Most requested pages/site areas
- Quality control metrics (percentage of server uptime, frequency of broken links, etc.)
- Compliance with look and feel, navigation, E-conomy policies

Accountability

We believe that a strong executive committed to the principles of Net Readiness is the best predictor of success for an organization aspiring to succeed in the E-conomy. Furthermore, we believe that the optimum reporting structure is for the E-business leader to report directly to the CEO or another senior executive responsible for value creation. Reporting structures that assign the E-business activity to the CFO or CIO send the wrong signal.

Establishing definitions and maintaining control are the critical elements for all Net Ready relationships precisely because accountability is so dispersed among strategic partners, outsourcing suppliers, members of the supply chain, agents, and other outside constituencies. Net Ready organizations must maintain accountability as a hedge against interlopers inserting themselves at vulnerable points of the supply chain. The constellation of electronic systems that support all the alliances among various members of the supply chain is the very essence of Net Readiness. To implement these new systems, you must assemble and manage teams from very different businesses that are geographically dispersed, and you must ensure that all the links know what they are responsible for and what their roles are. Peter Drucker sums up this critical step by asking: "What information do I owe, and to whom do I owe it; and what information am I owed, and who owes it to me?" We can generalize this question to, "Who is accountable to me and to whom am I accountable?"

Trust: More than Skin Deep

Trust is an essential lubricant of all virtual business transactions. Net Ready organizations must evolve, that is, earn trust, while recognizing that nothing on their corporate chart of accounts is more fragile. There are landmines in all the arrangements that define Net Ready organizations. For example, sharing networks with alliance partners is almost a guarantee that people from other organizations will access proprietary information. Temporary employees may be on your team one day and work for your competitor the next. But that competitor may well be your partner in a limited sense.

Trust is the key. It doesn't matter how many rules you put into place or how much oversight you engage in. Your company's success depends on the nature of the relationships it builds with its new partners and employees. The solution is ethical values that are clearly articulated, communicated, and enforced.

Principles of Governance

Our observation of the most successful Net Ready organizations shows that they have evolved mature and flexible governance models. These models support the ability of the best-of-breed organizations to execute around the following governance principles. Based on the experiences of dozens of organizations navigating to Net Readiness, the following governance lessons stand out:

- *Establish cross-functional teams.* Deliver a cross-functional effort that embraces a business component and a technology component that tightly focus on a market need. E-business initiatives, if they are to have a strategic impact, need to extend beyond all previously respected boundaries to focus laserlike on only one thing: what matters most to customers.

- *Demand near-term E-business results.* Your E-business projects should take three to six months with three to six people, or you should do something else. The idea is to start small (but not insignificant). Focus on high-impact, quick wins first. Break up long-term goals into short-term projects with defined, measurable goals. Validate as you go: rapid prototypes, constant user feedback.

- *Actively promote use of E-business applications.* This view is the diametric opposite of the "build it and they will come" model. Simply throwing an E-business application to the world is worse than doing nothing because it presents the illusion of progress. Net Ready governance requires an active conversion of behavior among customers, partners, suppliers, and employees. Consider establishing a group whose sole purpose is advocacy, education, training, and whatever is required to have people adopt new and sometimes threatening E-business behaviors.

- *Make E-business a business-driven line activity, not a technology-driven staff function.* Line managers should be on the hook for selecting, implementing, and realizing benefits of E-business. A business executive, not an executive identified with IT, should have the ultimate decision-making responsibility.

- *Make E-business funding decisions resemble all business funding decisions.* E-business funding decisions should be made on the basis of value. Net Ready companies reject the idea of funding E-business initiatives on the basis of last year's spending and this year's budget objectives. Nor is every project equally important. Evidence from Net Ready successes suggests that the best strategy is to treat E-business investments like any other capital decision, blending business judgment with some form of return on investment metric.

- *Establish a cross-functional governance council with E-business, technology, and evangelical components.* To drive Net Readiness at a large enterprise, develop a high-level E-business council, led by a business executive, to market Net Readiness cross functionally in three dimensions. First, ensure that customer-focused business goals drive everything. Second, infuse every business process with E-business processes. Third, actively evangelize the benefits of getting on board. Promote, market, cajole, bribe, and threaten people, as appropriate, to get them squared with the vision and to persuade them that resistance is futile. One of the tasks that the governance council should be charged with is to make the tough decisions about projects: go (fund it), no go (don't fund it), and kill (stop funded projects).

- *Make IT take on a free market fulfillment role.* IT works well when it is allowed to play the role of E-business enabler, acting as teacher/consultant to the business with respect to technology issues. In this role, it should determine and drive enterprise-wide standards.

Competencies

Net Ready companies shine in the coordination of the relationships between leadership, governance, and technology. We call the ability to navigate among these values "competencies." Competencies determine the way Net Ready organizations respond to changes in the world, exploit available resources and opportunities, and accommodate themselves to emerging realities. Organizations that display Net Ready competencies either have or can readily develop answers to the following questions:

- Is the enterprise capable of dealing with rapid and ongoing change?
- Can we adapt and drive change quickly across the organization?
- Do we have the implementation competencies to execute ruthlessly (three months or less)?
- Do we have the technical competencies to support Internet initiatives?

- Do we have the operations capabilities required to support our Internet strategy?
- Do we have experience managing multiple relationships (both internal and external)?
- Can we form and dissolve relationships/partnerships quickly (building and managing an E-cosystem)?

Net Ready competency requires a deep understanding of the complexity underlying the E-conomy. Net Ready executives must be able to think concurrently about the effects of numerous events. The ability to multitask is essential for success in the Net Ready world. Also required is an understanding of the mechanisms that help the organization maintain coherence and maintain its status as a recognizable entity. Net Readiness also places demands on connectivity; a company must be able to exchange information on a real-time basis about developments within and without the organization. Finally, the Net Ready organization must evolve ways to coordinate these elements if it expects to deal successfully with the complexity it encounters as a result of the waves of economic, technological, political, and social changes.

A useful way to think about competencies is by considering the five Cs that, together, make up our understanding of competency as an actionable concept. (A fuller discussion of these issues can be found in *Corporation on a Tightrope* [New York: Oxford University Press, 1996].)

- Complexity
- Concurrency
- Coherence
- Connectivity
- Coordination

Let's look at each of these attributes in the context of Net Readiness.

Complexity

Organizations in today's global business environment must deal with challenges that were unthinkable even five years ago. The business challenges facing leaders today are accelerated by issues of globalism, real-time activity, ever-demanding customers, scarcity of critical skills, and unprecedented levels of competition. Traditionally, business competition consisted of a given industry whose boundaries were stable, even immutable. No more. The Net blurs the very boundaries between markets. It also redraws the definition of winning. Traditionally, a stable pecking order defined the storefronts in an industry. With the Net, the distance between No. 1 and everyone else is growing bigger and bigger. Today, as Cisco's CEO John Chambers has observed, if you're not No. 1 or No. 2, it's tough to stay in business. The complexity of the Net makes such increasing returns possible. Net Ready organizations, unconcerned by constraints such as geography, raw materials, or the cost of getting new customers in far-off places, find that further growth becomes easier, not harder.

The Net replaces physical constraints with the constraint of complexity. On the Net, economies of scale yield to the limited ability of humans to manage increasingly complex, interrelated, and fast-moving activities.

Pricing on the Net, for example, has become much more complex and fluid than what they still teach in business school. Net-based pricing is more than just a tactical component of marketing and the sum of product costs plus a little profit. On the Net, pricing is about creating long-term value. It's more about capturing market share than capturing costs. Net Ready companies always see a tension between pricing strategies designed to optimize either present or future performance results. In many ways, the Net eliminates the issue of pricing for individual organizations by setting values across a market space. In any case, why worry about pricing when someone will eventually give away the product or service that you are trying to sell?

Microsoft's incorporating a free browser into Windows is just one example of how what used to be sold is now available at no cost. E-mail companies are reeling because thousands of sites offer free E-mail. The Net Ready auction services such as Onsale and eBay now find themselves faced with Yahoo!'s free auction service. Some organizations have learned to navigate this complexity. Netscape successfully shifted from relying on browser sales to emphasizing the content on its Netcenter Website, parlaying its strategy into a winning lottery ticket courtesy of America Online (AOL). Other companies won't be so fortunate.

Organizations in this business environment must learn how to adapt to rapid change: changes in customer and consumer buying habits; markets that evolve literally overnight and disappear as quickly; and the notion that conducting business is a $24 \times 7 \times 365$ activity. In order to become Net Ready, organizations must acquire competencies for working in complex, adaptive systems. This undertaking is not easy but is essential for Net Readiness.

Concurrency

In the Net Ready economy, everything happens at the same time. Beginnings, middles, and ends are landmarks that no longer signify anything of note. No longer can you assume that what you got is what you'll get. Discontinuities rule the day; processes are nonlinear. Instead, the five Cs that we're discussing here push against each other and create a fluid mix of variables that only the most relaxed and savvy of managers can hope to navigate. Multitasking, then, becomes a prime virtue of Net Ready managers.

Coherence

Coherence defines the integrity of an enterprise. Boundaries keep an organization from veering off and permanently losing shape. A Net Ready organization may be extremely fluid, with its structure and constituencies fluctuating as a function of the markets it serves from time to time, but it nevertheless has an anchor around which it twists within its allotted space. Organizations are defined by many boundaries, external and internal. External boundaries, including legal and regulatory rules, often define an organization and give it legitimacy. Other external boundaries are defined by the will of the organization's owners. Internal boundaries are centered around the ethical governance of the leader as informed by the owners, stakeholders, partners, and customers.

Organizations become coherent through their exquisite connectivity, both external—between the organization and the state, or between the organization and its owners—and internal—between individuals and among groups, teams, alliances, partners, and outside suppliers. These networks are responsible for many of the shifts that take place in the organization's shape. At the same time, these networks, by ensuring that the shifts that are taking place are understood and responded to within the framework of defined rules and boundaries, prevent the organization from crossing the line into chaos.

Connectivity

Managing knowledge is a prerequisite for Net Readiness, and connectivity is a prerequisite for managing knowledge. The issue is not the technical aspects of connectivity. Human attitudes and biases always lag behind the introduction of new technologies, limiting the full potential of investments in bridging the distance between people. A central issue for many workers confronted by new connectivity is the loss of power and autonomy as the products of their work slip out of their control. Many workers are loath to give away what they know until the see the value of what they get from everyone else. Net Ready organizations must have the leadership in place to model how connectivity actually increases power and autonomy by enforcing a value of sharing knowledge and expecting everyone else in the organization to do the same.

Knowledge management—a fledgling discipline dedicated to a more effective way of discovering, creating, and distributing knowledge within organizations—has fallen on hard times because of a fundamental problem. And although the collaborative database and groupware that underpins knowledge management can and will be improved, the technology is not what has relegated knowledge management to its present ineffectual status. The problem is that people prefer to hoard knowledge rather than share it. We have studied centuries of human organizations and have found that people are addicted to accumulating information, much as they are addicted to accumulating wealth and power. People have found little percentage in sharing information or giving it away. In most organizations, knowledge management initiatives shrivel in the face of unrecognized human aversion to sharing what is known to be true and, even worse for the organization, sharing what is known to be false. People will always share knowledge of victories before they share knowledge of where the bodies are buried.

Until the attitude of hoarding knowledge changes, knowledge management—and connectivity—will be limited. Fortunately, the more successful Net Ready companies, such as Cisco and AOL, have discovered that, unlike wealth or power, knowledge can be sold or given away and still be retained. Bits are persistent.

Net Readiness in the context of connectivity is a question of attitude. Attitude starts with the leader. So ask yourself some hard questions. Are you willing to share information with your subordinates? Are you willing to open the books to them? Why not? How about sharing information with your partners? Suppliers? Customers? Why not? What are you protecting? Do not assume that robust connectivity is without risks. Trust can always be abused, and extreme connectivity can be a threat to an organization without a keen sense of its own integrity. Our point is merely that Net Ready companies lean toward openness and consider the benefits of connectivity before they look at the downsides.

Because the downsides are obvious, let's take a closer look at the benefits of connectivity and of sharing the details of business with an ever-
widening range of long-term allies, aligned partners, and associates. The
best model we know for demonstrating these benefits is Silicon Valley,
where an environment of unabashed, almost over-the-top knowledge
management leads to a brazen set of benefits. Silicon Valley has evolved a
culture that, while supremely individualistic, acknowledges the critical importance of sharing information—the good, the bad, and the ugly—in as
near real-time as possible. The results are usually chaotic, sometimes
shameless, and often painful on a personal basis. But this connectivity has
generated the greatest concentration of Net Ready wealth in the history of
the world.

Coordination

The robustness of the relationships between E-business initiatives and
other entities across an enterprise's business channels helps determine a
company's Net Readiness. To create powerful win-win strategies, it is critical to have partnerships between emerging Net businesses and larger companies with established brand names. Exquisite coordination is required
for both sides to make explicit their objectives and contributions and to assign clear responsibilities within their networks.

Principles of Competencies

Operational competencies are key to an organization's ability to compete
in the Net Ready economy. Operational behaviors and norms are informed
by culture (see "Silicon Valley Competencies"). Net Readiness requires organizations to be competent in the following areas:

- *Have experience in managing multiple relationships.* Most complicated
  initiatives in the E-conomy require multiple partners, overlapping relationships, and concurrent development. Success requires critical capabilities in building, managing, and in some cases dissolving these relationships. Leverage relationships with partners so each can focus on its own
  core competence.

- *Be capable of dealing with rapid and ongoing change.* There's no resting
  on laurels in the E-conomy. All advantage is temporary advantage. The
  ability to respond, create, and manage change is an imperative.

- *Drive change quickly across the organization.* Every corner of the organization must be willing to abandon accepted and successful business practices in favor of something new.

- *Identify and prioritize E-business opportunities.* We emphasize throughout this book that there is a plethora of opportunities in E-business. A company's ability to identify and rapidly prioritize which opportunities to execute is critical. This competency is not an easy one to develop. Most companies take too long analyzing what is the right thing to do, and how to perfect the execution.

- *Be able to execute ruthlessly.* You must make meaningful changes in three months or less. You also must know when good enough is good enough. It's not executing ruthlessly to say a project is 70 percent done. Any project that requires more than three months to execute should be segmented into smaller chunks that can be completed in three months.

- *Be confident of having the operations capabilities and technical competencies to support Internet initiatives.* It's not all leadership and governance. Some workers have to do the heavy lifting, and they need specific skill sets to do it.

- *Know when to hold 'em and when to fold 'em.* A key competency is the ability to know when to kill projects. There's little room for loyalty in the E-conomy or in E-business projects. Build capabilities around identifying mistakes, putting an immediate stop to them, and then executing elsewhere. Know when to jump in and when to let go.

Silicon Valley Competencies

Competencies are inextricably linked to culture. Silicon Valley has evolved a cohesive set of competencies that support the biggest concentration of Net Readiness in the world. Attend to how it's done in Silicon Valley:

- *Failure is a badge of honor.* Somehow the Valley recognized that bankruptcy is no shame when you swing for the fence. Failure is a rite of passage and is recognized as the statistically unavoidable consequence of taking risks, to be neither scorned nor hidden.

- *Relish risk.* Swing for the fence and if you make it, you're on the cover of Fortune. If not, fold up the tent and try another team. Silicon Valley motto: If all else fails, you can achieve immortality by spectacular error.

- *Name it. Claim it. Let it go.* Never rest on your laurels. Net Ready companies are always looking down the road. If you come up with a cool idea, great. Milk it for a short while and move on while it's still hot. Mix your new idea with demonstrated pieces cobbled together from everywhere, and it's on to the next idea.

- *Show an exuberance for change.* An aversion for the status quo leads to constant self-cannibalization. The heralded quotations of the Valley reflect this truth: "Only the paranoid survive" (Intel's Andy Grove) or "We must obsolete ourselves or the competition will" (Hewlett-Packard's Lew Platt).

- *Call a spade a spade.* Stay as close to pure meritocracy as human organizations allow—you'll see no social promotions in the Valley. In general, enterprises there are so lean and things are moving so fast that there is no room for pretense, double-talk, or hiding out.

- *Be obsessed with speed.* Don't waste time on governance that doesn't add immediate value. Life cycles are measured in months. Don't reinvent the wheel; instead, use tested objects that provide functionality out of the box.

Technology

A key driver of Net Ready success in the area of technology is to build an architecture that is robust and comprehensive, one that enables organizations to rapidly develop and implement new E-business applications. With such a corporate-wide architecture, E-business leaders can easily and frequently deploy applications without having to justify the cost of incremental investments in infrastructure for every value-added initiative. E-business leaders who have such an infrastructure in place are in a much better position to launch initiatives rapidly and to exploit emerging opportunities. (Cisco Systems is a good example of a company that has embraced such a model of architecture. See chapter 8, page 237.)

To measure their Net Readiness along the technology dimension, organizations should be able to answer the following questions:

- Do we have standards across the enterprise?

- Can we buy it? (If so, don't build it.)
- Do we have the technological infrastructure (network services, hardware, software, security) required to develop and scale?
- What do we need to do to create a business-smart technology organization and a technologically smart business organization?
- Do we insist on simplicity, standardization, and flexibility in every corner of the E-business environment?
- Are the talents of the people across the enterprise optimally harnessed?
- Are our solutions flexible enough to accommodate change?
- Are solutions customizable to our customer's needs?

We cannot overstate the importance of having your enterprise infrastructure in place (figure 1-1). Once the architecture—networks, data security,

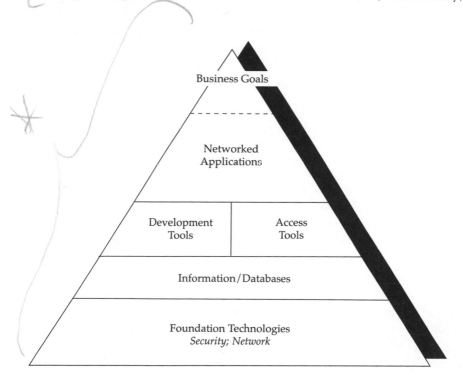

Figure 1-1. E-business Architecture. Net Readiness requires an architectural foundation that encompasses a standards-based, enterprise-wide technology platform, on top of which the organization can deploy a variety of value-added applications and networks.

databases—is established, choices about what technology to build on top of it become less critical. Traditionally, managers looking to the horizon have overemphasized the importance of the technology layer above the infrastructure. Tools, to be sure, are important, and without the right technology those companies most progressive in governance, leadership, and competencies will be frustrated in their progress.

We believe, however, that companies aspiring to be Net Ready should readjust their priorities. Don't get us wrong. Technology issues cannot be ignored. It's just that Net speed renders technology decisions—whether they are inspired or half-baked—irrelevant in no time. In other words, it's hard to make a bad technology decision because the technology has such a short shelf life. Consider the acquisition by the music site CDNow of its competitor N2K. The integration of the companies' incompatible technologies called for some hard decisions. Each company had built proprietary commence engines that could not be integrated. After evaluating the two systems, the company retained the CDNow architecture because it had a better database structure and would be more manageable and scalable as the site grows. This decision probably won't make a big difference to the company's strategic prospects in the long term. "On the Web the technology investments are so quick and so superficial, you can't make a wrong decision," says Mike Krupit, CDNow's vice president of technology. "You just pick something and move on. Two years from now, you're going to pick something different anyhow. Technologies aren't very long-lived in the dot com world."

If a company does not have a standards-based technology platform, Net Readiness becomes very difficult because the company's infrastructure needs to be redesigned for every application. With standards, organizations find it easier, cheaper, and faster to deploy new applications. Each step is easier because an established platform already exists, duplication is minimized, and scalability is promoted. It is cheaper because standards often improve reusability of modules. And it is faster because standards allow a business to adapt to changing business needs even as new technologies and changes in business process are more easily integrated enterprise-wide.

With some exceptions, Net Ready companies are always better off acquiring technology and process than developing it from scratch. By customizing existing packages or frameworks, organizations lower risks, save money, and gain time. It's the latter benefit that is the most compelling. The only exception to this principle is when new technology needs to be so tightly linked to an existing, closely held process that shoehorning in commercial alternatives would dilute the company's strategic advantage. (See chapter 7, page 213, for the discussion of Amazon's decision to develop its own auction technology rather than buy it.)

The most critical competency for any Net Ready company is to be business-smart in technology and technology-smart in business. You probably have an IT steering committee and processes for integrating IT with the rest of the business. Those steps are not enough. Senior managers of Net Ready companies carry on a lively debate about IT among both business and technical managers. What's essential is to make this debate subordinate to a strong business leader who welcomes the input of technical managers but who keeps all eyes on the prize: creating value for the business.

Organizations displaying high levels of Net Readiness insist on simplicity, standardization, and flexibility in every corner of the E-business environment. Plenty of companies preach standardization; few are able to make it stick. Net Ready enterprises drive simplicity and flexibility through every E-business project by setting architectural standards and closely scrutinizing the true costs and benefits of exceptions. They tackle complexity by reducing the number of technologies and platforms they deploy.

In the Net Ready world, it is true that soft stuff is really the hard stuff. What we mean is that the most challenging aspect of managing an organization, as most leaders know, is marshaling the will and talents of the ultimate software assets of an organization: its people. Winning the loyalty of a team, aligning its strengths with the mission of the organization, maintaining a sense of dedication, installing agreements about ethics and values, measuring the effectiveness of a team, compensating individuals appropriately: that's the hard stuff that keeps managers up at night. The task of developing or selecting and deploying the right technology, while difficult and challenging in its own right, is comparatively trivial.

Because managing the soft stuff is so hard and because efforts in this direction are so difficult to measure, managers have reflexively paid inordinate amounts of attention to aspects of management—deploying hardware and software, developing applications, creating tools—that are easier to articulate and measure.

Realize that the relationship of information technology to the Net Ready organization is critical. An organization's choice about technology raises complex issues about accommodating many governance models to ensure responsiveness to an organization's current and future strategic needs. Technology also addresses the role of the technology leader as enabler of the electronic network that holds together the many disparate parts of the Net Ready organization.

Access to Information

Net Ready organizations are witness to an irrevocable shake-up transforming the global economy. Regardless of what product or service they deliver, organizations participating in the E-conomy space are refocusing their efforts around access to information. Until a few years ago, most centralized organizations relied on access to capital and marketing to stimulate growth. Today, with the increasing emphasis on decentralized business units and with the rate of technological change in the global economy, technology and information have become as critical as capital, research and development, marketing, and other previous drivers of success. Companies that thrive and survive in this global marketplace will be information based. Billions of dollars and the survival of the company are on the line to a much more intense degree than ever before. Without immediate and accurate access to information, companies are more at risk for every decision that must be made.

Technology issues here converge with issues of governance. For at least the last decade, senior business and information systems executives have struggled with how to bring IT and business into closer alignment. As business needs multiplied and as the gap widened between the solutions IT offered and the business challenges facing managers, enlightened representatives of both camps redoubled their commitment to ending the disconnect. The ideal they have been striving toward is an alignment strategy that will optimize the provision of IT and service to the user community.

The focus of information systems has changed from automating internal (backroom) processes to enabling multifaceted mechanisms for directly delivering products or services to the customer. The increased complexity of these systems is compounded by the fact that many are used for competitive advantage, giving them life-or-death urgency. The central argument now becomes how to organize IT to achieve higher levels of competitive advantage.

With today's shorter product cycles, the old IT culture leads inevitably to large development backlogs and missed delivery targets. Corporate efforts to hold down total IT costs also are symptomatic of the old mentality and can be problematic, given strenuous business unit competition for available, sometimes even scarce, IT resources. Notwithstanding a greater melding of IT and business units, alignment efforts must maintain professional IT work and systems standards and allow IT professionals practical career options. If you can offer opportunity and technology together, you have a better chance of identifying competitive-advantage systems.

Companies that have internalized these new realities have substantially eliminated the disconnect between IT and corporate management. Whether these governance models are termed learning organizations, or virtual organizations, or something else, they promote opportunities to access and process information on global competitive intelligence, new product information, research and development, market trends, and environmental and regulatory impacts.

Principles of Technology

Even the best technology, by itself, is helpless to make a company Net Ready when the other elements of Net Readiness are missing. Yet without access to technology, Net Readiness is elusive indeed. In summary, Net Ready proficiency in technology requires organizations to adhere to the following principles:

- *Ability to build and drive standards across the enterprise.* These standards embrace all aspects of the infrastructure, including applications, network, and security. Create a ubiquitous, enterprise-wide connective and electronic publication model.

- *Demonstrated scalability.* Ensure that existing infrastructure (network services, hardware, software, security) is ready and can be scaled both up and down to meet emerging requirements.

- *Business-driven technological strategy.* Maintain an enterprise view of business and technology. Net Ready companies know what they need to do to create a business-smart technology organization and a technologically smart business organization (cohabitation, mutual accountability, and common management by objectives [MBOs] between IT and the business are critical).

- *Insistence on simplicity.* There are many pressures on organizations to move toward complexity, nonstandardization, and proprietary rigidity. Net Ready companies have learned to resist these forces. They often have what we call a "benevolent dictator." Someone in the organization (the CIO, perhaps) enforces simplicity (e.g., "You can use any database you want as long as it's ORACLE").

- *Human resources that are aligned with business goals.* Successful companies ensure that the talents of the people across the enterprise are optimally harnessed.

- *A mature build versus buy model.* A critical success factor is to overcome the "not-made-here" syndrome that prompts organizations to develop what they can more expeditiously purchase.

How Net Ready Are You?

To help companies determine the Net Readiness of their organization, we have developed the Net Readiness Scorecard or Internet Quotient (IQ). The Net Readiness Scorecard is designed to assess an organization's ability to migrate to an E-business world. It is comprised of a series of E-business statements mapped to the four pillars of Net Readiness. The term *e-business* applies to all Net-based business applications for businesses to businesses, businesses to consumers, businesses to suppliers, and businesses to employees.

We invite you to complete the simple version of this scorecard shown in table 1-3. This abbreviated version offers you a rough estimate of your organization's Net Readiness at the present time. Each statement in the scorecard asks you to agree or disagree on a five-point scale.

Table 1-3. Net Readiness Scorecard

Instructions:

For each statement, indicate to what extent you either agree or disagree that the statement is currently true of your organization. If you strongly disagree or disagree somewhat, circle 1 or 2, respectively. If you agree somewhat or agree strongly, circle 4 or 5, respectively. If you are neutral about the statement, circle 3. If you are not sure, just leave the item blank and go on to the next one. Good luck.

Scoring Key:

1	2	3	4	5
disagree strongly	disagree somewhat	neutral	agree somewhat	agree strongly

Leadership

Senior management is attuned to the opportunities/threats enabled by the E-conomy.	1 2 3 4 5
Our current E-business activities are well integrated with our business strategy.	1 2 3 4 5
Our organization exhibits a culture of enterprise-wide information sharing.	1 2 3 4 5

Table 1-3. Continued

Our organization has a published, well-accepted twelve-to-eighteen-month road map or journey for E-business success.	1	2	3	4	5
Our E-business efforts emphasize strategic/value creation rather than operational efficiencies.	1	2	3	4	5

Governance

Our organization has a standard administrative process for developing a business case for E-business initiatives.	1	2	3	4	5
We have established metrics for assessing the impact of our E-business initiatives.	1	2	3	4	5
We have clearly defined roles, responsibilities, accountability, and control for E-business initiatives.	1	2	3	4	5
We have staffed our E-business projects with the proper resources and incentives to reach our goals.	1	2	3	4	5
IT is viewed as an E-business partner that provides Internet consulting services to the business units.	1	2	3	4	5

Competencies

The enterprise is capable of dealing with rapid and ongoing change.	1	2	3	4	5
We exhibit ruthless execution when implementing E-business solutions (e.g., three to six people, three-month time frame).	1	2	3	4	5
Business management has Internet knowledge and IT has business knowledge.	1	2	3	4	5
We have experience managing multiple relationships (both internal and external) simultaneously and effectively.	1	2	3	4	5
We can form and dissolve relationships/partnerships quickly (building and managing an Ecosystem).	1	2	3	4	5

Technology

We have an established, standard IT infrastructure across the enterprise.	1	2	3	4	5
We have the necessary technological infrastructure (network services, hardware, security).	1	2	3	4	5
Our solutions are flexible enough to accommodate change (internal and external).	1	2	3	4	5
Our solutions are customizable to our customer's needs.	1	2	3	4	5
The vast majority of our new application development is E-business oriented.	1	2	3	4	5

Subtotals   – – – – –

Total Score   _____

Scoring

Add up the total point value of all the items you answered. In other words, every time you circled a 2, add two to your total. Every time you circled a 5, add five to your total. Add all your column subtotals together. The following scores suggest your organization's current level of Net Readiness.

(continued)

Table 1-3. Continued

Above 180:	*Net Visionary.* Your enterprise is displaying best-of-breed Net Readiness. Your E-business initiatives should be flourishing.
150–179:	*Net Leader.* The level of Net Readiness at your organization is impressive, but some important pieces are missing. This book should help you fill in the gaps.
120–149:	*Net Savvy.* Your organization displays a higher-than-average level of detachment from the issues and vocabulary of Net Readiness.
90–119:	*Net Aware.* Your organization is more Net Aware than Net Ready. Rethink the seriousness of your E-business effort. Major foundation work is required.
Below 90:	*Net Agnostic.* E-business is far from a concern of your organization. Whatever efforts you are undertaking will be fruitless. Better understanding of the impact of the Net and your role is required.

For a more sophisticated and accurate calculation of your organization's Net Readiness (IQ), you will find an electronically scored instrument on the Net Readiness Web site (www.netreadiness.com). The Web-scored version of this instrument gives you a more complete evaluation of your organization's ability to navigate the E-conomy. It is designed to help you profile your company's current state of Net Readiness and assess your Net Readiness relative to leaders within your industry, and it provides a prescriptive set of recommendations. A complete version of the Net Readiness Scorecard is also included in the appendix to this book.

2

Net Readiness Trends
Enabled by the E-conomy

This chapter explores eleven trends of Net Readiness. As these eleven drivers of the new economy converge, they redefine the very foundations of business behavior. The E-conomy makes the old rules of orderly processes, static measures of supply and demand, segmented pricing, and mass production null and void. In short, these drivers create nothing less than a framework for operating in the E-conomy.

Trends of Net Readiness

To date, the traditional economy has emphasized the manufacture and distribution of tangible goods and services. This emphasis on static attributes of supply and demand is changing faster than our ability to describe it. Nevertheless, let's try to articulate some of the strategic shifts the E-conomy imposes on those who would exploit it.

Every period of human history has been organized by sets of economic forces that have eventually yielded to new sets of forces. Before humans understood the principles of agriculture, for example, hunting-and-gathering economies dominated the world. The principles of hunting and gathering were simple and perfectly understood: people consumed what they hunted or gathered and then moved on. Economic planning, such as it was, restricted itself to considerations about the next meal.

Another example is the information era, which challenged the industrial age at some amorphous point in the 1950s. At first, the economics and assumptions of the industrial economy limited the possibilities of information processing. Computers were big and centralized, just like the mightiest machine tools of the day, and were locked in glass-walled rooms to do long division. The computers attacked back-office operations such as sorting and collating. They were administered by technicians with their own language who promoted the idea that computers were complicated and somehow dangerous, like a blast furnace or refinery. It was only with the personal computer (PC) revolution in the early 1980s that the information economy was put into the hands of end users who, taking advantage of "insanely great" tools, changed the world in an incredibly short period of time.

The Internet, finally, ties the industrial and information economies together to create the E-conomy, an environment with a brand new set of operating principles underscored by a whole new set of economic realities. The eleven trends of Net Readiness are:

1. Content and container: The value is in the migration
2. Processes are transforming from *simple* to *complex*
3. Industries are shifting from *static* to *dynamic* as products and services mutate from *tangible* to *intangible*
4. Customization: Constituents are becoming *less forgiving* and *more discerning*
5. Distribution channels are becoming more adaptable
6. New infomediaries are extracting value
7. In convergence, there is opportunity
8. Digitization: Separation of form and function
9. Informatization: Smart products are proliferating
10. Compression: Transaction costs are being reduced
11. Advantage is becoming more temporary

Content and Container: The Value Is in the Migration

The E-conomy creates exciting opportunities for those executives who recognize that the Net is transforming traditional concepts of products and services into new measures of economic value in terms of *content* and *containers*. Based on our experience with successful companies as well as with companies that have failed, we believe that success comes to those companies that understand the difference in adding value by providing *content* or by providing a *container.* We believe that if a company wants to create value in the E-conomy, it must provide a compelling argument for either the content or the container. Many successful enterprises offer both, but are specifically focused on offering them separately.

We have argued that the E-conomy operates by very different rules than does the industrial world that most companies are used to. Economies may be looked at from two key axes: *economic outputs* and *markets.* In the industrial marketplace, economic outputs were viewed as products and services; markets were viewed as a mass of people or customers onto which these products and services were pushed. Perhaps a Net Ready example would be of help here. If we apply these industrial-world definitions to, say, Hewlett-Packard, the economic outputs become test and measurement equipment or Laserjet printers. Under the old model, the economy postulates users (that is, the market) who are prepared to buy these outputs.

In the E-conomy, this type of relationship simply doesn't exist anymore. Customers in the E-conomy are becoming not only more empowered but also more granular from a segmentation standpoint. In the E-conomy, markets can be individuals, affinity groups, enterprises, and communities of interests (COINs). By the same token, our economic outputs become either containers or content.

The marketplace makes a clear distinction between content providers and container providers. Companies generally provide only one, and it can be quite traumatic for a company to migrate from one to the other. In the E-conomy, by contrast, the distinctions between the two strategic areas— content and container—are much more slippery and dynamic. The essence of competing in the E-conomy is a function of the nimbleness a company displays in navigating the relationship between content and container. Before we go too much further, let's pin these terms down.

The content, or the message: Information, data, experience, or knowledge that provides value or a framework for action.

A company that provides content is one that generates information, data, methods, knowledge, or wisdom in any form—print, broadcast, text, or multimedia. Content is value. In this book, we look at a number of content companies and how their business models operate.

The container, or delivery vehicle: The infrastructure by which content is transformed, accessed, delivered, or applied; community is built around that content, and commerce is enabled around that community.

Containers can represent products, services, transactions, industries, value chains, and many other entities by which value can be created in various business categories. Let's examine the content-container continuum in the context of Hewlett-Packard.

Although Hewlett-Packard may be best known for its printers and PC products, it is also a leader in the multi-billion-dollar test and measurement industry. The company manufactures some of the most highly regarded test and measurement devices in the world. In addition, it invites engineers and technicians to visit its Web site (www.hp.com) by providing a wealth of materials related to Hewlett-Packard offerings. The engineers and technicians have become the focal points for the company's Web site. Many engineers have bookmarked this site to learn more about Hewlett-Packard test and measurement equipment. Presumably they have also bookmarked the Web sites of Hewlett-Packard's principal competitors, most likely Tektronix. At this point, Hewlett-Packard's test and measurement products are best characterized as containers. These containers are useless unless filled up with content (test and measurement data and applications).

In figure 2-1, we locate Hewlett-Packard on the E-conomy map. There are no surprises. In its test and measurement market, the company has a business-to-business model. It is placed in the upper left quadrant because its equipment is squarely a delivery vehicle (container) for test and measurement functionality. As if in recognition of the fact that the company is a behemoth that needs to better present its value proposition in E-conomy terms, Hewlett-Packard is being broken up into separate organizations for computers, imaging, and test and measurement.

Hewlett-Packard is well positioned on the E-conomy map based on a traditional view of competition and competitors. Now let's see what happens when we place Test and Measurement Online (www.testandmeasurement.com) from VerticalNet's Electronics on the E-conomy map. Test and Measurement Online, a born-on-the-Web COIN, has positioned itself as the Internet's leading source of cutting-edge technical information about the test, measurement, data acquisition, data analysis, and instrumentation equipment industries.

Test and Measurement Online operates in the business-to-business model. Any engineer, designer, system integrator, or technician working in this field now has instant access to a comprehensive database that delivers the latest technical information on a wide variety of pertinent topics.

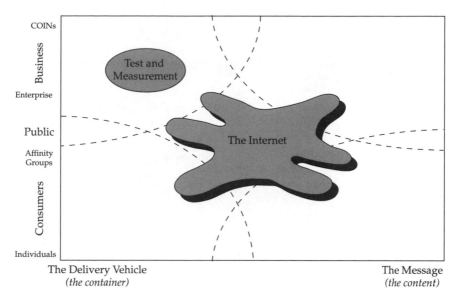

Figure 2-1. In the test and measurement market, Hewlett-Packard delivers test and measurement products in the form of containers in a business-to-business model. After buying the container, users must fill it up with data or applications to make it useful.

Clearly, Test and Measurement Online (TMO) functions as a content aggregator. For that reason, we position it on the content end of the E-conomy map (see Figure 2-2).

But Test and Measurement Online is not satisfied to remain just a content aggregator. It aspires to be a channel enabler, a force that exploits the Internet in new and creative ways. We discuss channel enablers in detail in chapter 7 (see page 217). At this point, the Test and Measurement Online Web site functions as a portal for the test and measurement community. By aggregating content, it offers standards, unbiased information, and one-stop shopping for test and measurement equipment. Moreover, VerticalNet has recently partnered with Onsale (a leader in online auctions and one of the few successful online businesses) to provide the commerce component of the COIN. In other words, Onsale is the commerce engine within VerticalNet, which provides business-to-business commerce for a wide set of industrial goods.

If such a Web presence did nothing else, it should provoke Hewlett-Packard and Tektronix into asking themselves some important questions:

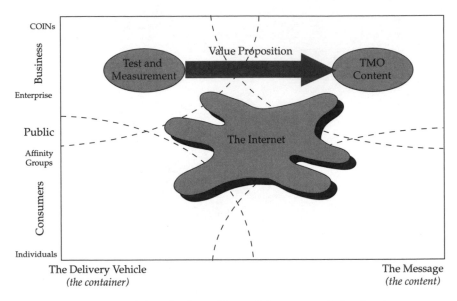

Figure 2-2. By one time-click in the future, Test and Measurement Online functions as a content aggregator in the test and measurement industry. Here the service leverages the functionality of the test and measurement boxes with value-added information and applications.

- Why should engineers visit a half dozen individual sites when they can get comprehensive, comparative information from one site and then conveniently get the equipment from one trusted source?
- How could such a model impact our business?
- Could this model impact our revenues or margins?
- To what extent will this model impact the way we come into contact with our customers?
- Should we build our own COIN based on the Test and Measurement Online model?
- Should we buy Test and Measurement Online and exploit it?
- Should we buy Test and Measurement Online and kill it?

But Test and Measurement Online is positioning itself in a way that is far more threatening than the diversion of some product sales from traditional sales channels to the Test and Measurement Online Web site. We believe that Test and Measurement Online will soon be in a position to provide what its name implies: the ability to actually deliver test and measurement services online. E-business and its ability to separate function from form could very well enable test and measurement transactions and functionality to be offered through a Web site. Imagine having the ability to obtain needed functionality without having to have a physical device (container) in the room. Imagine being able to obtain the necessary test and measurement functionality on a just-in-time basis completely divorced from a physical device. The impact on the test and measurement market space would be staggering. When test and measurement services can be offered on a virtual basis, what happens to

- Cost of goods sold?
- Distribution channels?
- Pricing models (pay per usage, renting, time-sharing, etc.)?

Such an event could very well rock the industry to the core. That is the result when a new channel enabler enters a market. In two time clicks from figure 2-2, Test and Measurement Online will have advanced to become the one-source experience for buyers and sellers in the test and measurement space (figure 2-3).

Currently, Hewlett-Packard controls the test and measurement market. But the E-conomy map foreshadows scenarios in which Hewlett-Packard may have to behave quite differently in order to maintain leadership. Locating an organization's E-business initiatives on the E-conomy map forces the company to ask itself critical questions:

- Where are we on the map?
- What value is there in migrating from one quadrant to another?
- What are our options?
- Should we sit back and see what happens?
- What competencies would we need to migrate?
- Who should we partner with to build such competencies?

Let's examine how other container companies are exploiting the opportunities in the map. Computer manufacturers have the right idea when they partner with online service providers to share the revenues from customers who are channeled to the online service provider through the com-

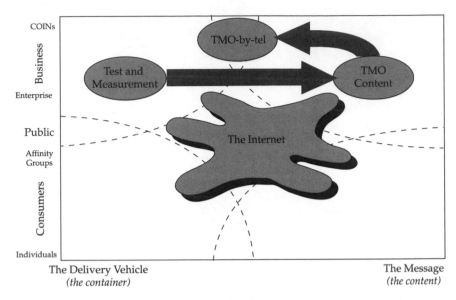

Figure 2-3. When Test and Measurement Online begins providing virtual test and measurement services (TMO-by-tel), its position on the E-conomy map shifts to the left because the company would offer both content and container.

puter hardware. In these cases, the online service providers share the wealth by giving the hardware maker a slice of the revenues that come from their users. The business model here is quite similar to the cellular phone business, in which the "box" is given away and revenue is made on the service. This process follows a clear migration from container to content.

Content and Container: What's the Difference?

Content and containers are another measure of economic value in the E-conomy. The traditional economy manufactured products that were either predominantly containers (machines such as printers or movie projectors) or content (value-added intelligence, such as Adobe print fonts, software, or videos). Without the added value of content, containers generally have little value. A printer is not useful without something to print; a movie projector is useless without a movie to project.

The E-conomy does away with this bifurcation, blurring the distinctions between containers and content and insisting that success usually requires plays on both sides of the equation. Companies in the E-conomy must take a hard look at themselves to see if they are participating in the container or content space. Then they must ask themselves if that's where they want to be. Maybe a content company can do better in the container space. Maybe a container company can add more value and reap greater rewards by becoming a content provider. In most cases, companies do not have to abandon one space to embrace another; they can often reap rewards by doing both well.

The key point is that although a container can be a tangible component, such as a PC or a microchip, its most valuable manifestation is as an intangible, a mechanism for delivering something of value, such as an application, an architecture, a channel, a platform, or an infrastructure.

Get the Message

Increasingly, the E-conomy favors companies who look for opportunities to migrate from one side of the E-conomy map to the other. Those who identify such opportunities can then hope to lock in success by innovating wildly and executing flawlessly. The point is that the E-conomy has a bias for action; it seldom rewards stasis. Moreover, although opportunities exist on both sides of the E-conomy map, most of the action seems to take place on the right side of the map. One reason for this shift is that margins for containers (delivery vehicles) are shrinking and containers are increasingly becoming commodity-like. PCs, for example, with their perpetually falling prices, are perfect examples of how the E-conomy treats pure containers.

Faced with deteriorating margins and more competition, what are PC manufacturers doing? To add value, PC manufacturers are adding content to their containers. But what kind of content? Should they bundle software with their machines? No, they are already doing that. The content to go after, PC manufacturers have concluded, is to bundle access to the Internet itself.

Processes Are Transforming from Simple to Complex

The E-conomy has no status quo. Every day is a new competitive arena, and the pace of change is now running at Internet speed. Table 2-1 shows the ways that internal business structures, industry boundaries, and cus-

Table 2-1. Customer Outcomes in the Marketplace versus the E-conomy

Notice the differences between the marketplace and the E-conomy in a number of dimensions important to the customer.

Marketplace	E-conomy
Marketing Messages	
Simple	Complex
Controlled	Open
Monologue	Dialogue
Distribution Channels	
Limited	Unlimited
Static	Dynamic
Velocity of Product/Service Development	
Slow	Fast
Methodical; linear	Continuous; version oriented
Evolution of Products and Markets	
Tangible	Intangible
Standardized	Customized
Emphasis on container	Emphasis on content and experience
Industry Boundaries	
Static	Dynamic
Owning	Leveraging
Competing	Partnering
Us against them	Us against us
Customer Expectations	
Forgiving	Discerning
Vendor driven	Customer driven
Broadcast	Interactive
One to many	One to one
Undifferentiated	Permission marketing

tomer outcomes and expectations morph when subjected to the vagaries of the E-conomy.

Industries Are Shifting from Static to Dynamic as Products and Services Mutate from Tangible to Intangible

By eradicating the distinctions between global and local, the E-conomy shifts industrial boundaries from the static to the dynamic. The result is global competition of a uniquely furious and unpredictable nature. Enterprises that formerly competed or partnered in different spaces now find themselves confronting each other.

The complicated relationship between Canon and Hewlett-Packard is an example of how the E-conomy creates complexity that threatens even the strongest of partners. For many years, Canon has manufactured the laser engines for Hewlett-Packard's laser printers. But now, Canon's copy machine business is threatened by Hewlett-Packard's marketing and product blitz aimed at replacing giant corporate copying machines with ubiquitous small printers. The effort is based on one terrifying insight (for copier companies like Canon) of the E-conomy: stand-alone copiers become a lot less useful when documents can be distributed by E-mail and turned into hard copies at a local printer.

In the same way, Kodak, the company that practically invented photography, missed the implications of Hewlett-Packard's networked printers. Kodak never registered Hewlett-Packard on its radar as a competitor in its core business of processing photographs. When it saw the way the digital winds were blowing, Kodak focused too much on the digital camera and missed the fact that what makes digital photography really come together is a system of products and networks that work together to take, store, manage, distribute, and display pictures, both on PCs and in familiar snapshot form. By the time Hewlett-Packard introduced its PhotoSmart printer, Kodak was too far behind to catch up.

This scenario should scare you because it will happen in whatever segment of the market you occupy. No longer can you monitor your explicit competitors. The E-conomy demands that you pay attention across a much broader spectrum of the competitive landscape. Paranoia has real survival value in the E-conomy because competition today is from anyone and everywhere.

E-conomy Ins and Outs

Out: Vertical Integration

Who cares about owning it? It's all about use and access. In the old days, it was about controlling a vertical supply chain. General Motors owned steel plants as well as iron mines and coal mines, all in a strategy to control every detail of the automobile manufacturing life cycle. And for a while, in a muscular, capitalistic way, the strategy even worked.

It's easy to own in good times. It's when the economy goes south that owning becomes problematic. Today, owning anything tangible just creates friction. You don't want it; you just want the rights to it. Part of Cisco's success stems from the fact that the company never touches 50 percent of the products it sells.

So outsource it. Negotiate rights. Partner. Owning it to take advantage of it is increasingly superfluous and often foolish because it frustrates nimbleness and consumes resources better applied elsewhere. Focus on your competencies and customer touch points, and outsource the rest. Formulating a business strategy specific to the E-conomy is key. Where, specifically, does your organization add value? How, specifically, does it touch the customers? Who, specifically, is in the same space, now or potentially? Only after you determine the answers to these questions can you make intelligent decisions about which processes are core competencies to be retained and which are available for outsourcing.

Then, once you have determined which competencies to outsource, comes the tough decision about whether to hand them off. When you outsource a process, you still have to maintain the competencies to manage the relationship and to dictate the rules of engagement with the outsourcing partner. Of course, the more you dominate an industry, the easier it is to do this. The less control you have, the easier it is for an industry leader to cut you out.

In: Horizontal Partnerships

We're talking linkages across the board, partnerships as quick to convene as disassemble. New strategy: define your core competencies and work side by side with the best partners you can find to exploit the fleeting opportunities the marketplace reveals. Then re-create yourself and your alliance structures to take advantage of the next impossible opportunity. The ability to recognize, exploit, and dissolve horizontal partnerships is an example of a new competency that companies will have to develop in the E-conomy.

Out: Physical Scale

Citibank's goal is to have more than a billion customers around the world and as few physical offices as it can get away with. This goal supports the argument that physical scale is becoming irrelevant when you can access the Net from anywhere. The E-conomy, however, can leverage physical scale in new ways. Barnes and Noble, for example, has one advantage over Amazon.com: its network of physical stores gives Barnes and Noble consumers an extra channel. Whether this advantage will translate into a meaningful competitive edge remains to be seen.

In: Network Scale

When you are part of a network, you can relax your grasp. Your power comes not from being strongly connected to any one resource but being loosely connected to many resources. Although the network can be global in scope, the elements of the network (that's you) can be specialized and limited, able to focus on core competencies, that is, the competencies required for the opportunity at hand.

Out: Hierarchical Organization

There's no room at the top of the pyramid for bloat. The buffers between executive decision makers and the contributors at the bottom are disappearing. Systems that link decision makers with the people closest to the customers—as well as the customers themselves—are the way to go.

In: Network Organization

Net Readiness requires that decision making be diffused from the top to the nodes closest to the customers and, in some cases, to the cus-

tomers themselves. Networks are the media for diffusing power because they are, at the same time, mechanisms for aggregating power.
The power of the networked organization is in the intersections between the nodes as much as in the nodes themselves.

The E-conomy today is filled with examples of the mutation of formerly
tangible products and services to intangible ones. The process is often so
seamless and natural as to be transparent. This mutation is as old as hu-
manity. At first there was barter, a mutual exchange of tangibles. Money,
with all the benefits of intangibility, quickly replaced barter. Today, electronic commerce is turning the country into a cashless economy. The
process, therefore, is hardly new, just accelerated. Here are just a few examples:

- *E-tickets.* You used to go to the travel agent and receive a paper airplane
  ticket that you would present to the boarding agent. Today, you visit a
  Web site and receive an E-ticket and a personal identification number
  (PIN) that lets you generate your boarding pass from a kiosk at the gate.
  Soon you will need just the PIN,

- *Software sales.* You used to distribute software on tangible diskettes or
  CDs. Increasingly, software is downloaded from Web sites.

- *Reference works.* You used to visit libraries to consult tangible reference
  works—encyclopedias, dictionaries, and so on. Increasingly, these resources are available online, where they are always accessible and always up to date.

Customization: Constituents Are Becoming Less Forgiving and More Discerning

Mass customization is the organizing principle of business in the E-conomy, just as mass production was the organizing principle of the traditional economy. Mass producers dictate a one-to-many-relationship. Mass
customizers take advantage of information technologies that create the
type of products and services that cannot be compared to a competitor's.
Why? Because these products and services are unique, the result of an ongoing, one-on-one dialogue with each of a company's customers. The results, as we will examine in more depth, often take our breath away. Dell,

for example, is a company that has a one-on-one relationship with customers, both companies and individuals, and builds only PCs that have actually been ordered. The range of possibilities for E-conomy entities built around customization are limitless.

Customization allows an organization the power to give every customer a unique view of the organization. Services such as "My Yahoo!" or "My eBay" allow each user to configure a unique relationship with the company based on the interests and desires of the customer. Literally millions of people have not only the illusion, but also the reality, of a customized encounter. A core theme of customization is the assumption that everyone should have the equivalent of a My Yahoo! across the spectrum of products and services. Consumers increasingly want more power to define what they consume. Every consumer strives to create a unique and custom-tailored point of encounter with the organizations that supply products and services for his or her personal consumption. In the E-conomy, every company should consider this concept as an invitation—no, a demand!—to create a "personalized" version of their product or service offering.

Almost every company leading in the E-conomy has created these kinds of customized silos of interactivity for its most important customers. Companies, whether they like it or not, will be forced to customize interaction with their key constituents. Every day, the incremental costs to customize unique encounters with a prospect or customer are getting smaller. Going after targets that were previously too low-volume suddenly starts making sense when the costs are so low. Customization of interactions in the E-conomy is no longer a luxury or even a nice-to-have; it's a must-have.

Why should you take a vitamin formulated for someone else? Now you don't have to. Acumin (www.acumin.com), a Web-based vitamin maker, blends vitamins, herbs, and minerals based on recipes selected by each customer, compressing up to 95 ingredients into a handful of pills. The result? A nutritional supplement that is just right for you as an individual. It harkens back to the days when pharmacists actually formulated compounds instead of just counting pills into bottles. To accomplish this customization, Acumin provides an online diagnostic test, dubbed Smart Select, to determine your needs. The questionnaire encourages you to state the particular health issues—fatigue, stress, high cholesterol, and so on—that you want to address through your personal formula. The company then matches your health needs with a unique mix of vitamins, minerals, antioxidants, and wonder workers, drawing from a group of nearly 100 components (and millions of potential formulas) to create the tailored pill offering.

The customer's formula changes over time to reflect expressed health needs and concerns—and those interactions only serve to strengthen loyalty. Of course, customers pay handsomely for customization—typically about sixty-five dollars per month (which is probably about the same amount many people pay for the different jars and bottles they assemble themselves from the health food store). However, customized products of this sort "engage customers extremely well," explain Acumin CEO Brad Oberwager. Should these customers defect, he adds, they would have to make a "conscious decision to buy an inferior product."

Customization is impossible without digitization. The E-conomy is ideal for creating customized catalogs that present visitors with an environment tailored to their specific needs and interests. One way to do that is to give individual visitors different interfaces based on their history at a site. For example, a purchasing manager who uses the catalog every day could handle a sophisticated set of tools, whereas a first-time visitor might need to be walked through the features. In addition to navigation aids, customized sites could provide visitors with a history of past purchases. Catalogs that associate visitors with their companies can support special pricing and other buying or promotional incentives.

The E-conomy has turned traditional one-to-many marketing on its head. As technology makes it affordable to track each customer, marketing shifts from finding customers for products to finding products for customers. This new mandate for business has been popularized as "one-to-one marketing" by Martha Rogers and Don Peppers in their book, *The One to One Future: Building Relationships One Customer at a Time* (Doubleday, 1993). The book argues that in the one-to-one future, sellers will use new technology to gather information about, and to communicate directly with, individuals to form ongoing, intimate commercial relationships. (For more information about Rogers and Peppers, visit their Web site at www .1to1.com).

That new, more intimate commercial relationship combines all real-time drivers—speed, value-chain integration, new infomediaries, permission marketing—to create fundamentally new relationships between traditional mass marketers and buyers. The best small businesses have always enjoyed one-to-one relationships with their customers. Did you ever have a neighborhood bookstore that took a one-to-one interest in its customers? "Good to see you. Did you enjoy that biography of Thomas Jefferson I recommended? Great. Then you might appreciate this new book on Churchill that I put aside for you." That kind of one-to-one interest makes any consumer feel special.

Traditional mass marketers (Crown Books, for example) identify a product (the best-seller list) and then try to find customers for that product (value-conscious buyers who respond to discounts). They aim for maximum share of a narrow market. But now, with the rapidly declining cost and increasing power of information processing, one-to-one marketers (such as Amazon.com or Barnes and Noble) are able to remember every detail of each transaction with each customer. Thus, such companies are able to offer tailored communications, personalized service, and mass-customized products.

One Customer at a Time

The catalyst for making one-to-one marketing possible is exquisite information about buyers' buying habits and preferences. Many privacy groups start to worry about such information being collected and disseminated. And they have a right to be. But such information already exists and is being used, generally without the consent of the buyer. There is often an adversarial relationship between sellers and buyers in the traditional economy.

In the E-conomy, good one-to-one marketers become jealous guardians of their customers' privacy. Unlike mass marketers who see the value of a name only as part of a list that can be sold, a one-to-one marketer understands that the most valuable thing he or she can produce is a customer and information about that customer. United Airlines recognizes that its crown asset is its database of information about its MileagePlus and credit card customers. It will treat this information gingerly.

That's not to say United won't share its information. It will. It will share information about buyers' preferences and desires in an attempt to package goods and services of interest to individuals. But sharing information doesn't mean that the company has to share the *identity* of its buyers. By partnering with many organizations, United can create targeted offers from a variety of companies. If a company doesn't have what a buyer needs, it can scout among other companies and, without ever giving away names and addresses, find what's there and package it for sale.

Customization is not without risk. If you don't do it perfectly, customers will defect, and they will never come back. On the upside, customization eliminates customer sacrifice—the compromise that consumers make when they settle for less than what they need because it's the closest they can get. Customization offers consumers the possibility that they can get their automobiles, computers, clothes, eyeglasses, vitamin pills, CDs, books, and anything else exactly how they desire. The downside of customization is that when you are making units of one, there is zero margin for error. Customer expectations cannot be higher, and returned merchandise, precisely because it is designed for a market of one, is a total loss.

The E-conomy has created a growing class of consumers addicted to the thrill of being able to get perfect products, perfect service, and perfect information almost as a matter of course. Customers increasingly expect perfect service and products delivered instantly. Today, E-business storefronts are called on to deliver a level of service that until a few years ago was considered impossible. Now that service is routine, and woe be to those companies who cannot keep up.

The E-conomy shifts the balance of power from sellers to buyers. Buyers are increasingly calling the shots, from telling sellers what their products are worth to dictating the way the sellers format their catalogs. Most of all, consumers expect to be presented with the highest levels of operational excellence. They insist on being treated as valued partners, as discerning members of a community in which they have a right to be well informed. The reciprocal of being more demanding is being less forgiving. Customers become less forgiving of sellers who, by virtue of execution or philosophy, do not embrace the new customer-driven model.

Each new level of achievement in delivering products and service simply raises the bar. E-conomy customers quickly become impatient if the execution of a commercial transaction is not absolutely flawless. Discerning customers have a low threshold for anything that hints of sloppiness or exploitation. For many years, customers have heard the lip service that they were valued. In the E-conomy, customers believe it, and they expect to redeem that value.

E-conomy Ins and Outs

Out: Seller-Centric Economy

Organizations have always employed technology to lower the cost of traditional sales processes. But the emphasis was always on making transactions slicker for sellers. That emphasis is changing. Technology now aids the buyer—and any seller who disputes this point will soon understand how less forgiving and more discerning buyers behave. It's not pretty. Just look at the gnashing and wailing among travel agents, even among E-conomy travel agents. In a bid to control Internet ticket sales, the airlines are cutting commissions and restricting the number of tickets that travel agents can sell. They are succeeding. In the last two years, U.S. carriers have more than doubled their share of online ticket sales, from 21 percent to 48 percent, according to the Internet Travel Services Association.

In: Buyer-Centric Economy

Buyers occupy the driver's seat in the E-conomy. Customers want solutions any time and any place; if not now, they will go elsewhere. Companies that accept this fact work to tighten the relationships with existing customers by having iterative dialogues with them in an attempt to empower buyers. Companies embracing the buyer-centric model have developed a number of ways for doing business in the E-conomy, each focused on the buyer.

Distribution Channels
Are Becoming More Adaptable

The E-conomy is driving a revolution in distribution channels and corresponding channel management strategies. We call it channel mutation. In the traditional model, distribution channel strategies were commonly organized and implemented based on market size, geography, or applications. Product and service suppliers designed and attempted to control the lowest-cost path of least resistance to reach their target markets. Buyers were forced to accept whatever channels relevant products and services were pushed into.

At the same time, suppliers had to make significant investments in new channels in order to gain uncertain access to potential buyers in new markets. The cost of establishing such new channels, given the uncertain returns, was enough to dissuade many entrepreneurs. A rigidity was imposed on the market because many competitors found the cost of entry to be prohibitive.

The E-conomy changes both sides of the equation. Not only will the E-conomy reduce the costs of establishing new channels, it will increase

the certainty of making sales because customers willingly identify themselves as prospects. By allowing customers to pull on the channels they
want and even create new channels that better suit their needs, the E-conomy will redefine the relationship between buyers and sellers. In this
sphere, sellers attempt to develop and support a rich and varied system of
distribution options in order to offer the greatest number of E-conomy interfaces to customers. There are countless access points to customers, and
accessing microsegments is now possible using cut-and-paste E-conomy
development tools. The infrastructure is in place. The most successful suppliers make it easy for a broad range of third parties to bundle, augment,
and resell their products and services, often with only a one-time, ad hoc
distribution agreement.

Key Questions

- What are the implications of customization for your business?
- Where do you fit in the value chain?
- What is your channel equity?
- Who controls the dominant share of channel equity?

Companies such as Hewlett-Packard, 3M, Mead, and Microsoft, for instance, independently encourage Staples, the office retailer, to assemble its
Web site from elements of their own sites. In this context, infomediaries
are organizations that embrace and extend the distribution system by
bundling the offerings of various suppliers into total solutions designed for
their own targeted customers. Some infomediaries bundle products (such
as office supplies), while others focus on specific office supply products
(such as laser printer cartridges). Sellers leverage this E-conomy channel
strategy so that their products have a presence or link to every logical Web
site that a prospect might encounter. The most successful suppliers have
positioned this new strategy so that traditional distributors see their participation as an opportunity for partnership instead of a threat.

The pull of many previously underserved markets creates opportunities
for a wide array of specialized resellers and value-added service providers.
These new infomediaries address microsegments that manufacturers might
never have identified, understood, or been able to reach. Suppliers acknowledge the value of their merchandising and logistics expertise. Soft-

ware supports the redistribution of goods and services through these new buyer-defined channels while maintaining the terms, conditions, and pricing set by the original manufacturer and all the infomediaries in the channel. One of the greatest challenges for suppliers is deciding which segments to support and which to outsource and let others manage.

New Infomediaries Are Extracting Value

One of the most durable myths of the E-conomy is that the Web systematically eliminates all intermediaries by squeezing out of the economy the inefficiencies that third parties such as brokers now exploit. Disintermediation, a nice piece of jargon, refers to the eradication of a layer or function that exists between two other layers or functions. There's just one problem: it's not going to happen, at least not in the way some experts believe. Although some intermediaries may disappear, the very nature of the Web opens up new niches to add value. Companies quick and agile enough to detect opportunities in complex markets will prosper as infomediaries. The new niches that are created are part of what we call the value web. If you can find a niche, you can be a storefront in a new value web.

Wait a minute, you say. What about all those celebrated examples of disintermediation that you've read about in *Business Week?* Doesn't Amazon.com eliminate the layer between consumer and bookseller? The answer is an unequivocal no. Amazon.com has changed the way certain segments of the market consume books, but what you see is a new channel replacing old channels, not disintermediation. Amazon.com is a perfect example of how the Web has added another value-added retail channel. Real disintermediation occurs when Viking, McGraw-Hill, or Random House start making a major effort to sell their books directly to consumers. Although it's possible to order books directly from the Web sites of publishers such as McGraw-Hill or Prentice-Hall, the orders are processed through an intermediary, a book distributor that is transparent to the buyer but is nevertheless an intermediary. Similarly, Amazon.com uses a book distributor to fulfill its distribution services. Amazon.com offers customers many compelling benefits, but those benefits are not in the area of disintermediation.

Today's intermediaries are on a tightrope. They can either take advantage of the space they currently occupy, or they lose. Travel agencies, for example, were supposed to be squeezed out by the Web, but most consumers still prefer to deal with a intermediary rather than to negotiate directly with airlines, hotels, cruise ships, car rental companies, and so on. The real issue, though, is this: Will consumers be willing to pay for the services of intermediaries? And if so, can the intermediaries adjust their cost structures to keep their business models viable?

Let's face facts. The business models of the online and brick-and-mortar travel services are identical. In both cases, a robust value-added channel sits between the customer and the actual service provider. Although both United Airlines (www.ual.com) and American Airlines (www.americanairlines.com) can now make unsold seats available on their Web sites, they have always sold tickets directly to customers. What's new is that their sales model is shifting from the airline ticket office or telephone to the Web. That shift is good for the connected customer because it reduces costs, but it's not disintermediation.

The automobile dealer has become a dinosaur now that Autobytel.com lets you purchase a car on the Internet, right? Not as long as there's an established automobile dealer network. Autobytel.com is a lead broker, and a good one, taking advantage of the inherent information discrepancies in the auto industry. It has carved out a lucrative niche to bring car buyers and sellers together, but the transaction is still between the customer and the car dealer. Autobytel.com eliminates some tire kicking and price haggling, but General Motors, Ford, and Chrysler tread gingerly so as to avoid antagonizing their main sales channel, the dealers.

The E-conomy is starting to shake up the ties between the Big Three automobile manufacturers and their independent dealers. Ford, for example, is experimenting with a Dell-like model in which consumers can "build" the car of their choice (body style, motor, interior, color options, etc.). Ford would then manufacture the car for that individual consumer and deliver it via a convenient dealer. But while Ford dealers may be gratified to take commissions for transactions to which they add no value, they should ask themselves this question: If Ford can take orders directly, what's to stop them from delivering the product directly?

As *Net Ready* went to press, Microsoft announced a joint venture that melds its CarPoint online automotive service with the resources of leading car manufacturers, led by Ford Motor Co. The new entity—which continues to be called CarPoint—has pledged to develop the automotive industry's first online build-to-order car-buying system that directly links consumers to manufacturers. Open to all makes and models, the system will let consumers purchase various brands of cars built to their precise specifications, at a variety of Web sites, beginning with CarPoint.com and Ford.com. This tentative step still preserves the role of the dealer. But if a consumer can customize a car online, price it online, and use the Web to direct the factory to manufacture it, how soon will it be before the manufacturer starts asking, Why are we letting the dealers take a cut of the action?

Lubricate the Spaces in the Value Chain

The lesson is, if you want to compete in the E-conomy, occupy a niche that, through the use of information-rich interactivity, lubricates the space between a customer's requirements and available products or services. Buyers and sellers are more than willing to pay for value-added services that eliminate the channel noise or friction that keeps a transaction from being completed. Such success is available more to new infomediaries, designed specifically to exploit opportunities as they develop. Existing infomediaries are always at the risk of being made irrelevant by incessantly innovative enterprises offering to provide for free what used to be provided for a fee. If you don't understand when the currency changes, you are out of business. For example, companies that offer electronic mail services for a fee (e.g., Prodigy) have been squeezed out by organizations that provide E-mail at no cost (e.g., Geocities). These new companies have calculated that the value of securing "eyeballs" (attention that advertisers will pay for) exceeds the potential revenue of a traditional Internet service provider.

Anyone standing between producers and consumers needs to move up the food chain, or the risk of being disintermediated is total. Any entity that occupies the space between a customer and an information appliance that can fully meet a customer's requirements will eventually be out of a job. On the other hand, the picture is not totally bleak for intermediaries. If they understand the space in which they operate and can add value to customers, they can squeeze respectable profits out of such opportunities. However, third parties who only provide fulfillment capabilities had better be prepared to change their business model and develop competencies that enable them to move toward value-added services and support.

Thousands of telephone operators were disintermediated when the public switching network allowed consumers to dial their own phone numbers. More recently, bank automated teller machines (ATMs) make it possible for customers to take on the work—getting cash, checking balances, shifting funds from one account to another—formerly handled by bank tellers. Automation such as voice response systems and the public switching telephone system eliminated tens of thousands of intermediaries.

Nor are unskilled workers the only ones at risk. Knowledge workers formerly insulated from the march of automation are no longer secure. Levi Strauss, for example, has a process that takes precise computer measurements of the customer to create perfect-fitting jeans. Using the Internet, retailers transmit that information directly to the factory, where automated systems manufacture a custom-designed pair of jeans for a perfect fit. What's missing here? The skilled tailor is no longer in the picture. Also disintermediated is an entire value chain of store buyers, inventory workers, stock clerks, and other functions, because the customer's needs can be fed directly to the production worker who can meet that need without intervention. This trend is true for both consumer markets and enterprise markets.

These new infomediaries are emerging in almost every industry. Take, for example, the electronic components distribution business. Companies like Arrow and Avnet have traditionally dominated the market. However, new players like NetBuy and Fastparts are trying to subtly penetrate this market. We see this happening in markets that exhibit certain of the vulnerable characteristics that we described in our introduction: high fragmentation, digitizability, inefficiency, asymmetries of information between buyers and sellers. Companies must become cognizant of these elements; they must ask themselves where in their value chain (upstream or downstream) do some of these opportunities exist, either for them or someone else?

In Convergence, There Is Opportunity

Convergence describes the phenomenon in which two or more existing technologies, markets, producers, boundaries, or value chains combine to create a new force that is more powerful and more efficient than the sum of its parts. Convergence is not a new dynamic; it has been going on as long as human beings have been developing and refining technologies, roles, and markets. We can discern at least three general areas of convergence that are of interest to the E-conomy: technology and infrastructure, information appliances, and markets and economic partners.

Convergence of Technology and Infrastructure

For the first time, the various components of the infrastructure of the E-conomy have converged to create the World Wide Web. This convergence gives users reasonable confidence that messages will get through the various nooks and crannies of the Internet and that all information appliances—notebook computers, personal digital assistants, cell phones, fax machines, and so on—are able to participate. The critical thing to remember is that it's less the reality of the situation than the perception that gives impetus to the convergence. The convergence of voice and data, for example, represents one of the most world-shaking transformations. Today, the country's switched telephone networks carry a mix of voice and data in roughly equal proportions. Within five years, the data and video loads will represent 99 percent of all network traffic. Voice will make up an increasingly marginal piece of the bandwidth.

Convergence is occurring faster than the ability to manage it. More than half of all CIOs expect reliable convergence of voice, data, and video on their networks within the next three years according to a survey by *CIO Magazine*. The CIOs point to universal messaging services that integrate voice and E-mail as an example of disciplined convergence. The movement away from traditional circuit-based, voice-driven networks and toward data-driven, packet-based networks best illustrates the opportunities presented by convergence. But what's driving this convergence? Are the key drivers behind it applications such as multimedia and voice-over Internet Protocol (IP)? Or is convergence more an infrastructure play than an applications play, a desire to reduce infrastructure costs and maximize the productivity of IT operations? The answer to this fundamental question determines strategy for an organization ambitious enough to exploit the convergence.

Value-chain migration, as a strategy, supports the development of real-time systems that integrate supply-chain systems and customer-facing systems, so that the whole value chain is a single, integrated process. Integrated E-conomy systems improve the ordering, configuration, and manufacturing processes by controlling the cascade of parts orders, assembly schedules, shipper notifications, and related financial transactions. Knowledge gained from an integrated and complete view of the value chain allows suppliers to make informed decisions about where to invest and where to outsource.

Convergence of Information Appliances

Businesses have always benefited from the convergence of information appliances. This book is a result of the convergence of movable type printing and papermaking. Today, the union of several information appliances are giving birth to more sophisticated devices, which in turn will drive the convergence of people, processes, and networks. These appliances will become the ATMs and point-of-sale devices of tomorrow. They will allow users to access information, conduct electronic transactions, authenticate identities, and perform other functions undreamed of today.

The outcome of any significant convergence is never fully predictable. People sometimes believe that convergence operates by combining technology A with technology B and getting some hybrid that has some reasonably obvious elements of both. But that's not the way convergence works. When the technologies of the automobile and road building converged to create the interstate highway system, no one could have predicted the massive social disruptions—from fast food to population shifts—that a mobile society created. In the same way, when the technologies of radio and cinema converged to create television, no one could have predicted the unifying and disconnecting forces that are not fully understood today. The law of unintended consequences has a field day whenever significant technologies converge.

Convergence of Markets and Economic Partners

Ask IBM executives to name their competition in the PC business, and the answer will most obviously be Dell, Hewlett-Packard, Compaq. Competition in the E-conomy, however, becomes much more complicated because of the convergence of markets enabled by E-business. How could IBM executives anticipate that Wal-Mart would partner with a Korean original equipment manufacturer (OEM) to provide PCs that are built to order and sold directly to consumers? Convergence is happening in most industries and will continue to happen. We see it in financial services, networking, and many other areas. Changing the way you look at competition and competitive threat is key to navigating the E-conomy.

Rational markets, in which many suppliers act on these insights, become more efficient and more uniformly profitable. Customers benefit from the lower costs that result from more efficient ordering, lower inventories, less expensive supplies, and improved quality. Electronic commerce technologies emerging in the E-conomy have empowered buyers who "pull" on channels. This pull creates new micromarkets—a process of mass channel customization. In order to offer the greatest number of contact points with customers, sellers are then forced to develop a presence in as many network locations as possible. Suppliers win by allowing (and often even encouraging) any network reseller to represent their products. New infomediaries emerge by providing total solutions to these new micromarkets. For example, book sites such as Amazon.com and music sites such as CDNow (www.cdnow.com) and Liquid Audio (www.liquidaudio.com) strive for a conspicuous billboard on as many different Web sites as possible, each one representing a potentially lucrative point of entry.

The melding of previously unrelated technologies, products, and information to create compelling new products and services also underscores the concepts of container and content. In the traditional economy, offerings have either been predominantly containers (physical objects such as printers or cameras) or content (value-added intelligence such as software or film). Convergence increasingly means that products in the E-conomy combine the attributes of both content and container in novel ways to create new value chains. To make convergence work for your company, you face a triple task. First, you have to decide if your offering currently functions more as container or content. Often this decision is not as trivial as it sounds. Second, you must consider how you can add content to the containers you are offering. Third, if you decide you are in the content business, you must see what additional infrastructures you might provide to add value to existing content. Being conscious of the eleven themes described in this chapter will help you conjure up combinations of container and content that create real value in the minds of your customers.

Digitization: Separation of Function and Form

In the simplest sense, digitization refers to representing content in ones and zeros, the language of computers. But the ability to represent content—text, video, audio, images—in this way opens up the door to unprecedented opportunities. Digitization and the other themes enabled by the Internet collectively bring society into a culture of speed (compression), into marketing to units of one (customization), and into a brand new world that blends products and services (informatization).

Digitization by itself is not very useful. Only when it is combined with one of the other themes does it create value. For example, customization is impossible without digitization. Once customer information is digitized, it is ready to be put into a database, sorted, and broadcast over the Internet. The Internet makes it possible for companies to move data from an online order form to the factory floor.

The biggest implication of digitization is how it enables the separation of form from function. Separation of function and form involves the delivery of function by different means. As we pointed out in our discussion of Test and Measurement Online earlier in this chapter, separating the functionality of a value chain from its physical representation creates enormous opportunities. We describe many similar opportunities in subsequent chapters, but let's look at one more example here. By digitizing most aspects of its quality assurance processes, Cisco has successfully virtualized the testing of its components so that neither Cisco engineers nor test equipment needs to be physically present to conduct or supervise the testing. By digitizing the testing process, Cisco saves money and compresses the delivery cycles. (For more about Cisco's Autotest and how it separates form from function, see "Separate the Function from the Form," page 172 in chapter 5.)

Digitization enables service companies to separate the functions of their services from their traditional forms, creating new markets and opportunities in the process. For example, Computer Associates International (www .cai.com), like most large software companies, has a business unit that delivers professional consulting services such as systems implementation. Until recently, all such engagements required consultants to deliver the services on site, which entailed costly travel expenses and per diems. But with an appropriate infrastructure in place and after some initial goal-setting discussions, consultants have no compelling reason to be on site. In a bid to use the Net and associated technologies to separate function from form, Computer Associates' Global Professional Services implemented Remote Deployment Services. As with an on-site deployment, Remote Deployment Services provides all the project management and the planning and implementation materials to help ensure an effective system rollout. The only difference is that services are delivered digitally. Beginning with a comprehensive teleconferenced evaluation, implementation consultants guide clients through a project's planning stages. After successful connectivity testing, the software is installed throughout the client's network using Computer Associates' remote control and software deployment technologies.

Sea-Land Service (www.sealand.com), the largest U.S.-based ocean carrier and a leader in the global shipping industry, used Computer Associates' Remote Deployment Services through its network backbone in the United States to deploy a strategic networking system in regional data centers in Ireland and the Philippines. Sea-Land operates a fleet of ninety-four container ships and more than 220,000 containers and serves 120 ports in eighty countries and territories; it operates the most technically advanced terminal operations around the globe. "We were able to accomplish a ten-day task in three days by offloading planning, testing, and installation tasks to Computer Associates while eliminating unnecessary travel expenses," said Leslie Rowland, manager of technology architecture at Sea-Land. "This accelerated our rollout, enabled our global employees to concentrate on strategic priorities, and ensured we got the most value out of our software and staff investments."

On the consumer front, the Borders bookstore chain is looking to the magic of digitization combined with customization to help it squeeze more value out of its brick-and-mortar retail operations. By taking a stake in the digital book wholesaler Sprout, Borders hopes to be able to offer buyers the ability to print books on demand inside stores. Sprout's technology keeps books on computer files, which are then sent to printers to produce single copies of perfect-bound, paperback titles as customers request them. Just-in-time printing will benefit Borders by reducing the cost of storing and shipping books for publishers and retailers, increasing the number of titles immediately available for sale, lowering the threshold for keeping slow-moving titles in print, and eliminating the risk of returns. That's good for both Borders and its customers, but it means some risk, too. The risk is that just-in-time books bring into sharp relief a couple of obvious scenarios that ought to give all retail bookstores pause. First, what if 7-Eleven decides to install printing kiosks in its 20,000 convenience stores? Better yet, what's to stop Kinko's copy shops from horning in on the action? Thanks to KinkoNet, the company already has a Net Ready infrastructure in place, complete with the necessary high-speed printers. Second, if books can be printed on demand at a stand-alone kiosk or even in a consumer's home, what exactly remains for a bookstore to offer?

Unlimited Copies without Noise

Digitization changes the entire concept of copies. In the E-conomy, copies are virtually free and indistinguishable from the original. The implications are staggering.

Before we look at some of these implications, let's take a step back and consider the tyranny of copying in the traditional economy. In the marketplace, copies are expensive, often as costly as the original. Copying in the traditional, analog marketplace is also inefficient. Every time you photocopy a document, the copy deteriorates. The copying process adds noise.

We all know that a photocopy of a photocopy is often unreadable. The same is true of analog copies of recorded music. Quality degrades with every generation.

But with digitization, copies can be made on an unlimited basis. What's more, each copy is free or nearly so. Thus, the first copy of Windows 98 might have cost Microsoft $500 million, but the cost of every copy after that is the expense of the packaging. When a consumer downloads software from the Microsoft Web site, the incremental costs to Microsoft are insignificant.

Digitization creates enormous social and legal issues in terms of intellectual property and copyright law. The E-conomy has to come to terms with these issues. But the economic forces enabled by digitization are so powerful that an understanding of its implications is critical to success in the E-conomy.

Informatization: Smart Products Are Proliferating

Call it penetrating intelligence. If you can't find a way to add "smartness" to your products, your competitor will. In the E-conomy, products are "informated." Technology is embedded in and around products in ways that facilitate a steady stream of information about transactions and the use to which products and services are put. With most network software, customers turn features on or off depending on their preferences. The product itself is a primary interface between the end user, the manufacturer, distributors, and other parties with whom the customer wants to communicate.

Informatization streamlines troubleshooting of complex systems. If you think you have a problem fielding customer complaints, consider the case of Greenville, S.C.–based Hartness International (www.hartness.com). The company's products, case packing machines, do the workhorse job of crating assembly-line bottles in preparation for shipping. If a Hartness case packer falters, an entire production process grinds to a halt, costing clients thousands of dollars an hour. Hartness has responded to this predicament by anticipating customer needs and providing enhanced service. The company has created a Video Response System, a wireless camera product that can transmit detailed images from anywhere on a plant floor back to Hartness service technicians. This bit of common sense—using videoconference technology to respond immediately to technical problems—required imagination and the help of Picture Tel (www.picturetel.com) to implement. Now, when machines malfunction, on-site customer technicians guided by Hartness advisors fix 80 percent of glitches.

Hartness's innovation is an example of smart field service in the E-conomy. Customers are now engaged in an intimate dialogue with Hartness. The company has expanded its customer share by providing more products to each one. And the company has locked in loyalty simply by making it easier to depend on its products. The video system has even become its own business, Hartness Technologies, which attracts customers outside the bottling industry, such as Hewlett-Packard and Chrysler. The program is a good example of how a company can expand a customer's requirements by moving beyond its core product to enhanced services.

Suppliers now are able to spend considerably less on staffing for help desks, technical support, and customer service while actually improving customer satisfaction. New digital systems that collect, analyze, and respond to product usage and performance data replace the old analog systems. Regular information related to a specific customer's usage patterns signals the need for routine service, support, or replenishment of consumables. In-depth performance analysis can reveal the need for upgrades, reconfigurations, or advice on how to improve performance. In addition, new knowledge and insights from aggregate performance data can be used to help design the next generation of the product. In this way, customers are relieved of many common issues related to product use, such as determining when to replace parts, remembering to order consumables, and attempting (most often unsuccessfully) to improve product performance. Perhaps the most valuable benefit of smart, networked products is that they're rarely down or suboptimal.

How Much Carfare Do You Have? Check Your Watch

It's a case of convergence—fashion meets function. Schlumberger Ltd. and Swatch have launched a new watch that packs a smart card payment system for public transit fares. The two companies collaborated to produce the contactless, electronic-ticketing watch, which is now on the market and being used in Finland.

The watch, called Swatch Access, comes in four designs and is sold at Swatch outlets in Finland and through transit authorities. The watch incorporates the same electronic chip that is used in Schlumberger's Easypass contactless smart cards. To use the watch, a passenger pays a given amount of money to the transit authority, which stores that sum on the watch's smart card. The cost of the ride is then automatically deducted from the value stored on the card as passengers pass through an electronic turnstile. Eventually, the watch could be used as a multipurpose electronic purse in which stored value could be used to pay for newspapers, telephone calls, beverages, or other low-value items.

Products that communicate with manufacturers or infomediaries, also known as smart products, will improve performance, reduce costs, and promote revenues. The most obvious example of the proliferation of smart products is the pace of embedded computer chips in virtually every device in people's lives. Most people are well aware of the role of embedded computer chips in automobiles. Today, the dollar value of a car's smart electronics is overtaking the value of its steel body. Consumers know that chips inhabit electronic gear such as microwave ovens and stereos, but embedded chips also proliferate in such ubiquitous appliances as elevators, air conditioners, garage door openers, hotel door locks, ATMs, refrigerators, and soft drink machines. Let's take a closer look at these smart products. What do they have in common? They all use the Net as a collaborative platform to deliver value by automating or eliminating routine, manual processes.

Smart Hotel Locks

The idea that all doors in a hotel should contain a computer chip seemed ludicrous ten years ago, but now even rooms that rent by the hour have doors with blinking, beeping chips. If National Semiconductor has its way, every Federal Express package will be stamped with a disposable silicon flake that smartly tracks the contents. Bar codes add value, but bar codes are dumb; they speak in one-word sentences and don't listen at all. The proliferation of smart products means that all manufactured objects, from videotapes to running shoes to flashlights to packages of children's cereal, will have embedded in them a tiny sliver of intelligence connected, via an IP-appliance, to the Net.

Smart hotel locks should make it possible for executive road warriors checking into their hotel rooms late at night to use their credit card to open the door. If the door lock is a node on the hotel's reservation system, the same credit card used to guarantee payment for the room should be able to open it. The benefits of adding intelligence to this process eliminate the frustrating step of registering and physically taking possession of a key. The system has a number of privacy and security issues to be worked out, but we believe that this sequence of events is inevitable.

Smart ATMs

Everyone uses ATMs and the machines seem pretty smart, but most ATMs are as intelligent as Tupperware. As ATMs become commodities, financial institutions have an incentive to differentiate one ATM network from another. Perhaps the best way to garner customer loyalty is to deliver an ATM that learns. Say you use an ATM every week. You always prefer to get instructions in Spanish, you always make a deposit to checking, always get $60 in cash, always transfer $500 to savings, and always check the balance of both accounts, printing out the results. How attractive would it be to you if the ATM knows what you want without your having to ask?

No ATMs in the United States can do that right now. But why not, when customers of Natwest Bank (www.natwest.com) in the United Kingdom have access to cash machines that are Rhodes scholars compared to the stunted ATMs in the United States? With the new Personal Option service, customers can preprogram the ATM network to remember a preferred set of services. It's not self-learning by any means, but it's progress. Nor is it entirely unsound to require customers to do a little programming. Such programming represents an investment that imposes higher switching costs, helping lock in customers to Natwest's ATM network. Whenever you can get customers to invest time and effort in a relationship, it makes customers think twice about switching.

Smart Refrigerators

Are you really sure the light in your refrigerator goes out when you shut the door? A new generation of smart refrigerators can probably tell you. They can also monitor your family's consumption of milk and order a replacement carton so you never run out. The newest generation of refrigerators leverage the Internet, bar code scanning, and microchip sensing technologies to make sure that you never run out of food and that companies never run out of information about your consuming habits.

Smart refrigerators represent the latest battle in cyberspace, and it's coming soon to a kitchen near you. Grocery manufacturers, supermarkets, and online grocers are scrambling to figure out how to leverage emerging technologies so they can place their products directly into your home. By putting intelligence inside the refrigerator, grocery stores nail an age-old dream: knowing consumer demand in advance. Frigidaire Home Products recently introduced a smart appliance that includes a microprocessor, touch screen, bar code scanner, and communications port. The refrigerator—developed by Frigidaire and ICL, a London-based technology company—allows consumers to automate their grocery shopping. Whenever someone is low on a given product, he or she simply swipes the carton past the refrigerator's bar code scanner, which adds that item to a list. When the consumer is ready, the list can be transmitted to a partner such as Peapod (www.peapod.com), an online grocery-service provider. The groceries will either be delivered to the consumer's door or be packaged for pickup.

Smart Soda Machines

Vending machine sales are very efficient at the point of purchase but extremely inefficient from a total value-chain perspective. They are subject to considerable seasonal fluctuations and buying patterns that are sometimes predictable and sometimes not. As a result, distributors navigate a tightrope between dispatching trucks to refill machines that don't need it and allowing machines to lose revenues by running out of stock. Smart vending machines solve that problem: they are self-aware enough to know when they are running out of stock. Before that happens, an embedded computer chip phones or radios the distributor for just-in-time replenishment. In the same way, the machines are smart enough to know when they will need service and can call for maintenance before they frustrate a customer and get banged up or worse.

The strategy makes obvious sense. It optimizes the revenue from each machine, improves service to retailers, and avoids end user frustration. But our point is a deeper one. The real value of the smart system stems from the real-time information the system provides. Imagine how the data from thousands of these machines can be used in predictive modeling to measure the impact of individual events on machine sales. For example, is a machine more profitable at a rock concert or a football game? Does profitability depend on the outside temperature or other factors? How sensitive to price are vending sales? By being able to monitor sales on a real-time basis, distributors can find ready answers to questions such as these. The same information can also be used to measure promotional activities in near real time. What's the value of data that can be used to track the impact of multi-million-dollar marketing or advertising programs? Moreover, the data has enormous value to help the company rationalize soft drink production and distribution strategies. Now take the next step and consider how this information might be of value to vendors, say, of potato chips or personal items. It is not difficult to see the possibility that the value of the information exceeds the value of the soft drinks themselves.

Compression: Transaction Costs Are Being Reduced

Perhaps the E-conomy's most dramatic impact on commerce is its role in systematically reducing transaction costs. By steadily squeezing transaction costs out of the virtual value chain, compression will continue to transform every aspect of interacting with customers. In the traditional economy, it cost about one dollar to maintain information about an individual customer. Today, it costs considerably less than one cent per customer. Lower transaction costs allow companies to control and track information that would have been too costly to capture and process just a few years ago. Any assessment of the true impact of the E-conomy must include the lower transaction costs that are unleashing network effects, increasing returns, and creating economies of scope and scale. In this way, the E-conomy is remaking the structure of companies and industries alike.

Compression and the other Net Readiness trends discussed in this chapter work together to squeeze out many of the traditional costs of interactions—the searching, coordinating, and monitoring that customers and companies must do when they exchange goods, services, or ideas. Compression comes in a multitude of shapes and forms. In its most powerful form, it is not even recognizable as a separate force. But whatever shape it assumes, compression squeezes out or eliminates the most costly pieces of the marketing, fulfillment, and customer service processes. The more commodity-oriented the service and support components are, the more ruthlessly compression consigns them to history. Most of the successful companies we have presented in this book owe their success to their ability to drive out time and expense, greatly reducing transaction costs.

Compression squeezes distance and time out of the equation and eliminates most of the costs that the traditional economy has long assumed to be more or less fixed. Compression is the force that makes distance irrelevant. Geography, the consideration that up until now has always played a key role in determining who competed with whom, is massively limiting in the traditional economy. In the E-conomy, your business can connect instantly with customers all over the globe. Of course, compression enables the flip side of this benefit as well: you're exposed to worldwide competitors who have just as easy access to your customers as you have to theirs.

In just three years, for example, Autobytel.com has, in effect, become the second-largest auto dealer in the United States. Much of this success can be attributed to the fact that margins on purchases from the Web site are significantly lower than those of traditional automobile channels. One reason is that compression makes geography less relevant. Before services such as those offered by Autobytel.com, geography limited customers to a small number of dealers—usually only one for each manufacturer in a sales area. But in the E-conomy, customers can easily and cheaply compare the prices and options offered by a much larger universe of dealers. In effect, Autobytel.com and its online rivals are unbundling the sales and service roles of dealerships. For now, dealers' service and maintenance functions remain largely unchanged. But that will have to change if dealers are to stay in the game as anything more than car repair service facilities. As customers make more and more purchasing decisions on the Net, dealers will find themselves relegated to the sidelines of the value chain, providing commodity services such as tire rotation and tune-ups. For similar reasons, Microsoft's Expedia travel site has become one of the largest online travel agencies in a span of only two years. Traditional travel agents will have to respond with creative new services to combat Expedia's inherent cost advantages.

Things are no different in the business-to-business arena. Cisco, for instance, credits much of its success to its ability to leverage compression to transform the cost and quality of interactions with customers. Cisco has invested considerably in building seamless Net-based systems for facilitating customers who can find prices, simplify product configurations, and submit and track the status of orders through Cisco's Internet marketplace. In effect, this part of the company's business has been unbundled and outsourced to customers. Through its Manufacturing Connection Online (MCO), Cisco's relations with channel partners have been transformed as well. The company has used its online presence to integrate its suppliers with its manufacturing partners, turning over the assembly and fulfillment part of the supply chain to its manufacturing partners, who ship directly to customers. Meanwhile, Cisco maintains end-to-end control of the process.

Here's a good question to ask: What part of your business relationship and activities with customers, suppliers, partners, or employees can you outsource to these constituencies and have them thank you for it?

Time Is Money

By collapsing time and breeding accelerated change, the E-conomy has succeeded in further reducing transaction costs. Successful E-conomy players accept a culture of constant change and are willing to constantly break down and reconstruct their products and processes —even the most successful ones. In a world of instantaneous connection, there is a huge premium on instant response and the ability to learn from and adapt to the marketplace in real time. The implications of how compression drives a zero latency economic model are staggering:

The E-conomy has no patience. Immediacy is the key driver in the E-conomy. In the 1950s, technological developments such as xerography or instant photography ensured a revenue stream for decades. At the same time, designing an automobile literally took a decade from conception to production. In order to succeed today, enterprises must operate in accelerated real time, continuously and immediately adjusting to changing business conditions through information immediacy. Compression as a value of the E-conomy concerns itself principally with cycle time reductions. The typical life span of consumer electronics products is less than six months. Today it takes Chrysler two years, not ten, to design a car, although even that is too long by a year. We believe that within three years, more than half of the revenues of the companies we consult for will derive from products and services that do not exist today.

Compression drives new economies of scale. Compression of virtual value chains redefines economies of scale, allowing small companies to achieve low unit costs for products and services in markets dominated by big companies. The U.S. Postal Service, which still views the world according to an industrial paradigm, could never afford to build a post office in every one of the nation's homes. But Federal Express has done exactly that by allowing individuals with access to the Internet to track packages through the company's site on the World Wide Web. (Customers can also request software that allows them not only to track their parcels but also to view at any time the entire history of their transactions with Federal Express.) The new economies of scale make it possible for Federal Express to provide what are, in effect, mini-storefronts to each and every customer, whether the service is requested at any given moment by millions of users or just one.

Compression drives new economies of scope. In the E-conomy, businesses can redefine economies of scope by drawing on a single set of digital assets to provide value across many different and disparate markets. The insurance giant USAA (www.usaa.com), for example, dominates the insurance market for military officers with a 97 percent segment share, a scale of operations built on direct marketing. Now, through the new customer relationships made possible by its digital assets (the information it collected about its customers), the company is expanding its scope. Using its virtual value chain, USAA can coordinate across markets and provide a broader line of high-quality products and services.

Compression rewards the shift from supply-side to demand-side strategies. As companies gather, organize, select, synthesize, and distribute information in the E-conomy while managing raw and manufactured goods in the marketplace, they have the opportunity to sense and respond to customers' desires rather than simply to make and sell products and services. USAA senses a demand in its customer base and then connects that demand to a source of supply. In the E-conomy, in which supply generally outstrips demand, managers must increasingly look to demand-side strategies if they are to succeed.

Advantage Is Becoming More Temporary

How do you create advantage in the E-conomy? We cover that question in Part II of this book. For now, let's distinguish between old and new ways of conceptualizing advantage (Table 2-2). Throughout the industrial age, it was rational for managers to focus on achieving competitive advantage and, once having achieved it, to sustain it. When the basic building blocks of success were measured in the scarcity of raw materials, markets, capital, and labor, organizing these elements better than your competitors created value. When the economy is a zero sum game ("if we have one more of these, you have one less"), competitive advantage is probably something worth protecting. Unfortunately, the energy and resources spent protecting advantage cannot be applied where it really counts: innovating on behalf of your customers.

Table 2-2. Advantage Dynamics in the E-conomy

Advantage in the E-conomy is temporary and buyer driven.

Marketplace	E-conomy
Placement	Movement ←— e bay
Fixed	Flexible
Position	Migration
Seller determined	Buyer determined
Supply driven	Demand driven
Value by feature	Value by context
External pricing factors	Pricing negotiated
Adversarial	Cooperative
Zero-sum; "I win, you lose."	Win-win

In the E-conomy, we need to look forward, not back. History demonstrates that it's pure hubris to believe that organizations can plan for competitive advantage. Look at the most celebrated systems in corporate America, such as American Airlines' Sabre System or American Hospital Supply's ASAP ordering system. Although these systems did, in fact, generate significant competitive advantage for their creators, they had at conception a much less ambitious and much worthier goal. They were designed to make life easier for the companies' customers and partners.

As organizations entered the information age, their mistake was to assume that IT by itself could drive sustainable competitive advantage. It doesn't work that way, even though some IT initiatives move companies forward and help create value. Relying on technology to generate competitive advantage is counterproductive for a number of reasons. For example, it places way too much emphasis on technology at a time when technology can be quickly and easily duplicated. There's no advantage to having something that can be easily duplicated. Also, aiming toward competitive advantage misses the point. Competitive advantage should not be the goal. It should be the result of something much more basic: offering customers a product or service that saves them time, makes their lives easier, or enriches their relationships. Companies derive competitive advantage from doing that well.

It would be a mistake, however, to assume that because advantage is temporary, it is irrelevant. The reverse is true. Our research indicates that the most successful Net Ready organizations have been among the earliest adopters of Net technology and methods. Four main reasons account for this outcome. First, early adopters get to handpick the most profitable customers and, if the company is born on the Web, get preferred access to venture capital. Our experience shows that, all else being equal, successful early adopters end up capturing customers with higher margins and retaining higher market share. In the United States, 50 percent of all homes connected to the Internet have incomes above $50,000, and 50 percent of households with an income of more than $75,000 have Internet connections. The 80/20 rule points out that by capturing the largest and most profitable customers in many industries first, the Net Ready companies will have an impact that is out of proportion to their number in the economy. E-conomy models indicate that significant cost advantages of 15 percent to 20 percent will accrue to many successful first movers. Companies that wait too long to invest will have difficulty competing against those that move quickly.

Second, early adopters tend to consolidate the value of their brands early. The value of brand equity in the E-conomy is paramount. As the playing field gets more crowded and confusing, consumers will instinctively gravitate toward the confidence of brands they trust. Early adopters have a better chance of establishing their brands in an uncrowded marketspace.

Third, early adopters get first pick of premier partnerships. In the E-conomy, where no organization can go at it alone, the importance of developing alliances with preferred partners cannot be overestimated. Late entrants have to cultivate partnerships with second- and third-tier players. (For a fuller discussion of why partnerships are indispensable in the E-conomy, see rule 5, page 285 in chapter 9.)

Lastly, successful early adopters derive considerable competitive advantage because of the talent pool they attract. What we have seen in the job market is that top talent goes to the top players in each E-business category. The most desirable business school graduates often favor the early adopters who have carved out a brand. Late entrants in the recruitment competition will find that the best and brightest have already been engaged and will likely have to offer very aggressive compensation packages to be taken seriously. These challenges are serious ones for late entrants into a market.

3

Identifying
Strategic Options

The E-Business Value Matrix is an assessment tool useful for evaluating E-business initiatives. This chapter describes how organizations can map themselves against the background of Internet initiatives from a cross section of industries and how the assessment can suggest subsequent strategies.

One of the essential challenges of succeeding in E-business is deciding which initiatives have the best chance of giving you the high-impact outcomes you want. It's not easy. Net Readiness, it turns out, is very much an exercise in portfolio management.

Net Ready executives understand that the E-conomy is real. It's not a fad or an option. The difficulty is that although most companies realize they have to act, they have little idea about what to focus on or how to execute. The difficulty is not one of scarcity of opportunities. Quite the contrary. Opportunities abound. The problem, if anything, is that being pulled in too many directions overwhelms organizations. Our work reveals that companies are typically facing a situation in which the IT organizations have a backlog of initiatives that mitigates their ability to focus and execute. Compounding many companies' difficulty of identifying a course of action is the difficulty of making any change at all. To complicate things even further, management is being hit with a double whammy. First, they are inundated with urgent E-business requests from various parts of the organization. Second, they are at the mercy of E-business vendors who are constantly pitching solutions that the vendors claim will solve their problems.

The key question, then, is how do companies choose the set of E-business initiatives that will be winners out of a plethora of possibilities? We're overstating the obvious when we say that picking the winners, or a set of initiatives that will drive winning, is quite difficult.

Unfortunately, what we've seen in today's market is that companies (especially those not born on the Web) make their choices in a very ad hoc, opportunistic, and chaotic manner. Such ad hoc approaches to investments in E-business represent a poor use of resources. The problem is that the E-business efforts of most organizations have not been very successful. There is still a deep lack of understanding as to how E-business can help improve a company's standing. In our experience, a lack of rigor around making these critical choices creates an environment that invites failure. The failure takes the following forms:

- Islands of Webification
- Lack of clear benefits/impacts desired
- Lack of effort required to drive benefits
- Inability to leverage efforts across the organization
- Ineffective accountability
- Inadequate buy-in from key constituents
- Unattainable expectations
- Inability to make go, no go, or kill decisions
- "Two-year projects that will fix the world"

Where are you now and where do you want to go? What's important to you? These questions are fundamental to any company aspiring to a position in the E-conomy. Given that the E-business environment changes, the technology enablers change, and the players certainly change, understanding how to manage investments in E-business is fundamental to success.

The E-Business Value Matrix

To help frame E-business questions against the background of the E-conomy, we developed an assessment tool that our clients have found particularly helpful. The E-Business Value Matrix (figure 3-1) is organized into four quadrants along two dimensions: business criticality and practice innovation, or newness. We have picked these two dimensions from the empirical evidence accumulated from our work. As we looked at the drivers of Net Ready suc-

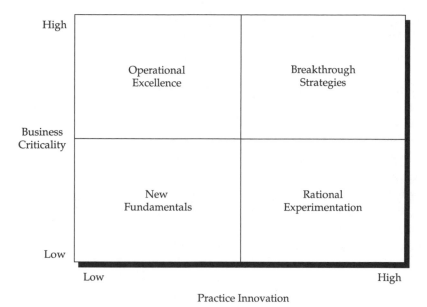

Figure 3-1. The E-Business Value Matrix. Our research has identified two core characteristics that drive the impact of an E-business effort: business criticality and practice innovation (newness). The framework created by these dimensions offers deep insights in the pursuit of Net Readiness. Against this framework, we can map the location of any Webified practice or process and thereby gain a better understanding of what needs to happen to maximize the chances for success. The E-Business Value Matrix is a tool to help companies make sense of a spectrum of possible initiatives in terms of the impacts those initiatives are having.

cess, we saw these two variables as most discriminating with respect to driving competitive advantage. We tried plotting other variables, such as cost, revenue, or market share, but none of these drivers, as important as they are, predicted Net Ready success with as much reliability as the variables of business criticality and practice innovation. Mapping E-business initiatives gave us the ability to understand the impact that such initiatives ranking high on both dimensions were having on the organization. All else being equal, it's better to deploy initiatives high in both business criticality and practice innovation. The problem is that all else is never equal.

We don't mean to imply that initiatives that rank relatively low in business criticality or practice innovation are undesirable. Such initiatives have real value to the enterprise. There is intrinsic value in Webifying almost any application. You reduce costs, add to responsiveness, bring the members of the value chain closer, and add to your store of Web experience.

All these advantages are tremendously desirable. So we encourage you to go after the low-hanging fruit and Webify your employee directory and 401(k) plan. It's not business critical, but you'll reduce costs and gain experience. Our point is that if you want to obtain real strategic advantage— the kind that truly drives significant impact—you need to have initiatives in every quadrant, including the top right. In other words, you must learn how to create strategic portfolios of E-business initiatives and to manage them well.

Briefly, the four quadrants of the E-Business Value Matrix are: New Fundamentals (the most basic operations of the business); Rational Experimentation (it's a new process, but it's not necessarily business critical; if we fail, the business survives); Operational Excellence (high in business criticality but pertaining to an existing practice); and Breakthrough Strategies (high in business criticality pertaining to a new initiative). We need to emphasize that there is absolutely no qualitative element in this analysis. One quadrant is not superior to another. Every company will necessarily have processes and practices that occupy each quadrant. Moreover, the decision on where to locate a practice is highly contextual. Different companies will evaluate similar practices in entirely different and valid ways.

The vertical axis of the E-Business Value Matrix measures the business criticality of the practice or process you intend to Webify. In other words, how critical to your business's mission is this practice or process or business model? Some practices will result in a higher impact. Others will be necessarily less critical. For example, the decision to Webify a bet-your-business application such as the customer billing system has high business criticality. First, the strategic benefits resulting from a successful deployment of a Web-based billing system are enormous. Second, the denial of the system to the business if the deployment is not successful would have drastic consequences. Hence, such a decision should not be made lightly. Most organizations start by Webifying applications that expose the enterprise to less risk in case of failure. When they have demonstrated competency to deploy Webified versions of tactical applications, such as the company phone directory or travel expense voucher system, then they can take on the more critical systems.

The horizontal axis—practice innovation (newness)—measures the originality of the practice, process, or business model. How new is this practice or model in your industry? Is this a new practice or does it already exist? Is it an incremental step over something that exists, or does it represent a more fundamental leap? For example, consider a company developing an Intranet to give employees access to their 401(k) portfolio information. Where would such a practice be located on the horizontal scale? From an industry perspective, it is certainly not a new practice. So we would locate such a practice on the lower left of the matrix.

Let's consider the same practice from the perspective of the vertical axis. How important is offering Intranet access to 401(k) information? Would the company be out of business if it did not have an Internet-enabled 401(k) program? Probably not. So we would locate that practice at the low end of both scales. We are not saying that Web-enabling the employee 401(k) portfolio information is undesirable. On the contrary, such an action is smart for many reasons that are obvious and probably also for reasons that are not yet fully understood. At the minimum, doing so gives employees the three attributes of the Web—independence, ownership, and control— that they most want. However, implementing this practice will not give the company any real competitive advantage.

Quadrant I: New Fundamentals

In this quadrant are Webified versions of existing tactical applications that tend to be of less critical importance. Everyone seems to be deploying Internet applications, but if you look closely, most of these applications are the more superficial kind of chores that all businesses attend to. These basic applications usually have a low level of investment and modest returns of a short-term duration. Nothing necessarily strategic is at work here: no attempt to create new markets or redefine business models. Usually, the applications attempt to add value in the form of cost avoidance or cost reduction. It makes sense to Web-enable applications for human resources or market research. Every company needs to complete a certain number of these applications before it can move on.

No room for complacency exists even in this quadrant. As time goes on, organizations that elect not to Webify the new fundamentals of their business will put themselves at increasing risk. There is no great strategic advantage, for example, in putting a company telephone directory online. Or is there? We can agree there is a tactical advantage and cost savings when a company can eliminate distribution costs and keep listings up to date by posting a directory on the Web. But at the end of the day, is that company in a better strategic position for having its telephone directory on the Web?

We believe it is. Such an application offers much more value than simply giving users real-time access to telephone numbers and E-mail addresses and simplifying the maintenance of the lists. Suppose this directory
offers the option of looking up individuals within the company using criteria such as areas of expertise, years of experience in a given application or
domain, or past membership on specific teams or projects? Suddenly the
intranet-based telephone directory does more than impact the bottom line
(cutting costs); it has the possibility of adding to the top line (creating
value). Much more important however, is that such Web initiatives have a
great impact on an organization's E-culture, or Web culture. Low-hanging
fruit such as Web directories go a long way in helping shape and drive future Web activities with higher impact. Having a Web culture is critical to
success in E-business.

Quadrant II: Rational Experimentation

Rational experimentation results when a company makes an attempt to
break away from conventional wisdom, often challenging its existing
business model. In this quadrant are initiatives that attempt to create
new markets and revenue growth in areas that do not necessarily rise to
the status of being mission critical. Any competitive advantage tends to
be of a short-term duration. More sustainable competitive advantage requires identification and execution of new E-business initiatives on a
consistent basis. Rational experimentation in E-business initiatives tends
to focus on:

- New organization practices and domains (for example, new customer
  segment, new product channel)
- Revenue increases more than cost reductions
- Less than business-critical applications (therefore lower in risk; if an ac-
  tivity fails, it will likely not imperil the business)
- New products or services that could become, if successful, a key part of
  the business
- Providing key learning opportunities for an organization

When a program that originates as a rational experiment really catches
on, it often moves to a breakthrough strategy or, in rarer cases, directly to
operational excellence.

Quadrant III: Breakthrough Strategies

This is the quadrant in which the celebrated players of the digital economy—Dell, Cisco, Amazon.com, Yahoo!—have made their marks. These companies have done a great job of creating breakthrough strategies—new and high in importance—and then dropping them into operational excellence. Initiatives in the breakthrough strategies quadrant tend to:

- Focus on business-critical processes
- Emphasize processes that impact competitive advantage (for example, new market creation, changing industry rules, changing the nature of competition)
- Emphasize growth, new value creation, revenue generation
- Accept high levels of risk
- Evolve to industry standards
- Be fleeting, as competitors play catch-up

We all know breakthrough strategies when we see them. E*Trade is an example of a company that changed the rules of how securities are purchased. Granted, its advantage was fleeting, but E*Trade took a giant risk and, by successful execution in Quadrant III, defined the online securities industry and forced all its competitors to play catch-up. But catch up they did, and now Charles Schwab commands a bigger slice of the online brokerage market.

Quadrant IV: Operational Excellence

In this quadrant are Internet initiatives that focus on transforming mission-critical processes and product features for sustained competitive advantage. For example, managing the organization's supply chain is critical for most businesses. An initiative to boost competitive advantage by applying the services of the Internet to channel management is an attempt to boost operational excellence. The high rewards of success are matched by equally high risks of failure. E-business initiatives in the operational excellence quadrant tend to:

- Focus on transformation
- Emphasize improvements along supply and demand chain

els of risk that are medium to high

itical to sustaining competitive advantage

An organization that intends to be successful and preserve a competitive advantage must perform well in this quadrant—stated simply, there is little room for failure in Quadrant IV.

Implications of the E-Business Value Matrix

Mapping a company's activities against the E-Business Value Matrix offers a number of insights (figure 3-2). The E-Business Value Matrix is powerful precisely because it is so predictive. After mapping hundreds of organizations to the matrix, we saw a number of conclusions emerge.

First, note that the left side of the matrix is focused on cost reduction, driving operational efficiencies, the bottom line; the right side is focused on new value creation, growth, revenue enhancement, the top line. Which

Efficiency	New Value Creation
Operational Excellence	Breakthrough Strategies
New Fundamentals	Rational Experimentation

Figure 3-2. By mapping business goals against the E-Business Value Matrix, organizations can begin to make some decisions about which resources will benefit them most. The left side of the E-Business Value Matrix (new fundamentals and operational excellence) is focused on boosting efficiency. Investments on the right side of the matrix (rational experimentation and breakthrough strategies) impact new value creation. Which goal is more important to your organization? Your answer will determine which cell gets the E-business investment.

is more important to your organization? If it's revenue enhancement or creation of new markets, you will have to ratchet up the practice innovation of the initiative and accept a lot more risk against a greater payoff. On the other hand, some organizations can legitimately decide to let others be the pioneers. The strategies of such companies are to streamline existing practices and reduce costs. The activities of these companies will be located on the two left cells of the matrix.

Second, the market exerts tremendous counterclockwise pressure to push breakthrough strategies into operational excellence and then down to new fundamentals. In other words, mapped initiatives are not static, they migrate over time. That means that competitive advantage is difficult to sustain. It further reinforces the fact that constant innovation and "versioning" is critical. For example, Dell broke industry rules by creating breakthrough strategies. But over time, the Dell model became a de facto standard for the industry. Through no fault of Dell, tremendous momentum pushed the activities it innovated into operational excellence and then down to the new fundamentals. The inescapable conclusion is that if your logistics are not as well executed as Dell's, you will have a tough time being a player in the same marketspace.

Third, our work and research has shown that companies who do indeed gain any type of competitive advantage play extremely well (although not only) in the upper half of the framework. Each organization must build a portfolio of initiatives and have significant activity in each of the quadrants, but if it intends to sustain a competitive advantage, it has no choice but to succeed in the activities located in the upper quadrants.

Using the E-Business Value Matrix as a business tool helps in a number of forward-looking ways, including:

- *Assessing initiatives by your partners and competitors.* Locate your initiatives on the matrix. Then locate the initiatives of your competitors and perform a gap analysis. Only when you determine if a gap exists is it possible to make intelligent decisions about applying resources.

- *Allocating resources among possible initiatives.* The matrix can be used as a tool to help finance those resources, knowing that the higher an initiative appears on the matrix, the higher is the risk but also the return.

- *Monitoring how impacts evolve and change over time.* Initiatives in the digital economy are never static. They always migrate from one quadrant to another, propelled by the realities of the E-conomy.

E-Business Portfolio Management

In order to drive E-business success, or at least E-business sanity, organizations must move away from the ad hoc allocation of resources and toward a strategy of actively building a portfolio of initiatives covering each of the four quadrants. This move requires a strategy of E-business portfolio management. Here are some basic principles:

- Map existing E-business initiatives on the E-Business Value Matrix to reduce the complexity of activities being undertaken and to help focus on desirable opportunities.
- Build value propositions for each E-business initiative that include cost, desired outcome (value created), business reason, degree of risk, and execution difficulty.
- Create a twelve-to-eighteen-month road map of E-business initiatives for your business.
- Strategically manage the portfolio across all E-business efforts by actively strengthening the portfolio and risk equation over time: fund/don't fund; continued support/program termination.
- Change and adjust the portfolio every six months as initiatives are implemented and new opportunities rise.

E-business managers need to accept that each course of action involves trade-offs between opportunity and risk. Furthermore, E-business initiatives in each quadrant are associated with distinct risk characteristics that form the basis for the type of portfolio a company builds (figure 3-3). Balancing opportunity and risk creates optimum opportunities for saving money and creating new value. Thinking about what's included in the portfolio gives organizations a semblance of control. It gives decision makers a high-level perspective of the competition for resources among the various E-business initiatives. The framework can help build a well-balanced portfolio of initiatives. Companies will ask themselves, "Do we have a sufficient number of activities in each quadrant?" How an organization builds a portfolio will depend on how risk averse the manager is, on the resources available, on the competencies of the organization, and so on.

Organizational Forms

Understanding risk trade-offs and the potential impact they may have on a business sheds a little light on the types of organizing structures that an or-

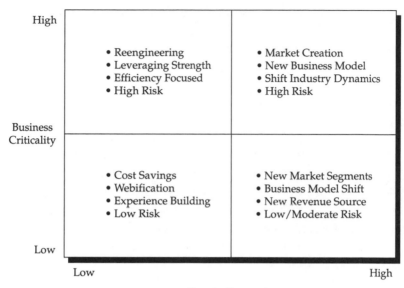

Figure 3-3. Risk characteristics of the E-Business Value Matrix. An organization's willingness to accept risk can be predicted by mapping its E-business initiatives on the E-Business Value Matrix. The more activity there is in the top right quadrant, the more the organization can be said to have a high tolerance for risk.

ganization may want to create to drive its initiatives. In our survey of companies participating in various forms of E-business, certain differences in organization were uncovered between Web-centric (pure plays) companies and established companies moving to the E-conomy. Web-centric companies benefited from:

- Being singularly focused on E-business and the customer
- Less complexity in their operations
- Less bureaucracy and flatter structure
- Speed in decision making and execution

Established companies moving to the E-conomy tended to:

- Be more concerned with channel conflict
- Take more time to analyze and make decisions
- Be slower in execution because of inertia
- Focus on issues they deemed more important than E-business

A number of companies we've worked with, however, have recently taken a different approach; they organize their E-business efforts according to the kind of change they expect to see. Using the E-Business Value Matrix helps companies think about new structuring methods for their E-business efforts. As the scope of change and business impact increase or decrease, different organizational forms become more appropriate.

Figure 3-4 illustrates the four basic organizational forms:

- *Grassroots.* This form empowers and motivates the existing organization to redesign processes around E-business. Most companies start here by allowing their people to plant E-business seeds. As organizations mature, they migrate to the integrated model.

- *Incubated.* This form creates a dedicated team of people to singularly focus on an E-business initiative (new business, product, or service) with corporate resources. This form is helpful in catalyzing change in companies, because they are able to mobilize quicker than through grassroots efforts. Often inspired by new incentive schemes and focus on E-business, these entities break the established rules and build, in

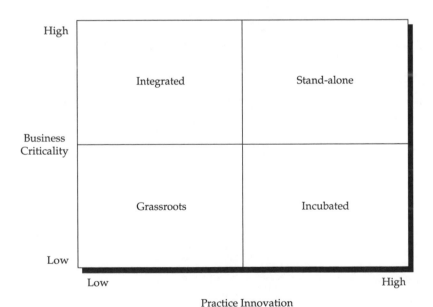

Figure 3-4. The four basic organizational forms of the E-Business Value Matrix.

some cases, conflicting initiatives. These initiatives, if successful, often migrate to the stand-alone or even the integrated model. This model works well for traditional companies trying to jump-start E-business.

- *Stand-alone.* This form creates a separate entity, apart from the existing organization, that is solely focused on building and driving the new business. This group is made up of top talent within and outside the company and has the freedom to run the initiative as it sees fit without the constraints of the "parent." It may very well spin off to a separate company (dot-com), and even be located in a different geography. These forms also have accounting implications on an organization (e.g., new valuations, tax write-offs, etc.). Most important, they have the focus they need to drive the stand-alone enterprise. In some cases, an established company may create a threat to itself in order to benefit from it later. Companies can choose from several forms—the joint venture or partnership (buy.com), the subsidiary (e-citi, HP.com), the buy-out (Kbtoys), or the dot-com (wingspan of BancOne).

- *Integrated.* This form drives E-business to be a core component of what the organization does. Leverage across the company is a key theme here. Creating executive ownership and accountability that is understood and managed programmatically is critical. For established companies who are trying to scale their E-business efforts across the organization, this model is most important, and requires governance policies discussed in chapter 1.

Choosing the right organizational form will be different for each organization, depending on where it is in its E-business efforts. In many cases, stand-alone and incubated forms become integrated forms within a company over time, as was the case with Charles Schwab's eSchwab initiative. However, governance models are not and should not be static. Companies need to think about what is the proper form for today, and when they will need to migrate to another form.

Also, depending on how Net Ready an organization is, different governance models make more sense. For example, companies that score low in their Net Readiness may want to incubate first, especially those who score very low in leadership. Companies who are more Net Ready are better able to integrate their E-business initiatives into the organization and manage them.

Mapping Web Initiatives to the E-Business Value Matrix

We have attempted to locate the E-business initiatives of a number of organizations on the matrix. Arrow Electronics' Web site (www.arrow.com), for example, is a good example of brochureware. We are not criticizing Arrow; this placement is an indication that the Web site is in the early stages of evolution. That's why we position storefront efforts in the new fundamentals quadrant.

The Dell and Cisco core E-business efforts (commerce engines) are squarely in the operational excellence quadrant. Both companies have attacked some very mission-critical pieces of business and, just as important, have done it successfully. Figure 3-5 maps on the E-Business Value Matrix the locations of many of the initiatives we have discussed.

The E-Business Value Matrix in Action

Let's see the E-Business Value Matrix in action by mapping the activities of two companies, one born on the Web, the other a traditional company that

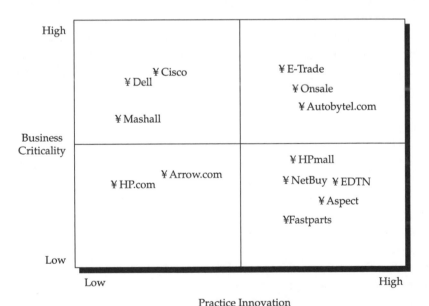

Figure 3-5. Mapping organizations to the E-Business Value Matrix. This figure shows examples of Net Ready organizations and their locations on the matrix.

has made the transition to Net Readiness: Dell and Fruit Of The Loom, respectively.

Dell Computer

Dell started off, like many industrial companies, in the fundamentals at the lower left of the grid. For a number of years it did a good job of moving product through the traditional direct mail channel. But Dell moved into rational experimentation when it considered whether the company could push its products online through the emerging Internet. It made some initiatives that, if they succeeded, would create a new channel whose importance was not obvious; if the initiatives failed, the company would not be in jeopardy, because its traditional channels would be preserved.

Dell's experiment succeeded, far surpassing any rational prediction. *The Wall Street Journal* recently gave Dell perhaps the highest honor possible in business. It spawned a new term: *to dell,* as in, "Three years ago, Amazon delled Barnes and Noble." It's true that Dell radically changed the nature of marketing PCs. But over time, its radical practices moved to operational excellence. In other words, the Dell model is now the de facto standard for companies in the E-conomy. Today, Dell's pioneering work simply represents the cost of entry for anyone wishing to compete. While the competitive advantage for Dell was real for a year or so, little competitive advantage remains. When competitive advantage is a function of increasingly less expensive technology, it is easy to catch up and even leapfrog industry leaders. Individual initiatives move over time, usually in a counterclockwise direction (see figure 3-6 for Dell's progression of Internet initiatives).

E-conomy Impact on Dell's Business

We are not saying that Dell has *lost* any competitive advantage. The company's success, and its willingness to take on pioneering experimentation, is based on two competencies it has built up over a decade. Dell's key success factor is the second-to-none supply chain management system it has developed and fine-tuned over the last ten years. To replicate that system is not easy. Putting up a Web site does not create a just-in-time inventory system. The second competency—Dell's ruthless execution of the fundamentals—is perhaps the most durable reason for its success.

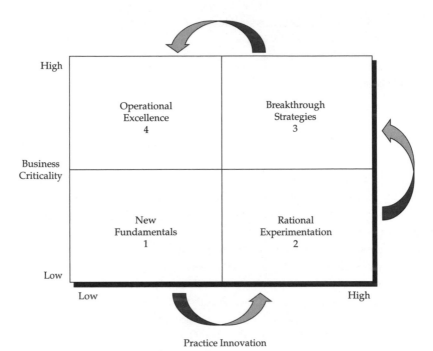

Figure 3-6. Dell's progression of Internet initiatives. Dell started off its Internet initiatives with the new fundamentals (1). Its efforts obviously clicked. Dell quickly moved into rational experimentation (2) by seeing if it could move its products and its customer-facing processes online. Once the concept proved popular, Dell combined its Internet channel with its logistics prowess and ruthless execution to create the breakthrough strategy (3) that made it the leading PC vendor. Its very success, then, changed the industry and created the de facto standard for doing business in the market, migrating its breakthrough strategy to operational excellence (4). Dell's effort shifted the marketplace so that its operational excellence now represents the cost of entry for any competitor.

Dell's Top Line: Revenue Enhancement

- Revenue growth of 20 percent per month
- Improved customer retention
- Improved lead generation
- Improved personalization (My Dell)
- New channels
- New revenues from partners

Dell's Bottom Line: Cost Reduction

- Increased sales per employee
- Reduced order and inventory management expenses
- Reduced service and technical support expenses
- Reduced supplier coordination expenses
- Reduced number of physical plants

Fruit Of The Loom

Dell's progression in the E-Business Value Matrix obeyed the traditional counterclockwise dynamic. But other models also exist. Fruit Of The Loom's Web initiatives, for example, follow a clockwise rotation. Let's see what accounts for this difference and how it impacts the company's business model and prospects for success in the E-conomy.

By the way, you won't find direct evidence of these initiatives at Fruit Of The Loom's consumer Web site (www.fruit.com). The E-conomy strategies of the most successful companies are never obvious from their Web sites alone because the public site presents the tip of the iceberg. Fruit Of The Loom, for example, has an exquisite E-conomy strategy, but its nucleus is hidden in the company's back-office operations and supply chain management. Like most companies born before the Web, Fruit Of The Loom started with the new fundamentals by establishing Web-enabled applications to communicate with its partners. It first set up a Web site that offered a lot of brochureware. But the company quickly attacked business critical processes, which in Fruit Of The Loom's case involved integrating its partners with its key distribution channels. Fruit Of The Loom sought a distribution channel that would give its distributors products on a just-in-time basis (see figure 3-7 for Fruit Of The Loom's progression of Internet initiatives).

Let's consider how a just-in-time silk-screening and distribution system streamlined the supply chain and eliminated inventory risks. Fruit Of The Loom has a huge business stake in sports-related silk-screened merchandise. The challenge was how to anticipate and stay ahead of the demand for merchandise that fluctuates with the fortunes of the various National Football League teams. If the Dallas Cowboys win on Sunday, demand goes up. If they lose, demand goes down. In a traditional supply chain model, keeping inventory on hand for the peaks becomes very expensive.

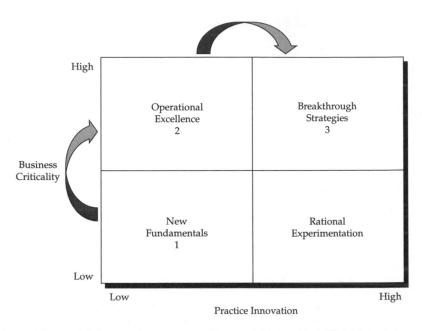

Figure 3-7. Fruit Of The Loom's progression of Internet initiatives. Fruit Of The Loom's Internet initiatives took a clockwise progression. To enable the new fundamentals, Fruit Of The Loom built an extranet (Activewear Online), which over time assumed breakthrough proportions. Activewear Online networks the company to distributors and suppliers. It includes a Web catalog, availability and pricing information, an ordering template, and even competitor information. Then Fruit Of The Loom took a strategic leap of faith. The company went to its partners and offered to build each one a Web site and host it on Fruit Of The Loom's platform.

Fruit Of The Loom solved this problem with its Activewear Online extranet system. Depending on the outcome of Sunday's games, distributors can have appropriate inventory on hand within hours to meet anticipated demand.

The Activewear Online extranet creates a value-added network of the company's distributors, suppliers, partners, and even competitors. In its most basic form, it presents a Web catalog of Fruit Of The Loom products with specifications, availability, and pricing information. The extranet makes it easy for the company's suppliers and distributors to do business with it. So far, so good. At that point, the company was still squarely in the new fundamentals quadrant. Fruit Of The Loom took off when it decided to take on the burden of creating individual Web sites for its hundreds of suppliers, distributors, wholesalers, and transportation partners. The Web sites feature an online order system, summaries of accounts, promotions, and up-to-date summaries. At first, the Web sites offered only Fruit Of The Loom products, but now Hanes (www.hanes.com) and other competitors are participating on the platform as well. Fruit Of The Loom has moved through operational excellence and is heading toward breakthrough strategies. It has strengthened all its relationships and increasingly locked in its partners. With this network in place, any competitor has to ante up an impossible investment to match Fruit Of The Loom's presence in the E-conomy.

Strategy: Lock In Members of the Value Chain by Raising Switching Costs

Lock-in, the art of capturing and retaining members of the value chain, is as old as Green Stamps and as modern as frequent flier programs. In fact, a new class of infomediaries is escalating the battle to lure away and lock in each other's best customers. Net Ready companies have an easier time locking in their customers. Fruit Of The Loom's strategy entrenches its customers so deeply into the web of services it encapsulates around its Intranet that considerable expense and upheaval will accrue to any participant who considers leaving. The choices that the participants make lock them ever tighter into Fruit Of The Loom's value web by virtue of the benefits they receive. Increasingly, the infrastructure works to align the interests of all parties. This outcome is beneficial to everyone, especially the consumer, who benefits from a more seamless value chain.

Any Web site with reviews, value-added services, chat rooms, auctions, branded E-mail, or recommendations is subject to the same phenomenon. Customers tell those early leaders how to improve their processes, and are often willing to shoulder some responsibility to get what they want. By doing so, they willingly lock themselves into a relationship. A competitor trying to replicate this experience will have an extremely difficult time.

Each of Fruit Of The Loom's Web sites is customized to each partner's needs and may include an order system, online catalog with search mechanisms, and account information with up-to-date summaries and promotions. Hundreds of Fruit Of The Loom partners could take advantage of this offer. The result is an infrastructure that strengthens the relationship between Fruit Of The Loom and its partners. To leave the relationship, Fruit Of The Loom's partners would now have to incur formidable switching costs. By the same margin, Fruit Of The Loom has also raised the barriers of entry into the E-conomy. Any competitor who seeks entry will now have to surpass Fruit Of The Loom's investment. Realistically, no competitor can do that.

Fruit of the Loom's investment paid off. The company decided that if its infrastructure were to have a high value over time, it would have to be broad enough to accommodate competitors. Otherwise, the platform would be accused of being biased and become vulnerable to someone else developing an unbiased, more desirable platform.

Activewear Online has been hugely successful. More than 60 percent of distributors are under contract to participate on the extranet. Some distributors who had actually invested in their own Web sites chose to be affiliated with Activewear Online instead. The first few distributors to use Activewear Online reported twice the volume of orders expected. Activewear Online is a secured extranet and is available only to authorized members. It's that membership that creates Fruit Of The Loom's return on investment. What is key here is that Fruit Of The Loom has brought to market a much stronger value proposition than simply selling apparel. It is now, in essence, both an infrastructure provider and an Internet service provider. The company has been able to build dependencies on behalf of its key partners by providing tremendous value and by changing the nature of competition in that market.

Project Prioritization Matrix

Building a strategic portfolio of E-business initiatives is only part of the success equation. As we discussed in the introduction, ruthless execution is a key driver of success and a competency that most organizations have yet to perfect. How does a company ensure that E-business initiatives are being executed the right way? How does it ensure that they are being implemented well? How does it ensure that the company will derive the expected benefits?

Companies need to drive a more granular implementation process. E-business initiatives should be broken down into key projects. These key projects are the E-business functionalities that will be delivered to the user (customer, supplier, partner, employee, etc.). To help companies drive rapid execution, we offer the Project Prioritization Matrix (figure 3-8).

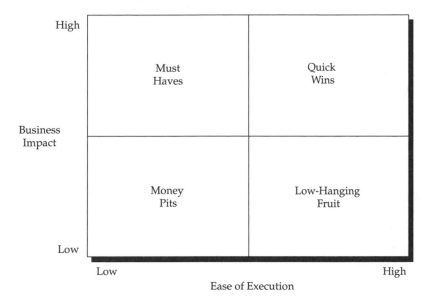

Figure 3-8. Project Prioritization Matrix. By locating your E-business initiatives on the Project Prioritization Matrix, it becomes evident which initiatives deserve first consideration for resources. The most attractive candidates tend to be clustered in the quick wins quadrant: high in business impact and high in ease of execution. Also attractive are the projects we label low-hanging fruit: low in business impact but easy to execute. Eventually, most companies will need to attack the must-have projects that are high in business impact but difficult to execute. If you get some quick wins and some good experience under your belt first, the must-have projects will not be so daunting.

The Project Prioritization Matrix is essential for portfolio management because it can quickly identify the initiatives that offer the most benefits. This matrix maps directly to the E-Business Value Matrix (figure 3-9). We used the E-Business Value Matrix to map a portfolio of E-business initiatives against the dimensions of business criticality and practice innovation. On the Project Prioritization Matrix, we map the constituent projects against the dimensions of business criticality and *ease of execution,* a format that offers prescriptive information. The Project Prioritization Matrix answers a basic question: Because even modest E-business initiatives are made up of numerous projects or tasks, not all of which are equally critical, where does a company begin?

The Project Prioritization Matrix tells you. Not all tasks are equal, either in terms of the business value they create nor the resources they consume. Not all tasks can be executed in three months or less. If they can't, they

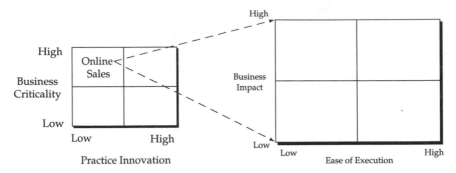

Figure 3-9. Mapping the E-Business Value Matrix to the Project Prioritization Matrix. By mapping the E-Business Value Matrix to the Project Prioritization Matrix cell by cell, managers can prioritize the various projects or tasks that comprise every E-business initiative on the dimensions of business impact and ease of execution. The goal is to identify the quick wins and go after those first.

must be disaggregated into smaller units. A primary responsibility of managers is to assign limited resources to the worthiest projects. The Product Prioritization Matrix is a tool that helps teams manage project interdependencies with a focus on the central issues of sequencing, or timing of deliverables, and project bottlenecks. In other words, the matrix allows managers accountable for delivery to concentrate on the projects that have the greatest business impact and are the quickest and easiest to implement. These tasks, which map to the upper right corner of the matrix, are quick wins, and most managers will want to pluck them first. Managers' second choices will be the low-hanging fruit projects (lower right corner) and the must-have projects (upper left corner). Projects that are clustered in the money pit quadrant (lower left corner) offer relatively little value to the business and are the most difficult to execute. Enterprises are well advised to put these projects on the back burner.

The ease of execution of a particular project is contingent on a number of factors:

- Level of information/database exposure
- Business process change required
- Change management required
- Competencies needed
- Level of interactivity

Let's take this mapping exercise one step further by considering a generic online sales application. Online sales applications are really complex E-business portfolios of many dependent as well as independent modules or features, such as

- Online ordering
- Service contracts
- Return merchandise authorizations (RMAs)/service orders
- Configuration
- Pricing
- Product upgrade
- Order status
- Notification
- Invoicing
- Returns
- Returns status
- Billing address change
- Lead times

Which of these modules or features should the manager of this application implement first? Figure 3-10 provides some solid clues. By mapping these individual projects against the dimensions of business criticality and ease of execution, the manager quickly determines which projects fall into the quick wins quadrant, the cell that commands first attention. Initiatives in this cell can be executed most easily and can provide the highest business impacts. This exercise reveals that the first projects to be to developed should be order status, pricing, lead times, invoicing, notification, and product upgrade. The projects in the low-hanging fruit quadrant (returns, returns status, and billing address change) should be developed thereafter. The projects in the must-have quadrant (online ordering, configuration, service contracts, and RMA/service orders) offer the highest business impact but also are the most difficult to develop. Many managers will want to leave these projects until they have a few quick wins under their belts.

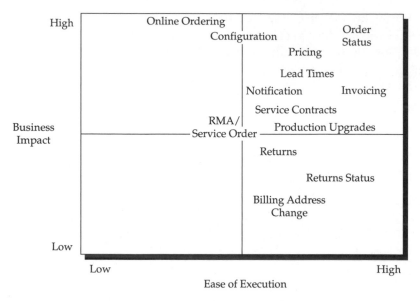

Figure 3-10. Prioritizing projects for a generic E-business application. The projects that comprise a generic E-business online sales application are mapped here to the four cells of the Project Prioritization Matrix. It is clear from the matrix that the projects mapped to the quick wins and low-hanging fruit quadrants deserve first consideration. Nor are all the projects in the quick wins quadrant equal. The matrix discriminates projects that are relatively high in business impact but relatively low in ease of execution. All else being equal, common sense dictates that these projects should be tackled first.

Principles of Prioritization

1. Identify key E-business initiatives to be funded.
2. Break down key initiatives into core user functionalities (projects).
3. Map core functionalities onto prioritization matrix.
4. Identify linkages/interdependencies.
5. Build project road map of deliverables.
6. Drive execution (three months, three to six people, $50,000 to $250,000).
7. Measure based on exception.

Conclusion

To maintain a viable presence in the E-conomy, an organization has to sustain significant activity in every quadrant of the E-Business Value Matrix.

For sustainable competitive advantage, however, successful execution in the top half of the matrix is pivotal. Why? Because without concentrating its efforts on breakthrough strategies and then rapidly migrating them to operational excellence, an organization can be quickly overtaken by the competition. "What have you done for me lately?" today's customers want to know. They are impatient for new products and services and will penalize organizations that do not respond quickly or creatively enough.

Here is an exercise that we frequently ask our clients to complete. We believe that it shows how the E-Business Value Matrix can reveal the strengths and limitations of a particular company or department aspiring to a greater level of Net Readiness.

Map Your Initiative

Locate a handful of your Internet-related business efforts within the four cells of the E-Business Value Matrix. Two caveats: First, don't get depressed when you do this exercise. You will most likely find that your E-business initiatives lie on the bottom half of the matrix. (That's okay; such a result is not a qualitative statement. Companies need to have initiatives here.) Second, be realistic. Unless the initiative is real and has changed the competitive landscape, it cannot by definition be a breakthrough strategy. Now, answer these questions:

- Where on the matrix are most of your initiatives concentrated?
- What is the business focus of your initiatives?
- What are your top three reasons for this business focus?
- Where are you versus the competition? versus another business unit? How do you close/maintain the gap?

By completing this exercise, you should have a clearer view of the alignment of your E-business initiatives in the context of the activities of other business units or competitors.

4

Extended E-conomy
Business Models

Opportunities abound for Net Ready organizations willing to focus on one or more of the five business models the E-conomy offers.

The E-conomy and the capabilities enabled by E-business technologies are driving the creation of new business models or roles that companies can take on. Our experience identifies five extended business models that are changing the way value is delivered. Successful Net Ready organizations take on one or more of these models. This chapter takes a detailed look at each of the five models in the Net Ready framework. Each of these models is being implemented in business-to-consumer and business-to-business environments. Furthermore, each represents a significant threat to existing companies who are slow to adopt. The five models are

1. E-business storefront

2. Infomediary

3. Trust intermediary

4. E-business enabler

5. Infrastructure providers/communities of commerce

The news media is full of stories about executives making overnight fortunes by taking on one or more of these roles. We want to make two points about this kind of success. First, high-impact success in the E-conomy is still very much the exception. As we have argued in this book, most E-business initiatives are haphazard and poorly integrated with existing value chains, and it is difficult or impossible to ascertain whether the initiatives offer a positive return on investment (ROI). Second, the news media focuses exclusively on consumers and on the well-known E-conomy successes that involve them. Ignored are the truly high-impact E-business initiatives that operate on a business-to-business level. That's too bad because the most exciting Net Ready work is happening in the business-to-business space. Throughout the remainder of this chapter, we illustrate each of the five business model opportunities with both consumer and business-to-business examples.

The E-Business Storefront

> **E-business storefront:** an entity in the E-conomy (business-to-business or consumer domains) in which commerce occurs, margin is created, and value is extracted using existing as well as new digital market channels. Often has a dot.com identity.

E-business storefronts are the online analogue to traditional ways of selling products or services. Similar to their industrial-age counterparts, E-business storefronts provide ultimate purchasing platforms to buyers; they also allow owners to cross-sell and upsell, maintain higher margins, and most important, compress the value delivery system by reducing transaction costs. But as much as E-business storefronts redefine the consumer value chain, they have a more profound impact on the business-to-business model. E-business storefronts create unprecedented value for business-to-business enterprises by creating new markets and brands, driving friction out of the process, and eliminating asymmetries of information.

The process of creating value in the E-conomy is often invisible, but the resulting value is very conspicuous. All the entities we have discussed so far—Amazon.com, E*Trade, Onsale, eBay, and so on—are, in one sense or another, E-business storefronts. They represent the intersection of the Net and E-commerce (table 4-1).

Forrester Research anticipates that business-to-business sales will increase to $1.3 trillion in 2002. The most significant segment of this sum is sales of electronic and computing components and products. The reason? Industries in which time to market is all-important find it immensely advantageous to use E-commerce to accelerate the buying process.

Intel, the leading semiconductor maker in the world, has a vibrant E-business storefront, the front window of which can be accessed at

Table 4-1. E-Business Storefronts

E-business storefronts are the storefronts of the E-conomy. When end users need to buy something, chances are they go to an E-business storefront.

Offerings

Products (product offering, order taking)

Services (fulfillment, customer service, and support)

Content (information on products and services)

Target Audience

Niche markets and buyers

Activities

Provide stand-alone network-based products, services, and content distributed in an E-conomy model

Competencies Required

Multiple relationship management

Ability to form/dissolve relationships rapidly

Robust/flexible infrastructure with plans for growth

Scaleable to meet evolving challenges/opportunities

Continuous innovation in product offerings and customer service

Goal

Dominate target niche

Revenue Stream

Product/service margin

Advertising

Examples

Intel

Amazon.com

E*Trade

United Airlines (UAL)

Cisco

Dell

Bluefly

www.intel.com. Intel established this Web-based business-to-business procurement application in an effort to streamline the transaction costs of supplying its customers with chips. Its largest customers have responded enthusiastically. Within one quarter of launching its site, Intel was pushing more than $1 billion of product *per month*. In development since January 1998, Intel's E-commerce program involves 200 customers, small- to medium-sized OEMs as well as distributors who have dealt directly with Intel all along. The company reduced the transaction costs of goods sold and cut cycle times for delivering products. Each of Intel's participating customers can check prices, receive product road maps, and purchase Intel products through a customized Web site. Moreover, errors in the administrative processing of offers have been significantly reduced. With the prices of semiconductors systematically dropping, any reduction in transaction costs goes straight to Intel's bottom line.

We see a similar erosion in the fees that securities brokerages can charge for transactions. The E-business storefronts of E*Trade and Charles Schwab have turned the business model of traditional full-service Wall Street brokerages upside down. Merrill Lynch, for example, grew fat on giving away research, advice, and service in exchange for commissions on overpriced transactions. Now, the transactions are basically given away, and the companies will live or die based on the value of their advice and the quality of their relationship management.

Nor can E*Trade rest on its laurels. The steady price erosion in transactions threatens E*Trade more than it does Merrill Lynch. Anticipating the day when transaction costs will no longer be the basis for a profitable business, E*Trade has to expand its range of services. One lesson of Net Readiness is that where there's friction, there's opportunity. In response, the E*Trade Group will compete in the emerging Net Ready banking space by its acquisition of Telebanc Financial for $1.8 billion. E*Trade's goal is to gain a more stable earnings stream by diversifying, anticipating the day when the securities trading market will no longer be profitable. That day is not far off, given the steady fall in the cost of processing securities transactions. We predict that firms such as E*Trade and even Merrill Lynch will soon be offering stock trades at no cost. Just look at the consumer and regulatory resistance banks received when they started charging a dollar per ATM transaction. Why should the cost of trading stocks be all that different? By compressing the delivery of banking services in the same way it compressed the delivery of securities trading services, E*Trade will drive out banking transaction costs and carve out a territory for itself. How better can E*Trade leverage its investment in infrastructure than by going after the Internet banking market?

E*Trade's decision to enter the cyberbanking space illustrates another lesson of Net Readiness. An organization can create value, as E*Trade is attempting to do, by migrating to another quadrant of the E-Business Value Matrix and thereby diversifying its E-business initiatives. Selecting the new

Net Ready challenge is the first decision. How the company chooses to migrate becomes the next critical decision. Should the company build the initiative from the ground up, or should it buy something that already exists? Both approaches have benefits. E*Trade bought Telebanc, deciding that it was better to put its development resources into beefing up the infrastructure of its securities business. By contrast, when Amazon.com entered the online auction space (see "Amazon.com's Entry into the Auction Space," page 213 in chapter 7), it could have bought any number of auction engines, but chose instead to build its own.

Infomediary

Infomediary: an entity that brokers content, information, knowledge, or experiences that add value to a particular E-business transaction; also known as content aggregator.

Infomediaries bring together buyers and sellers and provide value by offering content in the form of advice, personal service, or other benefits. Infomediaries can serve as aggregators of logical prospects or as buyer advocates. Unlike E-business storefronts, which have inventory to move, infomediaries typically own nothing. They have to rely on partners to succeed. Operationally, infomediaries focus on forming numerous partnerships, maintaining extensive content, and promoting their sites to buyers. Commissions, advertising and tenancy deals, and supply-side subscriptions are common means of generating revenues.

Reject the myth of disintermediation. Infomediaries generate a lion's share of the value in the E-conomy and will continue to do so for the foreseeable future. The infomediary, far from being eliminated by the E-conomy as myth would have it, is the most reliable source of generating new wealth. Infomediaries range from portals such as Yahoo! to Net start-ups that are creating unique markets on the Net—such as the travel aggregators Travelocity (www.travelocity.com) or Expedia (www.expedia.com). The business models that infomediaries are employing are as diverse as they are inventive. Some, such as Instill (www.instill.com)—which serves as a virtual order desk for restaurants and food-service operators—streamline an inefficient buying process. Others are consumer magnets, aggregating buyers by providing trusted information or services and steering them to manufacturers and service providers in return for a fee or a cut of transactions. These services include sites such as Autobytel.com and Autoweb.com, credit companies such as Get-Smart.com and E-Loan, and insurance services such as InsWeb.

NetBuy (www.netbuy.com) serves as a classic example of a business-to-business infomediary. In technical terms, NetBuy exemplifies an E-business initiative that enables real-time intercompany electronic supply chains. In operation, NetBuy is a comprehensive online service that allows buyers to point, click, and procure standard electronic components from an aggregated source of countless distributors. NetBuy is a catalyst. It does not own any products but rather matches buyers and sellers. It takes a commission for completed transactions. There is never a charge to buyers.

NetBuy features one-stop shopping for more than $2 billion in components from more than 2,000 manufacturers, all available for immediate inventory. Buyers simply indicate the part they want. NetBuy returns the matching part at the lowest price available. No need to search product directories or use the phone or fax. Quotes and orders are processed online for drop shipment, allowing buyers to track shipments and billing through a single source.

The value proposition that NetBuy offers revolves around rapid fulfillment of orders that buyers need immediately. Whereas traditional spot-market ordering in the electronics market takes two to five days or more and often requires the buyer to seek out hard-to-locate specialty suppliers, NetBuy can locate available inventory in seconds and process an order in just hours. NetBuy offers buyers the advantage of reduced time and cost of acquisition and provides distributors with an unprecedented opportunity to reach new customers at a cost that is far lower than a conventional spot-market transaction.

Some of the greatest opportunities lie in using the E-conomy to simplify complex and costly transactions. Realtor.com (www.realtor.com), a site for home buyers, is streamlining the nightmare of purchasing a home. Buying a home is a process that seems straight out of the Dark Ages; it involves a dozen or more intermediaries, from Realtors to title agents, each one imposing friction and adding cost. Realtor.com is affiliated with the National Association of Realtors and is up front about its bias: it directs consumers to one of its members. This E-business adds value by automating many other aspects of home sales, such as financing, surveys, and title searches.

Infomediaries aim to be the nexus of large numbers of buyers and sellers. The key dynamic: once the infomediary gathers a critical mass of buyers and sellers, more keep flocking to the site, because that's where the action is (table 4-2). Infomediaries can participate in various parts of the

Table 4-2. Infomediaries

Infomediaries generally do not buy or sell anything but rather facilitate transactions by providing aggregation services.

Offerings

Aggregation services

Match making (between buyer and seller needs)

Content (around a market segment, industry, part of an industry's value chain)

Product and service (fulfillment capabilities)

Target Audience

Members of a virtual community

Members of a value chain or part of an industry's value chain

Market segment

Activities

Aggregate buyers and sellers to facilitate transactions to be distributed in an E-conomy model

Competencies Required

Billing, order processing, invoicing, fulfillment, and other core processes with respect to product/service offering

Aggregation/brokering of end users and information

Partnership building

Management of relationships with other E-conomy partners

Goal

Capture dominant mind share or share of transactions

Revenue Stream

Advertising

Subscription fees

Partnership fees

Percentage of transaction fees

Examples

NetBuy

Autobytel.com

E-Loan

InsWeb

Travelocity

value chain, not just at the end. E-Loan (www.eloan.com), for example, attacked mortgage brokers, an element of the home loan process. Now E-Loan has aggregated so much demand that they act as a bank (see "Assume Another Role," page 188 in chapter 6).

Computer-Mediated Prices

From the earliest days of economic life, fortunes have been made and lost on the simple fact that prices for the same products and services can be radically different from place to place. Economists have called the factors for these price differentials "economic friction." As infomediaries reduce this friction by aggregating information about price, it is likely that for the first time in history buyers can have perfect knowledge of markets. When this happens, the same product will be the same price no matter where you buy it. Today, when you buy a digital camera, the camera costs one price at a department store, another price at a discount mail order house, and still a third price from the manufacturer's Web site. A number of infomediaries (see the discussion of CompareNet in the next section) have developed price comparison engines to help consumers locate the best possible value.

But these comparison infomediaries are skating on thin ice, because as more people use networks to obtain product information and prices, a particular item such as a digital camera or a pair of shoes will sell for the same price anywhere in the world. The concept is similar to a company's stock price, which is the same wherever it's purchased because of information available to stock traders using networks. The E-conomy will feature computer-mediated markets for everything, resulting in the complete elimination of price differentials for consumer products. Consumers are already seeing this phenomenon occur in communities such as eBay as the prices for similar goods—stuffed toys or digital cameras—seek their own level and take on commodity-pricing attributes.

The lesson of computer-mediated pricing for Net Ready companies is clear: a business strategy focused on delivering the lowest prices is not a sustainable value proposition. Net Ready companies will be forced to compete on the basis of innovative product design, exceptional customer service, or some other strategic attribute.

But here's a tantalizing digression: What if the E-conomy can rationalize the offering of products below cost? What if the value of the information about a transaction transcends the value of the transaction itself? The flabbergasting outcome will be that a company can actually offer a buck for ninety cents on the dollar. The magic of the Net and of the infomediary model actually makes the option of offering products below cost a reality. A number of Net Ready companies, such as Priceline.com and Buy.com, are experimenting with this intriguing strategy (see pages 131 and 202, respectively).

Buyer Brokers, Seller Brokers, Transaction Brokers, COINs

There are four types of infomediaries: buyer brokers, seller brokers, transaction brokers, and COINs. Before any company decides to participate in these spaces and take on one or multiple roles in the E-conomy (a concept that we discuss throughout this chapter), it must have or acquire certain competencies in order to be successful. As we discuss each type of infomediary in the sections that follow, we offer suggestions for competencies derived from our client assignments as well as from field research that we have performed over the last four years. Our suggestions represent the necessary or minimum competencies that we believe any company should possess if it is to be successful as an E-business storefront. Let us now examine each of these categories.

Buyer Brokers

Buyer brokers reduce transaction and search costs for the buyer by aggregating seller information, product information, and evaluative information.

The Internet is a perfect vehicle for comparison shopping, but mindless elements in the E-conomy persist in imposing biases on the process (see "Protecting Margins: The Internet Giveth; The Internet Taketh Away"). The big lesson of the E-conomy is that it punishes any attempt to bias the evaluation or buying process by restricting or manipulating information. One way to contradict the suspicion that a Web site is merely a pimp for a parochial set of commercial interests is to impose an arm's-length distance between the evaluation process and its fulfillment.

One of the most successful infomediaries buying into this philosophy is CompareNet (www.comparenet.com). CompareNet provides a powerful engine that searches out products by brand, features, or price, and then sets up elaborate side-by-side comparisons. But the real power of the site comes from the fact that all information is factual, not editorial. The Web site does provide links to discussion and opinion groups, but there is no attempt to review the products or otherwise influence buyers. Although CompareNet has partnered with product distributors like Crutchfields for fulfillment, the transaction is an arm's-length one that the buyer may or may not elect to pursue.

CompareNet buyers have access to comprehensive product information from start to finish. First, shoppers can research products ranging from automobiles to washing machines to running shoes by searching for key features and utilizing customizable brand-comparison charts. Users can then search, browse, and participate in thousands of Internet discussion groups to obtain product opinions and recommendations from their peers and to determine which product best fits their needs. These same shoppers can search classified ads posted by consumers from across the country to buy used merchandise at secondhand prices.

CompareNet sees the value of building a community around the shopping process. In 1998, it partnered with Classifieds2000, the leading classifieds service on the Web, and Deja News, the discussion network. These alliances enhance CompareNet's services by allowing consumers to not only research and compare thousands of products, but also seek opinions from other consumers via online discussions as well as shop for previously owned items posted within a network of online classified ads. CompareNet is magnifying its value to the consumer by adding a community-based (i.e., COIN) element to the company's comparison services. By combining objective product information with Internet discussion groups and classified ads, CompareNet offers an efficient shopping resource for today's most sophisticated buyers.

PackageNet (www.packagenet.com) exemplifies a buyer broker by aggregating information about package shipping that buyers can use to facilitate their package shipping requirements. PackageNet targets the package and express delivery market segment by developing a new category of services that depend on clever aggregation of heterogeneous shipping options. The service presents a variety of options for delivery times, costs, and route choices from several couriers, which saves buyers time and, by ensuring a thorough search of many possibilities, money as well. With more than 4,000 locations coast to coast, PackageNet is designed to make it easy for buyers to determine the closest location, store hours, fees, insurance services, and other policies. Buyers simply enter their zip codes to get a list of convenient locations. Clicking on a location brings up a map, store hours, and other information. The PackageNet nationwide rates page offers the rate and estimated delivery time for the user's package. Buyers can sign up for the PackageNet Preferred Shipper Program to get unique services such as extra package coverage, guaranteed ground shipments, and discount coupons. Finally, buyers can go to the Web site to track any package shipped via UPS, Federal Express, or Airborne.

The site walks buyers who are unfamiliar with package shipping through the entire process. Even if users don't know the address of the person they want to ship to, PackageNet can help. Clicking on the address page will help users find the address of any person or business in the United States. The catalog page provides links to catalog specials and catalog Web sites. PackageNet is slowly migrating to become a container, or infrastructure provider, for package shipping services. The site provides a retailers program, a private area for current and prospective PackageNet retailers. The PackageNet Web kit allows online merchants, retailers, and other sites to link to the PackageNet Web site to provide their customers with a complete shipping resource for personal shipments and merchandise returns.

Protecting Margins: The Internet Giveth; The Internet Taketh Away

In the wrong hands, the Net can be used as often to protect high prices as to rationalize low prices. For example, although airlines accommodate Internet-enabled fare shopping for the leisure traveler—principally as a way to move unfilled seats—they make sure that the business traveler has no such options. The fare and availability alerts that all major airlines now E-mail out on Wednesdays to identify excess capacity for the following weekend contain restrictions that are designed to make these fares all but useless for business travelers.

The Net makes comparison shopping easy, but shortsighted marketers can undermine even the best technology. For example, when Excite acquired Netbot, an Internet comparison-shopping company, the first thing it did was disable the user option to comparison shop for books and CDs. Before Excite's purchase, the Netbot agents would scour dozens of sites looking for the best price for a book. Now, Excite allows consumers to search only one bookseller, its partner, Amazon.com. According to Excite, these shopping categories were removed as a result of contractual obligations. A similar situation exists in other categories. Consumers need to look carefully when a site says it can help find a good price. The bargain it finds may not be the best price available.

The Internet's ability to rationalize prices, however, is so compelling that no industry can resist its pressure. Take set prices, for example. Better yet, forget about them. The Web will drive the last nail into the coffin on established prices. A combination of auctions and of intelligent software agents searching for the best prices will eventually determine the prices of all products and services. Marketers will have to find other competitive advantages besides price.

This outcome may sound risky or unworkable, but the truth is that Net-based markets may not be such a bad thing for sellers. What's the value of being able to predict the precise consequences of a pricing decision? What if enterprises can instantly calculate whether it pays to add more capacity? Two benefits are clear. First, companies will be able to slash inventory carrying costs because they will always know the market-clearing price. Second, they will know they have maximized the revenue yield on every sale.

Seller Brokers

Seller brokers reduce transaction and search costs for the seller by aggregating and providing information about customers and prospects.

Autobytel.com, perhaps the most conspicuous example of a seller broker in the E-conomy today, has one simple goal: to make car buying and car selling as painless as possible. To do that, Autobytel.com (www.autobytel.com) aggregates information about car buyers and, on behalf of its car dealer partners, wraps a streamlined set of services around the whole process. Autobytel.com is one of a growing number of services that gives consumers easy access to all facets of new and used car transactions, including financing, insurance, extended service agreements, and aftermarket options. (Autobytel.com participates in the E-conomy as more than just a seller broker. Later in this chapter we explain how Autobytel is also a premier example of an E-business enabler.)

When Autobytel.com founder Pete Ellis invented online automotive purchasing, he created a unique way to buy and sell vehicles and, in the process, revolutionized car buying and selling. Other services on the Internet act as conduits for traditional car sales by merely posting dealer Web sites and leading customers into the traditional car sales scenario. Autobytel.com has been credited by analysts with developing a program that has completely changed the automotive purchasing process. The company was launched in 1995 in Corona del Mar, Calif. Since then, Autobytel.com's growth has been phenomenal. In June 1997, Autobytel.com was named the fourth fastest growing new small business in America by Dun & Bradstreet and *Entrepre-*

neur Magazine. Since the company introduced its services in 1995, it has aided well in excess of one million car buyers.

Autobytel.com has used the attributes of the E-conomy to assemble a community of partnerships, information resources, and transaction services in an effort to lubricate every element of the sales channel. In turn, the company derives value from the myriad opportunities enabled by the aggregation of car buyers and the constituencies that have evolved to support them, all of whom are happy to share some of that incremental value with Autobytel.com. The site's simplicity of operation belies the subtlety of its concept and the razor-sharp focus on execution. On the simplest level, the site aggregates information about car shoppers and delivers sales leads to the dealers who pay for the privilege. On another level, the site aggregates content to attract car shoppers. In this respect, Autobytel.com provides tools and information to level the playing field on which car dealers have long held an insurmountable advantage. On behalf of customers, Autobytel.com surmounts this advantage, creating value for customers by eliminating the information discrepancies that have long kept them at a bargaining disadvantage.

Autobytel.com's aggregation model is relatively simple. A consumer visits, describes the car of his or her preference, takes advantage of some sophisticated search algorithms, and calculates the true costs of a purchase. Autobytel.com then sends the lead to a local car dealer that has subscribed to the Autobytel.com network. The dealer is then obliged to respond with a no-haggle price. Although the shopping Web site offers a cheap way to attract smart shoppers, the trade-off is that the site divulges information that dealers prefer to keep secret—namely, how much the dealer stands to make on each transaction. This is valuable information that shoppers can use as a sharp bargaining tool.

But the relationship with the customer does not end there. Autobytel.com is positioned to be a portal site into the Internet with coordinated services for every step of the automobile purchase. Car ownership has a long cycle: buy, use, repair, and sell. Autobytel.com wants to offer compelling services for every part of this cycle. The site already offers many aftermarket services. Does the consumer have a used car to sell? The site has access to Edmund's Buyer's Guides, Kelly Blue Book, Weekly AutoMarket Report, and other resources. Does the user need a quote for financing? Car insurance? All these resources are just a click away.

The service is completely free to the customer. Autobytel.com's revenues derive from annual fees paid by auto dealers who participate in the

Autobytel.com network. The site charges dealers annual fees ranging from $2,500 to $4,500 as well as monthly fees ranging from $500 to $3,000. The dealers are glad to pay because of the quality of the leads Autobytel.com delivers. More than 2,600 dealers have joined the Autobytel.com network, generating fees of more than $16 million last year. The Autobytel.com example illustrates the E-conomy rule that power gravitates toward the customer. All the value that Autobytel.com creates is aligned with the reality that an empowered customer is a more valuable customer. Autobytel.com is the poster Web site of the proposition that the more perfect the information a customer has, the better off everyone in the transaction becomes. Autobytel.com transformed the prevailing wisdom that automotive dealing is a zero-sum game: the car dealer loses a dollar for every dollar a customer gains. In fact, Autobytel.com demonstrates that in the E-conomy, car buying and selling can be a win-win proposition.

It's obvious that car buyers win. By having better information, including a good idea of the dealer's true costs, car buyers are in the driver's seat when it comes to negotiating the best possible price. But how about car dealers? Does Autobytel.com merely extract "excess" value from the car dealers and transfer it to customers? Absolutely not. No E-conomy infrastructure provider could sustain itself if it did not create new value, but instead merely transferred it from one party to another. Autobytel.com does create new value for dealers. Car dealers exist to sell more cars, for example, and the beauty of Autobytel.com is that it enables dealers to sell more cars while reducing marketing costs. In the traditional economy, car dealers have to pay marketing costs on average of $335 per car sold. By becoming a member of the Autobytel.com network, a dealer's marketing costs plummet to an average of $86 per car. It is primarily in this legacy of a very inefficient sales process that Autobytel.com can recover value for dealers.

Autobytel.com also creates value by providing the buying component for a growing number of automobile-related Web sites. For example, the Autobytel.com engine is used at Edmunds.com, AT&T WorldNet, CarPrice.com, and IntelliChoice.com. Autobytel.com further leverages its success as an E-conomy infrastructure provider with an aggressive branding effort to grow a customer base. While Autobytel.com has become a pioneer of online advertising—it practically invented the notion of exclusive deals with portals such as Excite, Infoseek, and Netscape—it hasn't neglected marketing in the traditional economy. The site even bought television airtime for the Super Bowl.

By acting as a rule breaker, Autobytel.com has revolutionized the way cars are bought and sold. It is a clear model of how technology, principally the Internet, can be used to blow up and then remake an industry, in this case, the $1 trillion automobile business.

Transaction Brokers

Transaction brokers reduce transaction and search costs for both buyers and sellers by bringing both parties together, helping match needs, and facilitating the resulting transactions.

Travelocity (www.travelocity.com) is the leading one-stop travel site on the Net. In June 1998, it announced more than $5 million in weekly transaction volume, a significant level of accomplishment for a site launched in March 1996. Travelocity consistently ranks among the top twenty-five Web sites in the workplace, and the site's 3.5 million registered members makes it a formidable presence in every corner of the E-conomy. These members tend to be well-heeled business travelers, a community of prime interest to everyone in the E-conomy. Travelocity recognizes the value of this membership, and is leveraging it with services such as

- *Air, car, and hotel booking.* Through the Sabre computer reservation system, schedules for more than 700 airlines, reservations and tickets for more than 400 airlines, and reservations and purchase capabilities for more than 35,600 hotels and 50 car rental companies.
- *Three best itineraries/low fare search engine.* A Sabre exclusive feature that automatically searches for the three lowest priced itinerary options based on a traveler's criteria.
- *Last-minute deals.* Deep discounts offered by various providers on last-minute travel.
- *Hotel maps and photos.* Street-level location maps and photos of selected hotels.
- *Flight paging.* A digital flight information service available free to owners of national alphanumeric pagers.
- *FareWatcher.* A free E-mail notification service offered to Travelocity members that keeps them informed when fares between their favorite cities go up or down.

In addition, Travelocity is building a COIN of people interested in travel and has partnered with a number of vendors for merchandise sales of books, luggage, maps, travel videos, and other wares.

COINs (Communities of Interest)

COINs reduce transaction and search costs for both buyers and sellers of a particular interest by aggregating both parties through content, community building, and commerce.

The COIN business model is emerging in industries from aerospace to food to solid waste. VerticalNet (www.verticalnet.com) has perfected this business model. One of the fastest-growing facilitators of industry-specific content and collaboration sites for business-to-business commerce on the Internet, VerticalNet handles limited sales transactions online. Its goal in each of its sites is to bring potential buyers and sellers together. Buyers can post requests for proposals and requests for quotes on the site and can solicit bids from sellers. By building communities of customers, vendors, and experts in the industries they serve, VerticalNet proved that high-value, industry-specific information can be published profitably on the Internet.

Net Ready Strategy

- *What:* Portal of COINs around business-to-business industrial goods and services
- *Company:* VerticalNet (www.verticalnet.com)
- *Offering:* Aggregates buyers and sellers in industry-specific communities, reducing fragmentation and leveraging opportunities for E-commerce and other value creating activities
- *Net Ready Strategy:* Community of Interest

The company organizes a Web presence for more than thirty COINs (see table 4-3). Companies use VerticalNet primarily as an online matching service in which sellers identify sales leads and buyers post their requirements for specific machinery or projects. Once a potential match is made, the parties typically finish their deal through the regular process of exchanging phone calls and faxes or meeting in person.

Table 4-3. Selected VerticalNet COINs and the Web Sites That Support Them

Each VerticalNet site is designed to deliver a well-defined audience—environmental engineers at wastewater treatment plants, for example—to advertisers willing to pay for access to their attention.

Process Group

Chemical Online	www.chemicalonline.com
Food Online	www.foodonline.com
Pharmaceutical Online	www.pharmaceuticalonline.com
Hydrocarbon Online	www.hydrocarbononline.com
Semiconductor Online	www.semiconductoronline.com

Electronics Group

Medical Design Online	www.medicaldesignonline.com
Wireless Design Online	www.wirelessdesignonline.com
Computer OEM Online	www.computerOEMonline.com
Photonics Online	www.photonicsonline.com
Test & Measurement Online	www.testandmeasurement.com

Environmental Group

Water Online	www.wateronline.com
Public works	www.publicworks.com
Solid waste	www.solidwasteonline.com
Pollution Online	www.pollutiononline.com
Power Online	www.poweronline.com
Property and Casualty	www.propertyandcasualty.com

VerticalNet's first Web site, Water Online (www.wateronline.com) is also its biggest, attracting nearly 100,000 visitors a month. At Water Online and other VerticalNet sites, suppliers to the specific industries can buy storefronts—a virtual advertising section owned by the supplier. Visitors to the VerticalNet site can find the latest news about their industry, drawn from a variety of newswire and editorial services, and can visit online directories of products and suppliers to locate needed information. When a supplier also has a storefront on the site, more detailed information can be provided to the visitor, all at no cost. The VerticalNet communities also feature résumé and job posting areas and an ability to post requests for proposals (RFPs) from companies seeking bids and responses.

VerticalNet creates value within a vertical industry using a five-point discipline: individualizing advertising; hosting sites; building and designing sites; sponsoring forums (with expert guests); and negotiating a percentage of each transaction that takes place within the online marketplace. The company now generates a relatively minor portion of its revenue as a "virtual distributor" of commodity products—everything from water valves to design software. But ultimately, the company sees big opportunities in electronic commerce as more and more trade takes place online.

Right now, VerticalNet is capturing a significant amount of valuable information on the interests and purchasing behaviors of its community members—using cookies and other technologies to track members' movements on the vertical sites. It charges its sponsors between $6,000 and $25,000 to deliver personalized Web advertisements and product announcements in its individualized, E-mail newsletters. As VerticalNet learns more about the individual members of each of its vertical trade communities and enables sponsors to deliver individualized messages to them, it enhances sponsor loyalty.

"We're a commerce facilitator," says VerticalNet president and CEO Mark Walsh. "It's about facilitation and acceleration of existing sales channels." In addition to RFPs, request for quotations (RFQs), and product postings, VerticalNet offers E-mail, chat sessions, and bulletin boards. Companies that have purchased storefronts on various VerticalNet sites include electrical engineering company ABB, petroleum engineering company Foster Wheeler, General Electric, Hewlett-Packard, and Sony. "The real impact of the Web is on how businesses will relate to each other as buyers and suppliers," Walsh added. "When that happens, the potential markets for online business are huge."

Some COINs help sellers link their back-end systems to the site, allowing for real-time inventory checks and fully integrated accounting. Chemdex (www.chemdex.com), a COIN for scientific research materials, has attracted 130 suppliers, according to CEO Dave Perry. Customers include pharmaceutical company Genentech and Harvard University, whose employees can order from a catalog of 300,000 products and pay for them online. A server-side Java application connects the Chemdex sites to suppliers' back-end inventory management systems.

The healthcare industry, plagued with inefficient processes, a lack of information available globally, and an inability to collaborate across its supply chains, is another industry in which COINS can be beneficial. The problems that are created—doctors who are unable to research new diagnostic equipment, hospital administrators who have trouble locating the best price on basic supplies, or vendors who can't easily reach new markets—translate into more expensive, lower quality patient care. The industry's historic lack of investment in information technology is clearly a significant source of its inefficiencies. However, numerous studies indicate that this trend is reversing, leaving the industry ripe for leveraging the Internet as the ubiquitous business connectivity tool. One response is Neoforma (www.neoforma.com), which brings together 13,000 suppliers of hospital and medical supplies and 70,000 buyers belonging to 7,500 health-care entities. A COIN of this scale has never been possible before the Internet. This pattern repeats itself across many industry groups.

COINs aggregate fragmented groups of buyers with equally fragmented groups of sellers in selected niche markets and charge commissions for the products they help move. The main shift that the Web has brought about is the transition of power from sellers to buyers in Net Ready markets.

Essential Functions of Infomediaries

As long as there is an industry with a fragmentation of suppliers or customer ignorance about prices and relative performance of products, there will be a profit zone for infomediaries. Infomediaries respond to a limited number of business requirements. Here are a few of the emerging characteristics that an evolving and sophisticated infomediary may need to offer:

- *Aggregation of needs.* Combines several existing needs into a new category of needs that did not exist before. Example: E-Loan (see "Assume Another Role," page 188 in chapter 6).

- *Aggregation of services.* Combines several existing services to create a new service or category that did not exist before. Example: Autobytel.com (see "Seller Brokers," page 112 in this chapter).

- *Bid/ask engine.* Creates a market-driven floating pricing system in which buyers and sellers negotiate, often by a computer-enabled process, to establish prices. Example: Onsale (see "Move the Product up the Food Chain," page 163 in chapter 5).

- *Consultative adviser.* Scours the Web to identify value-added services to leverage the products or services that the consumer is about to purchase. Examples: Firefly, Sixdegrees.

- *Hidden demand.* Takes orders for nonexistent category of services. Sources the services after sufficient demand is created for it.

- *Matchmaking.* Identifies and matches the requirements of buyers with products and services from sellers, on an ad hoc basis, without a priori knowledge of either one.

- *Negotiation.* Provides agents that can negotiate price, quantity, or features according to a set of parameters.

- *Notification service.* Notifies customers, often by E-mail or page, when the service becomes available or when prices change or reach a certain preestablished threshold. Example: CompareNet (see "Buyer Brokers," page 109 in this chapter).

- *Smart needs adviser.* Identifies buying opportunities or alternate products or services. Examples: Notification of weekend E-fares by Travelocity, United Airlines, or American Airlines; notification of weekend hotel room discounts by Holiday Inn.

- *Upsell.* Suggests an additional product or service so that a consumer who buys both is offered a combined discount or an additional benefit. Examples: Gateway, Dell.

Portals as Infomediaries

Portal is a term, generally synonymous with *gateway,* for a World Wide Web site that is or proposes to be a major starting site for users when they get connected to the Web or an anchor site that users tend to visit. Typical services offered by portal sites include a directory of Web sites, a facility to search for other sites, news, weather information, E-mail, stock quotes, phone and map information, and sometimes a community forum. Portal sites have attracted much stock market investor interest because they are viewed as able to command large audiences and numbers of advertising viewers.

Everyone in the E-conomy wants to get into the portal act (see "Electric Utility Plugs into Portal"). Today, portals in leadership positions include Yahoo!, Excite, Netscape, Lycos, Microsoft Network, and a few others. With its own private array of sites when you dial in, America Online could be thought of as a portal to its own Web portal at www.aol.com. A number of large access providers offer portals to the Web for their own users. Portal strategies can be examined from a number of perspectives, but from a value proposition standpoint, they exhibit all the characteristics of an infomediary. Their principal role is to aggregate buyers and sellers, making transactions more comfortable for the former and more efficient for the latter.

In one sense, portals are nothing new. In the traditional economy, catalogs such as *The Sharper Image* work on a portal model. Anytime an entity can aggregate and provide timely information for the benefit of buyers and sellers, it assumes portal status. Information has always been integral to commerce. What makes a portal an infomediary is that in the E-conomy commerce is increasingly and exclusively about information. The portal sites serve as infomediaries by putting content and audience together. They can also add value by amassing elective COINs, which then allows them to generate revenue in a variety of ways: advertising, referral fees, even garnering percentages of sales. The approach relies on the Internet to deliver information in a bottoms-up mode and to provide low-cost access to a critical mass of consumers.

But not every infomediary can succeed at being a portal site. In fact, most will fail, because they make a fundamental mistake. They understand correctly that portal sites have value because they can command the attention of large numbers of visitors to the E-conomy. But E-business storefronts who strive for success by single-minded pursuit of consumers are missing the point.

Here's the lesson: portals need business partners more than they need users. E-business storefronts that conclude that the portal site is the product and its users are the consumers are mistaken. They are looking at the situation through the wrong end of the telescope. As with other media businesses, "eyeballs" are the product, and the portal's advertisers, E-conomy partners, and content providers are the consumers.

It's one thing to attract eyeballs. It's quite another to retain them. And it's quite another still to determine that the eyeballs being attracted are profitable and worth retaining. In a world in which consumers are gaining control of what they see, the race is on to build relationships to keep customers coming back at a profit. America Online, for example, is constantly working to make its portal site "sticky." A sticky site creates customer loyalty by offering customers the three Cs: content, community, and context. America Online's home site, for example, offers members and nonmembers the ability to construct personal Web communities or access E-mail from anywhere. America Online calls these features *sticky applications,* in which customers make an investment by creating individualized content.

Successful portals have learned that a customer who invests time teaching a business what he or she needs will be less likely to go elsewhere. It's a way of increasing switching costs. The marketer wins loyalty. The customer wins individualized service. These learning relationships are the key to getting and retaining customers at a profit.

In the traditional economy, radio and television stations sell their audience size to advertisers. That's why there's such a fuss over Nielsen ratings: programming is just a way to hold viewers' attention between commercials. The E-conomy turns much of this tried-and-true equation on its head. First, portals don't really need more Net consumers. While audience growth may be a primary goal of the portal newcomers, most major portals sell out only a fraction of their advertising inventory. (And when you hear portals talk about advertising inventory, remember that you, as an Internet user, are the inventory.) The supply also continues to outpace the demand.

Second, the larger the portal audience is, the greater are its costs. Larger audiences require portals to invest in more hardware, bigger network connections, and more support staff to hold it all together. Therefore, increased traffic is meaningless unless a portal can derive revenue from it. The situation that prevails in the E-conomy is wholly unlike the television and radio model. There, the costs of broadcasting are relatively fixed once a station enters a market and begins broadcasting, regardless of its audience size. This situation is also unlike print media, in which subscription fees are the norm, and unlike early online services such as America Online and CompuServe, in which metered connection times were the norm.

In the E-conomy, the advertisers and the E-conomy deals are a portal's primary audience. Therefore, the battle over portals is less about fighting over eyeballs than about fighting over the business of potential advertisers and merchants. That market is unquestionably portals' chief source of revenue. Because of this relationship, portals will more often—if forced to choose—side with business partners over their audiences. This arrangement won't change until portals deal directly with consumers as a primary source of revenue.

Let's look at this situation from another angle. Few major portals generate their own content. Their content is typically syndicated from third-party providers or generated by their own users through message boards, chats, and free E-mail. In other words, the portal's role is that of an information infomediary. Successful portals use their power to create relationships, COINs, and communities to drive a variety of business activities from which they can extract value.

Electric Utility Plugs into Portal

Central Illinois Light Company (CILCO) is a small electric and gas utility based in Peoria, Illinois. Its first Web site, which went live on

Christmas Day 1995, presented 100 or so static pages of brochure-ware. Today, CILCO has one of the most advanced sites in the industry (www.cilco.com). "The present CILCO site was intended to be a portal site, one of the early implementations of this concept on the Internet," says Mark DuBois, CILCO's information technology services senior business consultant. "The idea was to build an electronic community and provide reasons for visitors to return again and again to the site."

To that end, the site not only offers the predictable menu of customer service options (reviewing electric bills, paying bills, signing up for service, etc.) but a palette of useful services. Visitors to the CILCO site can check on the weather or track packages shipped via Federal Express, UPS, or Airborne. The package works. More than half a million people—over 100 times the population in CILCO's service area—visit the site each month. This critical mass makes the CILCO site a valuable commodity, especially because all electrical power companies in the state will be completely deregulated by the year 2003.

At that point, consumers can buy electricity and natural gas from any one of dozens of providers. CILCO is determined to use its Web site to create and sustain the customer relationships it needs to preserve its competitive edge. In addition to being a portal site, the CILCO Web site provides consumers with the ability to negotiate power and gas prices. Consumers can lock in long-term rates for predictability or can negotiate spot rates to take advantage of fluctuating prices.

CILCO understands the value of economies of scale. Today, CILCO hosts the city of Peoria's Web site, and the same community events and information may be viewed from both sites. Ad banners are linked to the displayed information, so business banners appear on the CILCO site but consumer banners are shown on the consumer information pages. The company is building electronic commerce features into the site, and visitors already can shop online for CILCO-branded merchandise. CILCO is clearly an E-business storefront as well as an infomediary.

Attention Brokers

In the E-conomy, the quality of attention is strained. Every human gets exactly twenty-four hours per day. Time is nonnegotiable and nontransferable. The inviolability of time as a fixed asset leads inexorably to the emerging medium of exchange in the E-conomy: attention. The chains of the past still hold the E-conomy in tow. Companies are still trying to use traditional advertising and marketing gimmicks to secure attention. The first generation of Web sites and banner ads flashed and moved to get eyeballs to alight and mouse keys to click through. Devices such as ad banners and other forms of traditional advertising are based on the interruption marketing model because they interrupt a visit to a Web site, a magazine article, or a television program. But with a million sites added to the World Wide Web every month, buyers are less and less willing to give their attention away. These days, they want something for their attention, even if it's a little entertainment such as a game or a contest. Today, sellers are giving away prizes and services for the privilege of securing attention for a few seconds. Some companies are even paying cash for slices of attention capital.

Attention brokers are another class of infomediaries emerging in the E-conomy. Attention brokers rise to the challenge of building an audience of ready-and-willing consumers in the E-conomy. Incentive programs, which reward consumers for their attention, have shown some merit in this area and have given consumers a reason to be more active product purchasers and assimilators of online advertisements. In return, marketers get the promise of a new customer and, in many cases, a sale.

Like all infomediaries, attention brokers create value by aggregating content to bring together merchants and consumers. These brokers are unique in that they add something extra to the equation, namely a premium linked to attention. It all goes by the name of *permission marketing,* the concept that producers should be willing to pay consumers for certain behavior that the merchants want to reinforce. Such behavior includes visiting a Web site, completing a survey or questionnaire, or buying a product or service.

Permission marketing describes a business model emerging in response to the bankruptcy of seducing people for their attention instead of negotiating for it. Permission marketing says that everyone benefits when there are some explicit agreements in place between sellers and their audiences. The general agreement is: I agree to give you my attention in exchange for you giving me something of value. That something may be entertainment (a game), a contest with prizes, a product, or cash or some other token of value.

Permission marketing is not new and certainly not restricted to the Web. If you have ever been promised a free vacation, television set, or set of golf clubs to visit a time-share vacation complex, you have encountered a particularly heavy-handed form of permission marketing. The agreement is fairly simple: I give your salespeople my attention for an hour or so while they try to sell me on the benefits of the offer, and in exchange you give me something of value. I may or may not take you up on your offer, but since you got my attention, I earn the item of value.

Net Ready companies use attention infomediaries to refine this dynamic to unprecedented levels. Permission marketing is built around rational calculations by both parties. Let's start from the buyer's point of view. Buyers have money to spend on products, but they lack two things: one, the time to evaluate products, and two, trust in the companies that make them. Permission marketing is based on selfishness: buyers will grant a company permission to communicate only if they know what's in it for them. A company has to reward consumers, explicitly or implicitly, for paying attention to its messages. That's why the Net is such a powerful medium. It changes everything. Companies can use E-mail to communicate with people frequently, quickly, and unobtrusively—so long as they have permission to do so.

Now let's look at it from the seller's point of view. One of the problems with interruption-based marketing is that the seller has to assume that "no" means "no"—when, in fact, it often means "not now, maybe later." Interrupt advertising and direct mail do not allow a seller to distinguish between "no" and "maybe." The economics dictate that if buyers see the seller's message but don't buy the product, or receive a piece of direct mail but don't respond, then they have rejected the seller's pitch. The truth is that sellers just don't know for sure that their message has been rejected, but they can't afford to find out. It's just too expensive to create relationships using interrupt marketing. So sellers are forced to move on to the next batch of prospects.

The Net changes the calculus of marketing by eliminating the costs of revisiting the "maybes." With E-mail, frequency is free. Sellers can keep communicating with buyers, relating to them with education or entertainment in an attempt to turn them into customers. If you want to change people's behavior, a one-time message won't work. You have to get permission, create a relationship, offer a benefit, get in their face, and talk to people over and over again.

Trust Intermediary

Trust intermediary: an entity that creates trust between the buyer and the seller.

Trust is an essential lubricant for commerce, electronic or otherwise. In the E-conomy, trust assumes an even more fundamental importance because only the level of trust differentiates one anonymous trading entity from another. Without trust, companies in the physical world have a hard time growing beyond the boundaries of a family. That constraint limits not just their size but their ability to hire professional managers and share wealth and control.

In the E-conomy, trust minimizes the friction that gets in the way of transactions and information sharing, both outside and inside. Moreover, trust underlies the rules for self-organization. The old industrial model of the factory is a command/control environment in which central authority lays down the rules, and workers either follow them or not. The rules for self-organization are internalized; the organization has common norms and goals. It doesn't need to make all those rules explicit and you can interact freely. The question is, how can companies go about creating trust on the Internet? What can serve as a proxy for trust if it doesn't exist in a culture? Will companies end up doing commerce only within the equivalent of sponsored markets?

The high value that people place in brands is testimony to the need for objects of trust. Participants in the E-conomy will initially place their trust in the same E-business storefronts that they trusted in the physical world. That's why brands such as Citibank, Visa, Wells Fargo, and American Express have such value. These brands can leverage the carefully constructed security of their names to all manner of E-business initiatives. An appeal to brands is behind the claims of such E-business storefronts as Expedia ("powered by Microsoft") and Travelocity ("powered by Sabre/American Airlines"). These travel sites are attempting to leverage the brand equity of their better known partners (table 4-4).

Payment Enabler and Trust Enabler

There are two special types of trust infomediaries—payment enabler and trust enabler. Each has a unique function in the E-conomy. Let's consider each of these categories.

Table 4-4. Trust Intermediaries

Trust intermediaries provide a secure environment in which buyers and sellers can confidently exchange value.

Offerings
Secure environment
Escrow services
Privacy
Recourse
Brands

Target Audience
Buyers
Sellers
Affinity groups
COINs

Activities
Provide an auditable environment in which informed consent may be determined, value may be exchanged securely, and privacy maintained

Competencies Required
Billing, order processing, invoicing, fulfillment, and other core processes with respect to escrow or other service offerings
Securitization and customer trust building, for example, expertise in secure payment transactions, encryption
Exquisite attention to detail
Rich historical analytical capabilities to determine risks

Goal
Extract value from each transaction by enabling a safe, secure transaction environment

Revenue Stream
Licensing fee
Subscription

Examples
Verisign
CyberCash

Payment Enablers

Payment enabler: an entity that enables secure payment transactions and reduces risks to buyers and sellers.

The Internet is creating new opportunities for merchants, giving them the capability to reach millions of potential customers and to transcend traditional demographic boundaries. Financial institutions can expand their market presence as well, by providing solutions tailored to the needs of these online merchants. But all this E-conomy commerce effort is for naught unless secure payment schemes can be standardized. Enter payment enablers such as VeriFone (www.verifone.com), acquired by Hewlett-Packard in 1997 for $1.29 billion, and ICVerify (www.icverify.com), more recently acquired by Cybercash.

A significant enabler of electronic commerce has been the availability of secure and functional payment technologies. In particular, the ability to utilize the established credit card infrastructure for "card-not-present" transactions has supported the growth to date. As additional functionality is added and new security mechanisms are developed, the deployment of electronic commerce capability will only accelerate.

Sellers in the E-conomy share many needs. All seek easy-to-use, software-based solutions that provide robust credit card processing functionality. They want a secure solution that will give their customers the confidence to utilize their credit cards over the Internet. In addition, these businesses want access to the acquiring bank of their choice based on prior relationships or access to superior discount rates. Given the Internet's reach and pervasiveness, these businesses also want the ability to scale the payment transaction capability as market demands generate greater commerce throughput.

Trust Enablers

Trust enabler: an entity that creates a trusted or authenticated environment in which parties can interact with confidence and recourse.

How does a company build trust in the E-conomy? Ultimately, as in the physical world, a company does it by proving, one transaction at a time, that it can be trusted. Trust is an essential condition of a functioning economy, whether it be based on barter or software agent–driven commodity markets. Personal contact and trust are intimately related. The closer the proximity between seller and buyer, the easier it is to establish trust. The challenge for the E-conomy is to establish trust in the absence of any preexisting relationship between buyer and seller.

One piece of good news is that the E-conomy is very much based on credit, not cash, a fact that lowers the risks somewhat. The word *credit* means to "to believe" or "to trust." The E-conomy needs trust enablers to create an environment in which credit can be extended with confidence. What's needed in the E-conomy are branded symbols of trust on the Internet, analogous to the UL Labs' or Good Housekeeping's seals of approval that emblematize trust and accountability in the physical world. Entities such as TradeSafe (www.tradesafe.com), which protects E-conomy transactions in a safe cocoon called an escrow agreement, is a classic trust intermediary. Taking on the function of a trust intermediary as a strategic technique for creating sustainable competitive edge can be highly effective.

Intel Inside

Intel Inside is one of smartest and most successful examples of an initiative designed to build trust. We admire the position Intel has created for itself in the information technology field. Its financial success, market dominance, technological prowess, ability to innovate and lead, and astonishing operational skills have combined to make the company one of the most powerful and influential corporations in the world. In marketing, Intel has earned a place of honor for its early and aggressive grasp of branding, which the company has pounded home with its Intel Inside campaign.

The Intel Inside brand is one of the computer industry's best-known symbols. It has been used in more than $2 billion worth of PC advertising by the industry. It's also considered one of the most brilliant and enduring consumer marketing programs ever in the computing marketplace. What does the Intel Inside brand really mean? In essence, it gives the consumer the confidence that the PC they are looking at contains an Intel microprocessor—the computer's brain. The campaign establishes the proposition that the microprocessor is the most important component within the PC. Intel's Pentium processor has been the most successful microprocessor ever in the PC industry. So the logo brings with it certain brand values.

One value the Intel Inside brand delivers is safety. In other words, the consumer knows that this PC contains an industry-leading, high-performance processor—the Intel Pentium processor—and that a Net Ready company stands solidly behind it.

Anonymous Exchanges

The E-conomy allows for creation of competitive, anonymous markets for many industries. In these electronic arenas, buyers and sellers converge and competition pushes prices to near optimal levels. Anonymous markets cannot function without some level of trust established by channel equity. When channel equity is in place, the value of brand equity—so critical in other areas of the E-conomy—becomes less important and, in some cases, even irrelevant.

Anonymous exchanges, in which qualified buyers and sellers don't need to know the identity of the other party, favors buyers. The E-conomy empowers the buyers of relatively homogeneous services such as insurance, refinancing, travel, and other structured products. It does so by allowing for an anonymous market, which is unbiased by old-school selling techniques such as relationships and wining and dining. Perfect information will drive buying decisions, not personal relationships, and transactions will be cleared in a lean, efficient manner. Two companies pushing this model are E-Loan, which links mortgage brokers with lenders, and Fast-Parts (www.fastparts.com), which allows electronics companies to exchange components.

Anonymity tends to reduce prices. Margins may fall for sellers, yes, but their cost of sales will fall, too. When the day is done, sellers may actually come out better than they were before. Advertising costs should be reduced because brand awareness means nothing in an anonymous market. Lean-selling organizations will gain share and prosper. Organizations that count on an informationally inefficient market to keep buyers from obtaining key price data will be out of luck. Buyers win. Sellers win. That's one attribute of the E-conomy.

Auction Partnerships

Auctions are another attribute of the E-conomy that offers buyers clout. With the emergence of intelligent software agents that can interrogate the Web, buyers are in a position to render irrelevant a vendor's price list. Under this model, a buyer broadcasts on the Web the prices they are willing to pay for, say, a plane trip from Chicago to Hong Kong, an hour of video-conference time to Indonesia, or a Ford Taurus. In the next few minutes, the Web becomes a clearinghouse of software agents attempting to match buyers and sellers. United Airlines may well accept the buyer's bid if, in the estimation of the yield management agent, the airline will otherwise have empty seats on the day of departure. The software agent balances the probability that United can fill that seat with a higher fare against the possibility that the seat may generate no revenue at all for the airline if it remains unfilled when the doors close. In exchange for the buyers giving up flexibility, sellers willingly give up margin.

Sellers with fixed infrastructure costs, for example, telecommunications companies such as MCI or Sprint, may well accept a buyer's bid for an hour of videoconferencing services. The buyer's chances are increased if the bid represents periods during which the seller has historically been slow in moving product or service. At this point, the incremental revenue, whatever it may happen to be, offered by the buyer may well prove to be attractive to the seller.

In business-to-consumer commerce, one of the most radical rule breakers is Priceline.com (www.priceline.com), which has sold more than 500,000 airline tickets in the emerging buyer-centric environment. Priceline.com lets customers post prices that they are willing to pay for trips, backed up by a credit card as a demonstration that a demand really exists. Priceline.com then searches its proprietary fare database for flights. If an airline accepts the offer, Priceline.com makes a match and receives a commission or takes the spread between what the consumer offered and what the airline is prepared to accept.

It may look like Priceline.com merely aggregates buyers for airline tickets in the same way that Autobytel.com aggregates car buyers, but there is a big difference. Cars are not (not yet, anyway) a substitutable commodity the same way airline seats are. If you want to go to Denver this weekend, do you really care what airline takes you there? By contrast, if you are shopping for a BMW, you are not interested in taking possession of a Yugo. In fact, Priceline.com follows a demand collection model associated with a substitutable, commodity-like product. Priceline.com creates substitutable demand to get buyers substitutable product. The difference is that the demand must be certified up front by a valid credit card. The model then merely transfers that demand proxy to Priceline.com, which can then act as an infomediary. In effect, Priceline.com informs the sellers that "here is one customer with a substitutable range." An airline or hotel can choose to accept the offer or decline it.

Priceline.com is now expanding its patented business model to packaged vacations that include rental cars, plane tickets, and hotels. Travelers will state their price for a specific trip, challenging the businesses involved to cooperate to make the package work for all parties. Consumers are telling the travel industry, "You sellers work it all out and E-mail me in the morning. We're going to bed." Within the next few years, people will use software agents to help them sell demographic information about themselves to companies that are trying to get their attention to make sales. There will be auctions for attention, with the highest bidders winning the privilege of securing a seller's attention and getting paid for it.

As if on cue, as this book went to press Budget Rent a Car announced that it was jumping into the online auction frenzy. The number three car rental company launched an E-business initiative called BidBudget, which will give Net users the opportunity to digitally haggle over the price of a rental car in an auction format. The immediate goal is to move excess weekend inventory for recreational travelers. The new service, which taps Budget's existing yield management and Maestro reservation systems, gives customers price control and independence. The BidBudget Web site has an area in which customers can choose a location, select the type of car they want to rent, and then name the rate they are willing to pay. For example, a traveler headed to Cleveland looking for a midsize car could bid $18.85 per day for a model that regularly rents for $35. Successful bidders will be contacted by E-mail.

By allowing users to bid what they are willing to pay, Budget will be able to rent cars that would otherwise sit unused in parking lots. This development ratifies a number of points we make in this book. First, it's generally not the industry leaders (in this case Hertz and Avis) that take the bold, rule-breaking steps. Second, power is moving away from sellers to buyers. Third, a company must not be afraid to risk cannibalizing its existing channels to create new E-business opportunities. Fourth, the power of the brand on the Net should not be minimized. Budget's brand will boost its E-business initiative.

E-Business Enabler

E-business enabler: An entity that provides a component or functionality and adjunct services to enable and lubricate other E-business storefronts or infomediaries.

Another E-conomy role is that of E-business enabler (table 4-5). An E-business enabler uses its technology or competencies to facilitate or enable an-

Table 4-5. E-Business Enablers

E-business enablers create and maintain an infrastructure in which product and service providers can conduct transactions reliably and securely.

Offerings

Specialized functionality and ancillary services that allow members of a supply chain or COIN to extract value from transactions by adding value

Products for E-business applications and services to enable E-commerce and to support other E-business initiatives and services

Target Audience

E-business storefronts

Infomediaries

Activities

Support the opportunities of E-conomy product and service providers by delivering a robust, reliable functionality

Competencies Required

Emphasis on service; for example, billing, development, network management, maintenance

IT operations; for example, capacity planning, network strategy and operations, contract negotiations, facilities management, database administration, and so on

Support and infrastructure maintenance

Marketing and sales

Port infrastructure to target environments/vertical markets and to enhance value proposition

Goal

Extract value from each transaction by aggregating interested, willing prospects with merchants in an environment of explicit permission

Revenue Stream

Licensing fee for functionality provided

Partnership fee

Percentage of transaction

Examples

Federal Express

LoopNet

Onsale

Chrome.com

other set of business processes; to its end users it is frequently transparent. Thus when Federal Express provides the back-end outbound fulfillment logistics for an organization, it is playing an E-business enabler role. The same strategy is being used by DoubleClick as it licenses its advertisement-serving engine for customers such as Procter & Gamble.

E-business enablers frequently take shape as business-to-business trading hubs that cater to business constituencies ranging from aviation to zoology. These new trading hubs are typically extranets built and maintained by E-business enablers whose value proposition is that they can provide the extranets at cost. They allow individual businesses to leverage these sites to build their own extranet-based networks of suppliers and customers without requiring major investments in infrastructure. The idea is to give the businesses one-stop shops that bring real savings to customers while delivering vast markets to sellers. The E-business enablers occupy the middle and take a slice of the value of each transaction.

Onsale, a company that is discussed at length in chapter 5, is also evolving into the role of E-business enabler. Whatever competitive advantage Onsale derived from its auction technology is long gone. In response, the company extends its strategy by taking on another E-conomy role, in this case, the role of E-business enabler. For example, Onsale was the auction engine for Yahoo!, enabling this site to auction merchandise. Yahoo! users did not care that the auction in which they participated was administered by Onsale in the background. An E-conomy enabler seamlessly integrates itself into a partner's business operations to facilitate processes such as distribution, fulfillment, and a wide spectrum of channel logistics. Logistics management, in fact, is a prime area in which companies such as Federal Express and many others have found they can add value.

In their quest for new ways to establish a competitive edge, many companies are recognizing the unique types of customer value that can be created through logistics management. While firms such as Omaha Steak, National Semiconductor, L.L. Bean, and Frito-Lay would surely agree that product quality and consistency are important, they would also argue that the superior channel logistics create significant value for customers. Earlier in this chapter (see "Seller Brokers," page 112), we looked at Autobytel.com as an infomediary, which it assuredly is, but its strategy of being an E-business enabler to the automobile industry is the primary reason for its continuing success. Other examples of E-business enablers are Federal Express and CompuServe.

Federal Express Enables Omaha Steaks and National Semiconductor

Federal Express (www.fedex.com) started as a transportation company, but today it is assuredly in the channel logistics business. In other words, by linking tightly with its constituencies, it functions as an E-business enabler. To be sure, Federal Express still delivers overnight packages with its fleet of 40,000 ground vehicles and 600 airplanes. But behind the scenes is an infrastructure of IT systems and Net Ready connections that underpins Federal Express's transformation from package deliverer to strategic provider of E-conomy logistics, and other supply chain services.

Federal Express is using the E-conomy to provide end-to-end fulfillment logistics on behalf of its customers. Moving well beyond delivery services, Federal Express is increasingly a fully integrated corporate partner that picks up, transports, warehouses, and delivers all of a company's finished goods from the factory to the customer's receiving dock—with status data available every step of the way. By assuming a variety of strategic processes on behalf of its customers and by forging intimate links with their information systems, Federal Express has made itself an increasingly indispensable part of their infrastructures. The resulting links are so powerful, valuable, and costly to dismantle that Federal Express has made it very difficult for its customers to switch to UPS or Airborne, both of whom have followed Federal Express's lead. That's how an E-business enabler locks in market share.

A good example of this strategy is Omaha Steaks (www.omahasteak.com), which in 1996 chose Federal Express as its exclusive delivery service for mail-order steaks and other foods because UPS didn't offer two-day air delivery service. Although UPS has since started such a service, Omaha Steaks has stayed with Federal Express exclusively because of intimate IT links with Federal Express that let Omaha Steaks's customer-service employees easily track delivery status.

So seamless is the relationship between Omaha Steaks and Federal Express that it is difficult to perceive where one company starts and the other one ends. Consider that when orders—whether from phone, mail, fax, the Web, or America Online—are sent from Omaha Steaks's main computer to its warehouses, the data is concurrently sent on a dedicated line to Federal Express. While Omaha Steaks prints out a shipping label for the order, Federal Express is simultaneously printing out a tracking label. Omaha Steaks delivers the warehouse-fulfilled orders by truck to Federal Express in Memphis or to Federal Express regional hubs in Columbus, Ohio, and Indianapolis. Once Federal Express takes over, Omaha Steaks has full access to Federal Express data on delivery status, planned routing, and planned delivery day. Using a peer-to-peer connection over a Federal Express value-added network, Omaha Steaks's computer communicates directly with Federal Express's servers. Finally, to further blur the distinctions between the companies, Omaha Steaks, like many Federal Express customers, also lets customers track their orders on its Web site with a link to the Federal Express Web-based tracking service.

National Semiconductor (www.national.com) has handed over its entire logistics management to Federal Express, including warehousing and distribution. Today, virtually all the company's products, manufactured in Asia by three National Semicondctor factories and three subcontractors, are shipped directly to a Federal Express distribution warehouse in Singapore. The tight IT links between that warehouse and National Semiconductor exemplifies Federal Express's role as an E-conomy infrastructure provider. National Semiconductor's homegrown order-processing application, running on an IBM mainframe in Santa Clara, Calif., sends a daily batch of orders over a dedicated line directly to Federal Express's inventory-management application running on a Tandem Computers machine in Memphis. At that point, Federal Express essentially takes over, sending the orders to its warehouse-management application in Singapore, where they're fulfilled in the warehouse and shipped. Except for receiving an execution record back from Federal Express, National Semiconductor is done with the order transaction. Federal Express handles all the business processes preparatory to being handed the lucrative transportation component. That's the power of an E-conomy infrastructure provider and has helped make Federal Express the $11 billion business it is. The benefits to the customer are also compelling. Bottom-line savings for National Semiconductor include a reduction of the average customer delivery cycle from four weeks to one week and a reduction of distribution costs from 2.9 percent of sales to 1.2 percent. At the same time, the company also eliminated seven regional warehouses in the United States, Asia, and Europe.

Infrastructure Providers/Communities of Commerce

Infrastructure providers or communities of commerce: members aggregated across a set of complementary interests (products, content, and services) and markets; communities of enterprises organized around common interests through a common infrastructure.

The fifth E-conomy business model is that of infrastructure provider. Aggregating communities of interest around a common infrastructure is not a radical proposition. Businesses with common interests have long created communities in the forms of trade associations, cartels, guilds, and other legitimate and occasionally unlawful alliances. What makes infrastructure providers so compelling is that they apply the Net as a collaboration platform and value delivery driver. Because their value chains depend on the Internet as the underlying service infrastructure, infrastructure providers enable the creation of new value by reducing market fragmentation and leveraging an entirely new set of service opportunities.

Infrastructure providers bring suppliers, customers, and complementary services together and allow them to securely initiate and settle transactions on the Internet. These providers reduce prices and transaction costs, minimize inefficiencies, and make allies of competitors—because everyone in the value chain derives benefit from the completion of transactions. Let's look at two examples of infrastructure providers in action.

Chrome.com

Autobytel.com has been analyzed as a value-added infomediary (see "Seller Brokers," page 112 of this chapter). It also operates as an infrastructure provider by aggregating information about prospective car buyers for automobile dealers into a loose network of ancillary services such as insurance and financing. But Chrome.com (www.chrome.com) exploits the benefits of an infrastructure provider in ways that leave Autobytel.com at the starting gate. Chrome.com is a business-to-business, members-only digital automotive network. It facilitates vehicle transactions between consumers and new car dealers through value-added auto-buying assistance programs provided by a network of members such as credit unions, banks, and insurance companies.

Although we discuss Chrome.com in the context of an infrastructure provider, the digital automotive network is also an E-business enabler by virtue of licensing its configuration and pricing engines to be used as part of the car-buying areas of a variety of new environments, including corporate E-procurement tools, wholesale buying clubs, and consumer Web sites. Currently, Chrome.com technology is embedded in the Web sites of Costco (www.costco.com), Motor Trend (www.motortrend.com), Carsdirect.com (www.carsdirect.com), and name-your-price Web retailer Priceline.com (www.priceline.com). Chrome.com also placed its configuration engine inside the E-procurement tools of Clarus Corporation (www.elekom.com) to enable corporate purchasing of cars via the Web. By submerging its tech-

nology in these Web sites, Chrome.com enables the E-business of its partners. In doing so, Chrome.com streamlines complex transactions for power
users and creates a new class of market makers.

Chrome.com clicks on all cylinders because it understands that real
value is created at the point of sale, not at the point at which buyers and
sellers are introduced. By moving its intelligence to the network and
specifically to the point of sale, Chrome.com has become an infrastructure
provider that redefines car buying. Chrome.com has created an infrastructure and pricing engine that it can license to entities such as credit unions
and insurance companies that offer car buying as a value-added service.

Here's how Chrome.com works (see "How Chrome.com Creates Value"):
Car buyers go to Chrome.com's configuration and pricing engine to specify
the exact car they want at a price they are prepared to offer. Dealers in the
Chrome.com network then vie to see which one can deliver the features
and price requested. It is the only auto-buying system in which dealers bid
against one another for a piece of business. It throws the traditional relationship between car sellers and car buyers, including Autobytel.com's
model, on its ear. In the E-conomy, transactional control remains with the
consumer.

The Chrome.com infrastructure is made up of more than 5,600 car dealers, 250 auto brokers, 1,200 credit unions, 30 commercial banks, 500 fleet
administrators, and 250 leasing accounts. In operation, Chrome.com is a
password-protected extranet made up of a configuration engine and a
quote center, a separate application that matches buyers and sellers. The
company derives income from three main sources. First, it charges transaction fees for deals enabled by Chrome.com. Second, it charges subscription fees to every member of the COIN. Third, it licenses its configuration
and pricing engines to other sites.

In addition to its role as an E-business enabler, Chrome.com also operates as an infomediary and as an infrastructure provider. As an infomediary, it stakes out its place in the middle by leveraging a configuration engine that makes it possible for entirely new coalitions to be created and
offer additional service at point of sale. As an infrastructure provider, it will
succeed if it can get its service accepted by both car buyers and car sellers
and then create a critical mass of ancillary services willing to play on its infrastructure. Chrome.com has one big advantage. It makes room for the
members of the value chain who feel most threatened. For example, credit
unions and small insurance companies have been losing business to auto
dealers and larger insurance companies, respectively. Chrome.com now al-

lows these members to offer car buying as a value-added service, and they hope to retain the financing and insurance because, as members of the infrastructure, they are right there at the point of sale.

How Chrome.Com Creates Value

1. Using Web Carbook, which has a database of every vehicle make and model sold in the United States, buyers configure the options and price of their desired vehicle.

2. Quote Center generates a detailed vehicle quote request and transmits it to selected car dealers.

3. Dealers receive terms and conditions of the vehicle request and an electronic response form. Dealers check their inventory and respond with a bid.

4. Vehicle quote responses from dealers are received. The winning vehicle response is selected by the customer.

5. Vehicle "closing" is arranged with the successful dealership; at the same time, opportunities for cross-selling financing and insurance are presented.

In the E-conomy, each industry and value chain will be required to develop an infrastructure provider. An infrastructure provider combines the aggregation of information, technology, networking, and brand/trust management that together comprises an environment necessary to support the creation of new value. When the sum of all these elements comes together in a cohesive and integrated fashion, it creates exciting new opportunities for businesses to exploit.

The benefits that COINs bring to the table are difficult to underestimate. As a result of the integration of E-business initiatives, partners of an infrastructure provider find new ways to create value and growth. Note that the increases in value and growth cannot be accounted for simply by increases in efficiency, reductions in costs, or other bottom-line considerations. COINs create new value because streamlined interaction driven by new information sources fosters the availability of more individualized products and services. Suppliers garner new value as the network provides greater access to customers and increased demand for complementary

Table 4-6. Infrastructure Providers

Infrastructure providers create environments for exchanging value in which participants with common interests can interact.

Offerings

Seamless infrastructure across value chain

Explicit agreement between buyers and sellers

Tight integration between advertising, E-conomy, and fulfillment

Support of infrastructure maintenance

Replicable framework and methodologies

Target Audience

COINs

Complementary players in an industry

Service providers tightly integrated into a transaction (e.g., automotive manufacturers and dealers, lenders, car purchasers, insurers for automobiles, aftermarket part suppliers, etc.)

Activities

Aggregates information, technology, networking, and brand/trust management to create a seamless infrastructure to support the creation and exchange of value in a discrete vertical market

Competencies Required

Governance and coordination

Channel enabling

Platform provisioning

Ability to port infrastructure to vertical markets

Development and maintenance of infrastructure

Unbiased, open processes using standard platforms

Goal

Extract a piece of the new value created by providing infrastructure supported by value-added aggregation, information, and E-conomy services

Revenue Stream

Advertising

Subscription fees

Partnership fees

Percentage of transactions

Examples

The Sabre Group

GE TPN

ActiveWear Online (Fruit Of The Loom)

---

products and services. Most important, whoever provides or administers the infrastructure can extract a disproportionate measure of value (table 4-6).

Spawned from the Outside In

What opportunities are ripe for COINs and infrastructure providers to exploit? Net Ready organizations look for a number of clues to identify inefficient digital value chains. One common element is large markets with significant fragmentation, in other words, a multitude of independent buyers and sellers, few of whom have each other on their radars. Supply chains whose products come in complex configurations will favor a more uniform way to search for product and service information. Likewise, industries with complicated or expensive distribution processes will find value in a single, automated platform that concentrates information. Net Ready companies look for large asymmetries in the information controlled by buyers and sellers in a value chain.

COINS and infrastructure providers that succeed enjoy one durable edge over traditional distribution and manufacturing operations: they secure increasing returns rather than diminishing marginal returns. As a site becomes successful, the chances of its becoming ever more successful increase. The more buyers that are attracted, the more sellers will be drawn in; the more products that are available, the more customers will be drawn in. That, in turn, makes content aggregation easier—vendors must bring their content to the infrastructure provider, rather than the provider having to go gather it. Everything gets drawn to the center of the E-business channel, which the provider happens to control.

Remember that E-business value is created by taking on one or more of the five extended E-business models. The models are not mutually exclusive. The most successful Net Ready enterprises take on multiple business models concurrently. Enterprises that take on multiple roles and manage them well have a dramatic advantage in the E-conomy.

II

Techniques for Creating Sustainable E-conomy Value

Free fill-ups of gasoline for your car. Not just once but every time you need a fill-up. How's that for creating sustainable E-conomy value?

We believe it is possible to construct a business model that gives away gasoline. The trends and scenarios that make this concept possible, described in Part I of *Net Ready,* are aligned to make this delicious outcome not only possible but probable. Many of you may already be aware of where we are going with this scenario. If so, bear with us, because the business model driving the free gasoline offer will loom increasingly large in the economics of the twenty-first century. The analysis that follows parallels the way Net Ready entrepreneurs can begin to think about using the Net to exploit new opportunities.

At the time this book went to press, the price of gasoline was at its absolute lowest cost, adjusted for inflation, that consumers have ever seen. At one point in the spring of 1999, a gallon of gasoline cost significantly less than a gallon of bottled water. Think about it. What is possible when a commodity costs less than water? While you're thinking, let us ask you a few more pointed questions.

- How long does it take you, on the average, to fill up a tank of gasoline?
- What do you do during that time?

- Would you like to obtain free gasoline every time you fill up?

- Would you be willing to exchange some attention while the car is filling up for free gasoline?

- Would you be willing to, say, watch a short video that plays right on the gasoline pump?

- Would you be willing to exchange some personal information for even more benefits?

We have here the possibility of an exciting business model that recognizes the convergence of no less than seven of the eleven themes we have articulated in chapter 2 of *Net Ready:*

- Products and services are mutating from tangible to intangible

- Informatization adds value to transactions

- Smart products are proliferating

- Customers are becoming less forgiving and more discerning

- Personalization is the key to Net Ready success

- Attention intermediaries can insert themselves into a value chain

- The value of the information about the transaction outweighs the value of the transaction itself

In a world in which $500 PCs are given away in exchange for attention and advertising revenues, the idea of giving away progressively inexpensive gasoline suddenly begins to look interesting. Add to the mix the fact that filling a car with gasoline consumes five to ten minutes that otherwise is considered wasted, and the business proposition looks better all the time. Consider that the recipient of a free fill-up is in the satisfied glow of just having saved $10 to $20. Top off the cake with the fact that the consumer's credit card is inserted into a credit card reader ready for electronic commerce. Sprinkle on some icing in the form of knowing a fair amount of information about the consumer, including the anniversary and birth dates of the consumer's spouse, children, and parents, and suddenly we are beginning to develop a deeply compelling model.

Here's how it might work. To qualify for a free fill-up, you will have had to fill out an online questionnaire that notes detailed shopping or travel preferences. You would also provide the birthdays and anniversaries of your loved ones as well as their addresses. When you get to a participating gasoline station, you would insert a smart credit card into the pump. The pump would immediately download your consumer profile. As you were waiting for the car to fill, the system would send you personalized messages on a display right on the pump or perhaps for you to view from the comfort of your car. Is it your mother's birthday next week? Why not send her some flowers or a basket of fruit. Just $19.95. Well, you just saved that amount in gasoline. Just touch the screen here, and the system will save the day and make you look the part of the dutiful child. There's more. The system knows you like to ski. How? You either gave it that information or the system learned it by your behavior. So the system sends a message from your favorite ski resort on a promotion. Click here. Does your car need a tune-up? Click there. We understand, says the computer, that you like to travel to Bermuda. It just so happens that Delta has low-cost E-fares if you can leave this weekend. Hotels, too. Click here and here.

The business model generates revenues from a number of streams. One revenue component will be from advertisers eager to present personalized, one-to-one offers to a set of rigorously qualified and identified consumers. The other revenue component will be a piece of every E-conomy transaction enabled by the system.

Would it work? Who knows? The scheme has one significant fly in the ointment. There's a big difference between giving away PCs and giving away gasoline. Moore's law applies to the former, not the latter. We can bet the farm on the proposition that the prices of PCs will continue to fall and never be higher than they are today. Gasoline, unfortunately, follows industrial age rules of supply and demand as established by refineries and cartels. Price fluctuations are to be expected. Thus the unpredictable cost of the premium fueling this business model probably dooms the proposition, but perhaps one of our think-out-of-the-box readers will be able to turn the disadvantages—asymmetries of information, fragmented market, and fluctuating price of gasoline—into advantages.

We offer this thought exercise merely as a way to introduce you to Part II of *Net Ready*, in which we introduce strategic initiatives for creating value in the E-conomy. In Part I of *Net Ready*, we laid out some general operating principles of the E-conomy and invited you to map out where your current initiatives were located. In Part II, we present twelve specific E-conomy strategies for creating sustainable E-conomy value, strategies that our experience tells us will predict success. We have arranged these twelve strategies into three groups: product and market transformation,

Product and Market Transformation	Business Process Transformation	Industry Transformation
Reconceive the product/service	Unbundle and outsource processes	Redefine the basis of competition
Redefine the value proposition	Assume another role - E-business storefront - Infomediary - Trust intermediary - E-business enabler - Infrastructure provider	Become the channel enabler
Move the product up the food chain	Compress the value delivery system	Redraw industry boundaries
Separate the function from the form	Explode the price/performance ratio	Break the unbreakable rules

Figure II-1. The E-Business Value Transformation Matrix. You don't have to have activity in every cell, but every cell offers your organization the opportunity to create meaningful value.

business process transformation, and industry transformation (figure II-1). The twelve trajectories of the E-Business Value Transformation Matrix will move you and your enterprises closer to the enormous opportunities enabled by the E-conomy. In the next three chapters, we offer you a dozen road maps to guide you from where you are to where you want to go. At the same time, we try to mark the potholes, false trails, and remains of those businesses that were lost on the way. We delineate specific techniques and approaches that, when applied appropriately, executed ruthlessly, and backed up by leadership, governance, technology, and competencies—Net Readiness—and perhaps a little luck, will create the kind of competitive advantage that yields sustainable value in the E-conomy.

The behaviors and strategies delineated in the next three chapters to help you become Net Ready are not intended to be an exhaustive checklist. Nor do we suggest that you have to take on every strategy. What we are presenting here are merely themes worthy of your consideration and exploration. Not all will be pertinent to your goals, and even if they are, they are not all of equal priority. The determination of which techniques to embrace and in which order is completely context sensitive and will vary with each organization. It is here that your investments in Net Readiness— leadership, governance, competencies, and technology—will pay off. On the other hand, we believe that any significant E-business initiative will embrace one or more of these techniques.

5

Product and Market Transformation

If you don't like the constraints of the business environment in which you operate, create new constraints and make your competitors abide by them. There is nothing sacred about the constraints you inherit. Transform them and you may reveal an opportunity. Product and market transformation is the first critical dimension of creating E-conomy value.

One of the critical competencies for success on the highly popular U.S. television quiz program *Jeopardy* is the ability of the contestant to reframe answers in the form of questions. If the clue is, "The sixteenth president of the United States," the correct response is "Who is Abraham Lincoln?"

That ability to reconceptualize obvious answers and reframe them in new ways is also a critical competency for success in the E-conomy. The E-conomy does not reward "me, too" thinkers or those who accept conventional wisdom. Nor does it celebrate people with limited vision. It rewards those who challenge the why-fix-it-if-it-ain't-broken mentality? Those who break the shackles of business as usual—and a good way to do that is by asking questions that brand them as subversive to the organization—set the pace for the E-conomy. Such people are iconoclasts who question the status quo, cut through red tape, and challenge their organizations to greatness.

Any truly transformative vision is a leap into the unknown. It is very difficult to anticipate where such a vision will lead, although it is safe to say that the path will be more exciting and rewarding than any planner could hope to articulate. Whenever a great technology comes along, it must battle people whose vision is limited by the old technology. The development of the Xerox photocopy machine is a classic illustration of this myopia.

When Xerox was first developing the basic research on xerography and what would become the Xerox 914, the first commercial photocopying machine, the world was used to making copies using clumsy carbon paper and duplicator technology. IBM, to whom Xerox offered its patents, hired Arthur D. Little, the esteemed management consulting firm, to do a market research study. The consulting firm concluded that even if the revolutionary machine captured 100 percent of the market for carbon paper and duplicators, it would still not repay the investment required to develop a commercial copier. The consulting firm could be forgiven for failing to see that the Xerox copier would solve a problem that people didn't know they had. IBM passed, but Xerox decided to plow ahead anyway to the magnificent results it could never have foreseen.

Why? Because we now understand that the power of the Xerox copier did not lie in its ability to replace carbon paper—an obvious solution for an obvious need—but in its power to create a market based on latent or hidden needs. The Xerox machine uncovered an itch that office workers didn't know they had until they could scratch it. The Arthur D. Little researchers were right as far as they went. No office "needed" a Xerox copier. But they were wrong to the core of their pinstripes not to consider how a technology like xerography could enable new markets and opportunities. One lesson for the E-conomy is not to repeat the mistakes of the past. Whenever you evaluate a technology or business model, extrapolate beyond the obvious problem it seems to address. Ask at least three people totally outside your industry to help you. They will have different sets of blinders and may reveal the latent, unarticulated needs that you can exploit.

Everyone talks about the importance of thinking "out of the box." We agree that such thinking is important, but remember that the big problem with product ideas that come from out-of-the-box thinking is that to succeed in the E-conomy, you have to get those ideas back in the box. In other words, thinking by itself is not sufficient. Without flawless execution, the greatest ideas remain fantasies.

In Part I, we offered you a process to map your current E-business initiatives and invited you to consider in which general Net Ready directions you wanted to grow. In this chapter, we consider the four techniques that make up the product and market transformation arena of the E-Business Value Transformation Matrix (figure 5-1). We have seen that the advantages driven by technological breakthroughs are fleeting. We have seen tremen-

Product and Market Transformation	Business Process Transformation	Industry Transformation
Reconceive the product/service	Unbundle and outsource processes	Redefine the basis of competition
Redefine the value proposition	Assume another role - E-business storefront - Infomediary - Trust intermediary - E-business enabler - Infrastructure provider	Become the channel enabler
Move the product up the food chain	Compress the value delivery system	Redraw industry boundaries
Separate the function from the form	Explode the price/performance ratio	Break the unbreakable rules

Figure 5-1. The E-Business Value Transformation Matrix focused on product and market transformation. E-conomy opportunities are exposed when a product/service is reconceived, redefined, and moved up the food chain, and when form is separated from function.

dous momentum in moving today's breakthroughs to tomorrow's fundamentals. We described why moving up the E-Business Value Matrix framework represents sound strategic thinking. Now let's take a closer look at the four techniques.

Reconceive the Product or Service

Familiarity may breed contempt, as the saying goes, but it also breeds complacency. The hardest thing in the world is to rethink a product or service so commonplace, so ordinary, that a major effort is required just to consider that it may deserve a second thought. But in the reconception of the ordinary exists the possibility of creating real value. In this section we look at a few companies that have made such an attempt.

Your Card, Please

Is there anything more ordinary, more commonplace, and more frustrating than a business card? Everyone thinks the cards are needed, but everyone also believes they are a major pain. There are two parties to any business card transaction. Let's call them donors and recipients. For business card donors, the problem is to keep the cards current. In these days of area code roulette and E-mail address changes, keeping business cards up to date is an expensive proposition. For recipients, managing hundreds of business cards so they can be accessed is a daunting task. The biggest issue for both donors and recipients is keeping the information on these cards accessible and up to date.

One solution is to scan every business card that is received and manage them as a database in a personal information manager. A small industry supports just such a solution. But while recipients can now search through their business card database by name or company, there is still no reliable way to ensure that the data is current.

Tippecanoe Systems has considered this set of challenges and reconceived the situation by creating the virtual business card. It just might be the solution to the age-old problem of keeping business cards from going out of date. Its VBCard Web site (www.vbcard.com) links paper business cards to virtual cards accessible over the Internet. The linking is made possible by printing a user name and PIN on the business card, which will identify a single virtual card in the VBCard Web site.

"The problem with ordinary business cards is that a simple change renders them obsolete," says Mike Tyler, president and CEO of Tippecanoe Systems. "How many cards have you thrown away because your phone number area code changed? Or your title, or address? How many cards in your Rolodex are still valid? How many friends have you lost?" Visitors to the VBCard site can create new cards or update their existing card—while also having facilities to design and print paper cards using the print command on their Web browsers. The new cards will have the user name and PIN printed neatly at the bottom.

VBCard follows a paradigm common to most successful E-business initiatives. Begin with a common product and add a carefully focused service component to create a value-added E-business initiative. Here, this paradigm works like a charm. Donors have a business card that never goes out of date. Whenever they have to change their card, even when they change companies or careers, donors can go the Web site and update their information. Best of all, when people registered on the site update their cards, the site automatically notifies subscribers by E-mail. Thus, the site offers not only business cards that are always correct, but also the infrastructure for building communities and relationships that can create lasting value.

Net Ready Strategy

- *What:* Virtual business cards

- *Company:* Tippecanoe Systems (www.tippecanoe.com)

- *Offering:* Up-to-the-second information virtually; customers can create, update, print, store, and search business cards in a virtual manner

- *Net Ready Strategy:* Reconceive product; separate function from form

---

Clipping Coupons

In the beginning of the last section, we asked if there is anything more ordinary than a business card. How about supermarket coupons? These little pieces of paper clutter your newspaper and mailbox. The idea is sound, but who has time to organize coupons? If you smell an opportunity for an E-business storefront to reconceive discount coupons, you're on the money. The physical becomes the digital as paper coupons transmogrify into virtual, or Net, coupons.

Val-Pak launched Val-Pak Coupons online. Those who access the new Web site may miss out on the thrill of having coupons flutter onto the kitchen floor, but they now have the choice of searching for coupons by topic or geographical location and can print out only those coupons they will use. The site, free to the public, includes coupons for a wide range of merchants, including pizza parlors, hair stylists, and entertainment.

In one sense, the digital Val-Pak is very close in function to its brick-and-mortar incarnation. Merchants who wish to promote their products or services offer discount coupons as inducements for customers. The difference is how the E-conomy eliminates friction and wasted resources. On the Web, only people who opt in for coupons visit the site. Marketers increasingly have turned toward opt-in lists in an effort to entice people into receiving E-mail advertisements. Some companies offer giveaways in exchange for subscribing, while others offer incentives such as frequent flyer miles. Coupons can be carefully mapped to advertising programs and tracked against sales results. Net coupons can also be more carefully controlled to detect and avoid abuse.

Like many of the Internet companies whose ranks it is joining, Val-Pak is not yet making money directly from the Web. The business model that has made its offline operations a success, in which advertisers pay Val-Pak to design and print the coupons, insert them in envelopes, and mail them off, has not yet been translated into a viable online model. Right now the company offers the Internet coupon for free as a value-added service. The world is still waiting for an E-business storefront to successfully navigate a critical mass of the paper coupon industry to the Web.

Net Ready Strategy

- *What:* Virtual supermarket coupons
- *Company:* Val-Pak (www.valpak.com)
- *Offering:* Customer selects own value proposition; service aggregates discount coupons, allowing consumers to search and print paper coupons or redeem virtual coupons
- *Net Ready Strategy:* Reconceive service

America Online and Netscape

You may think that reconceiving business cards or coupons are trivial examples, but that's what makes them so enlightening. It's a little more difficult to comprehend an enterprise such as America Online (www.aol.com), a remarkable success story in a number of dimensions. Here, let us focus on just one strategy that the company used to achieve its undisputed position as the world's first $5 billion multi-brand media company. By reconceiving its service, America Online evolved from the Internet service provider (ISP) that it was as recently as 1995 to its current status as the leader of an industry providing branded interactive services and original content. It was first to evolve from an ISP to a media company, indistinguishable in fundamental ways from CBS or Disney.

With the acquisition of Netscape, America Online may have reconceived what it means to be an integrated Internet media company. A number of born-on-the-Web companies have attempted to build the Net Ready equivalent of the vertically organized holding company. Akin to owning all the components of a physical value chain—coal mines, railroads, steel mills, manufacturing plants, retail outlets, and so on—a vertical Internet company has holdings on all sides of the business, from E-conomy to connectivity to Web publishing to software development to advertisement serving.

For a variety of reasons, such a vertical company has never worked. But with the acquisition of Netscape and a number of other E-business storefronts, America Online has come close to becoming an integrated Internet media company. In this capacity, America Online's organization is similar to what Sony and Disney have attempted to do in the entertainment space. Sony has holdings in film, music, gaming, and consumer electronics. Disney has controlling interests in film, television, music, and theme parks. In the same way, America Online now has a connectivity business (America Online, CompuServe), a Web publishing business (Digital City, aol.com, Netcenter), a nascent E-conomy consulting business in the form of its new venture with Sun, a software and communications services business (ICQ, Netscape), and a new hardware enterprise in partnership with Sun. The combined company has about 35 percent of all Web advertising in its network and has the advantages of marketing and exploiting its software and traffic across a wide spectrum of platforms and demographics.

In reconceiving its product/service, America Online had to navigate two principal challenges. First, while Sony and Disney are kings of the hill when it comes to content providers, America Online's relationship with content is more problematic. Almost every Net Ready organization wants to offer strong content in their mix of services. Conventional wisdom has it that content is a magnet for the eyeballs that most companies want. The more compelling the content, the more "sticky" the site becomes. This condition of stickiness is universally acknowledged to be desirable in a Web site. Content can be purchased, created by users, or developed by professionals. But every successful Internet venture offers a mix of content. Even a pure service business like Amazon.com is selling the notion that content about books and reader-generated reviews gives it a competitive edge over traditional retailers and other online retailers.

For America Online, content like the Motley Fool investment series is crucial. But what's essential is not the service content on Netcenter, it's the valuable content generated by users on America Online. For the most part, America Online is amenable to buy content as a loss leader to attract a crowd into its showroom. That's why it paid Time more than $2 million for the online rights to People Magazine. America Online doesn't pretend to be able to recover the cost of this content through traditional advertising models. Until users kick their addiction to free content and show a willingness to pay for it, content will remain the loss leader come-on that the big service E-business storefronts like America Online use to get traffic in the door. For the most part, that means continued low fees and losses for developers of Net content.

Content is also tied up with process in ways that are not yet understood. Net Ready companies invariably encounter a tension between the way content is implemented and the content itself. In this tension, the content always wins. For example, right now most people consume Net content via a browser. That's why Netscape, a software company that develops a particularly popular implementation of a browser, was so attractive. But it is noteworthy to observe that it was the media company that gobbled up the software company, not, as some people might have expected, the reverse. The relative dominance of media over code is because software without content is a cheap commodity, almost without value in the Net Ready world. It turns out that the Net business is a service- and media-related environment. Software tools are crucial in the Net Ready world in the same way that printing plants and binding technology are crucial to the magazine industry. But readers don't buy magazines because of the offset process used for printing them, and consumers won't buy information services because of the software used to create and deliver those services.

America Online has had many ups and downs since it began operations in 1985, but under the leadership of its founder, Steve Case, the company has done a remarkable job of changing its service offerings. As a media company, America Online makes its presence felt in a number of ways. It is a portal site that creates a bundled set of E-conomy services from automobiles to sports. It is a content provider, most of which it buys but a substantial amount of which it creates. It puts all its offerings together to create communities. Its 18 million subscribers—not all of whom can be said to be satisfied, but all of whom have a stake in America Online's success—represent an inestimable asset. To its credit, America Online recognizes that only a media company can truly exploit such an asset.

Other media companies have had to swallow a lot of pride before they could accept America Online into their fold. But even CBS has acknowledged America Online's presence—it embarked on a nine-day, $10 million promotional campaign on America Online. The effort was designed to target America Online's subscribers, many of whom fall into the coveted young-and-affluent audience category that CBS has desperately sought in its fight to reverse its aging demographics. America Online featured the network in chat rooms, ad banners, and entertainment content areas, and most visibly, it previewed each night's scheduled programming on exit screens.

Unquestionably, the deal was a success for CBS. But for America Online, the campaign was an even bigger triumph. America Online has matured as a medium. The narrow casting capabilities of digital media have reached a point at which strategic alliances between television and Internet media companies are no longer merely exploratory experiments, but real necessities.

Reconception of an organization's value proposition is fraught with difficulties. Constituencies committed to the existing paradigm, especially if it is successful, resist mightily. Often the organization reconceiving itself finds it is now competing with its former partners and allies and cooperating with its former competitors. It takes a strong constitution to make the decisions necessary to reconceive a product or service. To its credit, this is just what America Online is doing. It is reconceiving its product and service in a number of dimensions. America Online is:

- Changing from an ISP to a media company
- Moving from a subscriber-based to an advertising-based and transaction-based revenue model
- Changing from a distributor of online content to a developer of online content
- Migrating from a closed, proprietary environment to an open, Web-based environment
- Moving from a consumer-oriented to a business-oriented medium

In reinventing itself, America Online is facing a paradox. As the company reconceives itself from a leading distributor of online content into primarily a developer of online content, it has to find a fine balance. The company must continue to court its traditional media partners in the short term while trying to replace them in the long term. HBO has made this transition effectively. For the first ten years of its existence, HBO took on, in Net Ready terms, the attributes of a container company: it broadcast premium movies. More recently, HBO has taken on the attributes of a content company by developing its own movies (content) for its own channel.

America Online continues to reconceive itself. The company acknowledges that it is primarily regarded as a consumer service. In an attempt to reverse this trend and carve out a niche for itself in the business services space, America Online purchased CompuServe, an online service replete with services for businesses. It also upgraded its enterprise unit in an attempt to sell remote access to large corporations. Late in 1998, it acquired Netscape.

The company is trying to leverage its network, which, as a consumer channel, sees that its peak usage times are in the evenings, generally from 8:00 P.M. to midnight, local time. The excess capacity represents an asset that can be offered to businesses. The more the company can balance its workload, the more economies of scale it enjoys. America Online recognizes that its weak link is security. In response, the company is partnering with a who's who of industry leaders, including Security Dynamics, Check Point Software, Aventail Corporation, and AXENT Technologies. Businesses demand comprehensive service agreements, guaranteed bandwidth, and network availability. Given its history, America Online is going to have a hard time overcoming its image as a consumer-focused operation, and an unreliable one at that.

Netscape's experience in reconceiving its product and service is also instructive. Unlike America Online, Netscape has done so not only to create value but as a matter of survival. Before it was acquired, Netscape had fundamentally shifted its business model. Once a provider of browser software, Netscape became an enterprise software vendor and portal service provider, with one business leveraging the other. With Netscape's business thus reconceived, customers could choose the strategy that made the most sense for them. For companies that wanted Netscape to provide portal services and technical expertise, the company's Netcenter site was an attractive solution for applications with high traffic volumes. If customers wanted to develop, deploy, and maintain their own Web-based applications, Netscape provided the tools to do it. If organizations wanted a mix, Netscape offered professional services and high-end software to devise workable solutions. And if customers wanted browser software, Netscape continued to offer that, too.

Netscape cornered the market on Web browsers after Jim Barksdale recruited Mark Andreesen and his colleagues from the University of Illinois, where they had created the first Web browser, Mosaic. Within a few months, the team developed the Netscape browser and launched the first real brand in the history of the E-conomy. For a year or so, the company's name was synonymous with the industry, and it enjoyed phenomenal success as its Netscape browser, distributed free for the asking, gave it entry to millions of homes and businesses.

The impetus for Netscape's decision was Microsoft's unexpectedly rapid acceleration and subsequent giveaway of its own Web browser, Internet Explorer. This development threw a wrench in Netscape's ambitions because it had recently begun to charge for its browser. As its browser revenue stream skidded to a stop, Netscape's other opportunities also ran into trouble. The company's entry into the collaboration and work group management space did not live up to expectations, because it failed to penetrate the work groups and departments that Microsoft and Lotus controlled. Similarly, its server strategy was diluted by the penetration of Microsoft, Compaq, Sun Microsystems, and others.

It's not enough for a company to reconceive its product or service. It must implement the reconception flawlessly. Now, Netscape's new stewards at America Online must make good on their new vision. Significant hurdles are in their way. The company's goal of becoming a world-class storefront in both the software provider and portal provider spaces is challenging.

Marc Andreesen's Five Strategies for E-conomy Advantage

Marc Andreesen, the preposterously smart twenty-something who headed up the team that created the Netscape browser, has crammed an enormous amount of the institutional memory of the Internet into his young career. He follows the E-conomy closely to determine how his company can best lead and, if necessary, best follow. A few days before America Online announced its acquisition of Netscape, Andreesen sat down with *Net Ready* in Chicago to share some of the lessons he has learned:

Net Ready: Is it better to lead or to follow?

Andreesen: Both have their places but it's not a decision you can really make. I like to quote Jim Clarke on leadership: "A leader is someone who sees a parade and gets out in front." I say you just have to keep trying and see if anyone starts a parade.

Net Ready: Can you articulate a few strategies that you see playing out in the evolution of the E-conomy?

Andreesen: Sure. Let me name five:

1. *Customer retention.* The trick is to retain customers at a profit.
2. *Create customer loyalty.* Use the E-conomy to upsell and cross-sell so that customers increase their relationships and commitment to the company and make switching costs a significant issue.

3. *Personalization.* If you can't provide one-to-one customization of your product or service, you will be in a great disadvantage because that's what customers demand. In the past, Netscape has sold the picks and shovels to the prospectors in the Gold Rush. With Netcenter, we are in the business of showing each prospector where to dig.

4. *Reduce time to market.* We need to reduce cycle times. We're seeing total end-to-end customization in the industrial sector. It requires exquisite levels of JIT, squeezing inventory out of the system, and it cannot be done without the E-conomy.

5. *Ready! Fire! Aim!* Keep building systems. If they buy it, it's a product. If they don't, it's market research.

We will leave to the market to determine Netscape's credibility as a provider of high-end enterprise software. Software development is outside the scope of this book. But as to Netscape's chances for success as a portal provider, there we have some opinions borne out of experience. It is true that Netscape's portal site has traditionally been one of the top five most heavily trafficked sites. But before Netscape tries to leverage the bragging rights from that statistic, it is important to remember that most of that traffic comes to the site by virtue of it being the default home page of the millions of browsers it offers. Unless Netscape can continue to develop excellent content for its Netcenter portal site, as Netscape's share of the browser market continues to erode, the traffic it can deliver to its portal site will erode as well.

To its credit, Netscape seems to understand that it must reconceive its portal site as a conduit to its many users with its growing stable of business partners. This is the real value of a portal service provider: to help its customers get customers. If Netscape can redirect to its partners the millions of hits that Netcenter gets every day (even if much of this traffic is by default) so that commercial transactions take place, the commissions Netscape receives will keep it viable. At the same time, it can also direct a logical portion of that traffic to its own business sites to provide organizations with enterprise software and technical expertise in deploying and managing their commerce-based Web applications that are, in turn, accessed through the Netscape portal. Now we are talking synergy!

Net Ready Strategy

- *What:* Browser and portal
- *Company:* America Online (www.aol.com)
- *Offering:* The ultimate portal to satisfy any requirement
- *Net Ready Strategy:* Reconceive service

Redefine the Value Proposition

In the traditional economy, value propositions are typically inward looking, focused on either product features or corporate operational processes. That's not good enough anymore. In the E-conomy, value propositions must have an outward perspective, taking the point of view of customers. Presenting customers with a value proposition means understanding what they are trying to achieve—even when they themselves may not be fully aware of it—and how the product or service will get them closer to that goal.

But even presenting customers with a clear value proposition is not good enough anymore. To really succeed in the E-conomy, you have to redefine the value proposition in the context of the new rules. You have to assume that somewhere out there is a competitor that will render your value proposition irrelevant. Competition today is not between products or even benefits; it's about competition between opposing value propositions. Some questions to ask yourself as you consider what your existing value proposition is and how it may be redefined:

- What are the dimensions of value our customers knowingly care about?
- What are the dimensions of value our customers may not be able to articulate yet?
- Where does the company stand relative to its competitors on each of these dimensions?
- What would customers perceive as unmatched value?
- What would customers perceive as knock-your-socks-off service?
- Can we deliver this value at a profit?
- How are the company's core competencies aligned with delivering these values?

- What would we have to change, abandon, or create to maintain a focus on new value disciplines?

- Extending our radar, from what other directions can competing value propositions emerge?

Free E-Mail

Under the business models imposed by E-mail leaders such as Prodigy, CompuServe, and America Online, E-mail services required a set monthly fee. Consumers accepted that E-mail services, like the telephone, should have a fee. But then along came Hotmail, one of the first enterprises—but not the first—that redefined the E-mail value proposition by offering E-mail for free. Free E-mail, or freemail, is possible when the companies realized that greater value is to be had from advertisers interested in a community attracted by the offer of free E-mail than from subscription fees. So successful is the concept that now there are hundreds of freemail services littered about the Internet.

As a concept, freemail is deliciously win-win. There's no cost to the customer, and because it's Web based, all a customer needs is an Internet connection and a browser to access and send E-mail anytime, from anywhere. The services are surprisingly robust. If your E-mail needs are routine—sending, replying, and maybe attaching an occasional file—just about any of the dozens of freemail services that have sprung up will give you what you need. Of course, you have to put up with ads scattered about the screens as you read and compose messages. But the ads are generally unobtrusive. They're also targeted to your business and personal interests, based on data you're required to provide when you sign up. Most services also offer to E-mail product information to you, but you can check the "no thanks" box and the E-mail services respect your wishes.

Hotmail, along with Juno (www.juno.com), pioneered the concept and carried it to maturity first. As a result, Microsoft was ready with $40 million in cash. It says a lot that Microsoft was quick to grab the leading freemail service, even if it didn't know quite what to do with it. Hotmail currently coexists with Microsoft Network (MSN) as a value-added service for MSN subscribers. Customers presumably use it as a supplemental E-mail account to avoid cluttering up their main E-mail inboxes or as receptacles for mailing list traffic. We believe Microsoft will continue to offer Hotmail as a freebie as part of its MSN portal strategy. For a discussion of why Hotmail has succeeded while Juno and the other freemail services are distant runners-up, see page 184 in chapter 6.

By the end of 1998, Hotmail had more than 30 million subscribers, according to Microsoft, and is growing at a rate averaging one million new accounts per month. Hotmail counts as an active member anyone who has used his or her account in the past 120 days, says Laura Norman, product manager for MSN Hotmail. Of the 30 million members, 15 million log on at least once a month.

Like other free services, however, Hotmail has one big downside. The paradox is that human beings all over the world seek what is free; but once they get it, they tend to dismiss it. People esteem more what they pay for. So it's no surprise that Hotmail has gathered such a huge audience. The strategic question is, How much does Hotmail's membership value the service? Some people have been abusing their free E-mail accounts for spamming or other unethical purposes. Some ISPs have retaliated by blocking or restricting traffic from Hotmail. Auction sites such as eBay have recognized that a disproportionate share of complaints have been directed against members with free E-mail accounts. The auction service has responded by requiring more identification from these customers. Unless Hotmail can distance itself from these difficulties, it will rapidly and irrevocably find its brand and value eroded.

Net Ready Strategy

- *What:* Free browser-based E-mail

- *Company:* Hotmail (www.hotmail.com)

- *Offering:* A free service that has a perceived value by the end user

- *Net Ready Strategy:* Redefine the value proposition from a transaction or subscription basis to an advertising model

---

Move the Product Up the Food Chain

Another technique for creating value in the E-conomy is moving a product up the product hierarchy food chain. Existing products take on entirely new attributes when complemented with elements of service and encapsu-

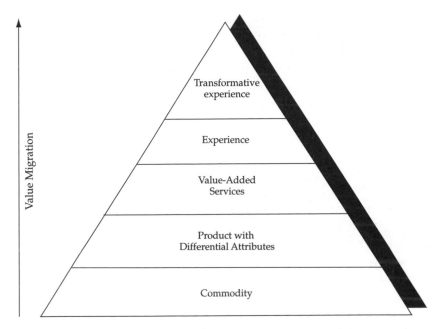

Figure 5-2. Product Hierarchy Food Chain. What does a transformative experience look like for your business? Moving up the food chain adds value by providing a differentiated product or service. The concept is to take a commodity (bottom) and move it up the E-conomy food chain to a product, service, experience, and ultimately, a transformative experience.

lated by information. Net Ready companies always strive to move their products or services up the food chain (figure 5-2). Advantage comes both in the differentiation that results from moving up the food chain and in the migration itself. In the E-conomy, enterprises that are in motion tend to be more successful that those in stasis.

Let's consider a few examples of E-business initiatives that follow this precept.

Onsale

Onsale (www.onsale.com), the online auction service, represented a revolutionary presence in the E-conomy when it was launched. As a start-up, its business model was not fettered by industrial age baggage. Onsale's challenge was how to create a new retailing experience that exploits the unique characteristics of the Internet. To do that, the company broke a number of retail myths. One myth was that products have fixed prices. In response, Onsale leveraged the concept of differential pricing. In its auctions, Online also took advantage of the concept of scarcity, which replaced the myth of unlimited availability, to create a more fevered competitive shopping environment. To squeeze out maximum efficiencies of scale, Onsale automated the entire operation, eliminating the person-to-person contact that traditional economies required. Finally, by generally not taking control of inventory, Onsale avoids the expense and risk of holding stock.

Onsale builds a lot of interactivity into the process. Bidders can see bids coming across in real time. An E-mail process lets customers know when they have been outbid. All this interactivity is an attempt to re-create the excitement of a real-world auction, in which the air can spark with competition. Moreover, Online combined commerce with entertainment by re-creating the excitement of a live auction in a geographically and temporally distributed format. Onsale has succeeded by bundling aspects of entertainment, gambling, and the stock market into the value proposition. Onsale's genius has been to take commodity-oriented products and move them up the food chain. Customers don't just buy, they win (table 5-1).

Auctions have been around since the beginning of economic history, and except for sales of Van Goghs at Sotheby's, they have a decidedly downscale and seedy reputation. Until Onsale came along to move the entire auction process up the value chain, auctions were the domain of people who frequented flea markets in search of cheap bargains. Onsale,

Table 5-1. Onsale Exploits the E-conomy Model

As a Net Ready company, Onsale's business model exploits the attributes of the Net in every respect.

Traditional Retail Model	Net Ready Model
Fixed price	Differential pricing
Unlimited availability	Scarcity
Physical inventory	Virtual inventory
Person-to-person contact	No person-to-person contact

in short, did nothing less than create a new metaphor for buying and selling: using the unique attributes of the E-conomy to bring buyers and sellers together to enable an entirely new auction experience. Encapsulated in an Onsale auction experience are attributes of Las Vegas, the stock market, the shopping channel, and the price club. Onsale went on to enormous success, breeding a cyberspace industry and a host of other entrants in the auction space, including the wildly successful eBay, which applies a commission-based model to its millions of auctions.

Onsale's insight was that computers could be used to convert the staid auction process into a sport or an entertainment. Its designers understood that men represented 90 percent of the auction market, so they created the Onsale environment to offer a twenty-four-hour window into the pursuit of scarcity. Onsale made a video game out of buying stuff by auction. The Web site responds to the primitive male hunting instinct: the testosterone-based need to turn life into gamesmanship. Onsale's perpetual auctions lure repeat buyers addicted on the skill and luck of playing a stock market–style auction game.

Looking back on Onsale's evolution reveals the mistakes and false starts that make up the history of any Net Ready company. Onsale's founder, Jerry Kaplan, was also the founder of GO Corporation, a company that attempted to move computers up the value chain by using a pen-based metaphor. As it turned out, GO didn't, teaching Kaplan a number of hard lessons, which he memorialized in his book, *Startup: A Silicon Valley Adventure*. He learned that being right doesn't necessarily translate into business success unless the timing is right, too. With pen-based computing, the timing just wasn't right.

But with Onsale, it was. One day, Kaplan joined his creative mind with Alan Fisher, a programmer who developed some snazzy online trading software for Charles Schwab. They started asking the central question for creating value: What else, besides trading securities, could the software be used for? "Why not auction consumer goods?" Kaplan brainstormed. Why not, indeed?

Well, funding, for one thing. That's another lesson. Even if the idea is right and the timing is right, if the funding is not there, there's no show. In 1995, the infrastructure of the Internet on which Onsale depended was not quite ready for prime time. The venture capitalists balked. Kaplan and Fisher were just about to hang it up when they hit on a way to show what the system could do. Kaplan seized on the fact that the Boston Computer Museum was planning a charity auction in May 1995. If they could make the Onsale software implement the auction, a critical mass of the most in-fluential movers and shakers in the industry would see it up close and per-sonal.

Industry people at the charity event loved it. They couldn't get enough of the real-time excitement of watching the bids fly. The two innovators got some funding, and within a week, Onsale opened for business. Of course, there still remained the delicate question of just what Onsale was going to sell. At first, it sold anything the company could get its hands on: sports memorabilia, movie posters, wines, cruises. Here's where they didn't quite have a full grasp. It took some experience to understand that what would really sell best on the Internet was stuff having to do with computers: PCs, peripherals, add-on boards, and memory chips. Techno-geek stuff was what was most interesting to the early adopters of the online auction busi-ness model.

Onsale then developed the model that has made it successful. Onsale avoids taking title or physical possession of goods (although it will if it has to). Most of the goods are bought or taken on consignment from blue-chip companies such as Hewlett-Packard, IBM, Toshiba, and Sony. Thus, Onsale serves as an asset manager for suppliers, a champion that streamlines the logistics between buyers and sellers. Onsale is increas-ingly targeting businesses to buy systems for organizational use. The scheme seems to be working. The company reports that 30 percent of its computer-products bidders are purchasing for their organizations, with business buyers accounting for more than two-thirds of its revenue from sales of high-tech gear.

Onsale's Progression of Internet Initiatives

As is true of most born-on-the-Web organizations, Onsale started opera-tions in quadrant 2, rational experimentation (see figure 5-3). Its experi-ment was: is it possible to create an auction format on the Internet and to sustain the trust that is necessary for viable cyberspace auctions? The com-pany started by auctioning off sports memorabilia online, but almost by accident saw that there was a bigger demand for computers and peripher-als. What started as an experiment clicked, and the activity quickly blos-somed into breakthrough strategies. Soon, excellent follow-through carried the activities into operational excellence. Today, online auctions are so ubiquitous that any contender that cannot execute operational excellence from the start doesn't stand a chance.

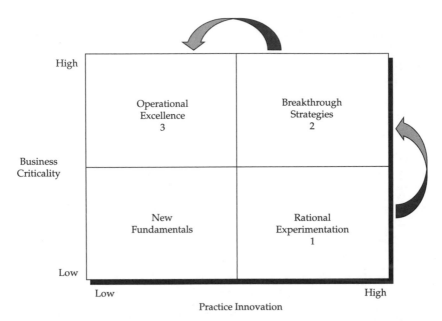

Figure 5-3. Onsale's Progression of Internet Initiatives. Onsale's business model and experimentation broke a number of retail myths. Starting with rational experimentation, the progression of Onsale's Internet initiatives quickly moved counterclockwise to breakthrough strategies and then to operational excellence.

Net Ready Strategy

- *What:* Online auction

- *Company:* Onsale (www.onsale.com)

- *Offering:* Creating a transformative experience for buying; originally, aggregating refurbished and end-of-line electronics for budget-conscious buyers by overlaying elements of entertainment and gambling; more recently, selling new stuff, corporate sales

- *Net Ready Strategy:* Move the service up the value chain to create a transformative experience

eBay

Let's take a closer look at eBay, the market leader in the online auction space and one of the few profitable category-killers on the Net. If Onsale is vulnerable, it is because the barriers to entry into the auction market are so low. Dozens of entrants are now competing for the excess goods and services market, of which PCs alone total about $11 billion a year. Virtually every major E-conomy portal—including America Online, Yahoo!, and Excite—now offers a classified auction service.

eBay's business is reminiscent of a nonstop virtual flea market with a mix of standard garage-sale fare, distressed merchandise, and genuine antiques, all varnished with the slight risk that the merchandise is not quite as represented. Any eBay visitor can browse among more than two million items for sale, many of which are unique or otherwise hard to find, organized across more than 1,600 product categories. Sellers register their items by paying a fee from 25 cents to $50, depending on placement. The site then solicits bids for an item starting with a seller-specified minimum bid. At the end of the auction period, usually about a week, eBay notifies the highest bidder and the seller via E-mail, and the buyer and seller consummate the transaction on their own. So far, that's the weak link in the process. If and when the deal closes, eBay charges the seller a commission from 1.25 percent to 5 percent of the closing price.

Moreover, with more than two million items for sale at any one time, eBay, like the Web itself, can get overwhelming. This situation is a classic challenge of asymmetries of information creating friction. In an effort to battle Amazon.com's auction service, eBay has now made it easier for collectors to stay up to date on their bids with a service called Personal Shopper. Personal Shopper is able to filter through new items of interest and notify each of eBay's three million registered users via E-mail when an item that that user wants comes up for bid. Personal Shopper also allows users to track individual items by keyword, description, and price range and to specify whether they prefer daily, weekly or longer intervals between E-mail notifications for new listings. In a clear example of customization at work, Personal Shopper uses change detection, or "minding the store," software, which helps Web users track any Web-based information at any level of detail and notifies them via E-mail, pager, cell phone, palm-held computer, or the Web when the information changes.

eBay's application of this change detection technology is on a consumer basis, but organizations can use it on a business-to-business basis to create strong customer lock-ins. As customers make their auction preferences known, businesses can observe what an individual customer is willing to pay for a particular item or how long he or she is willing to wait for it. They can then use that information to configure just the right price or offer other initiatives to increase that customer's purchases. The technology also enables businesses to remember each customer's characteristics by providing ongoing reports about his or her purchasing patterns and behaviors.

The price for entry is low enough that dozens of storefronts in the traditional as well as digital economies are joining in. In the traditional economy, the Times Mirror Company, publisher of the *Los Angeles Times* and other newspapers, launched its Auction Universe site. Even Sotheby's, the most prestigious real-world auction house, is getting into the game. Don't look for Sotheby's to emulate the eBay model. Sotheby's needs to protect its brand, so it insists on a high level of authentication for the property that it auctions. But the venerable auction house does conduct limited online auction of original manuscripts and first edition books—one manuscript fetched $30,000.

It's inevitable that virtual auction houses and brick-and-mortar auction houses will simultaneously target each other's markets and create strategic partnerships to leverage the unique value propositions that each brings to the market. Online auction companies want to leverage the brand and confidence the established houses have created. The brick-and-mortar auction houses want to exploit the E-commerce and fulfillment competencies that the online auction companies have developed. eBay needs to promote brand equity because it recognizes that, in many ways, the eBay brand represents the ultimate competitive barrier to entry in the marketspace. "The eBay brand provides a real emotional benefit that works at a lot of levels," says Meg Whitman, eBay's CEO. "On one level, the auction format is great fun—the excitement of the hunt, the agony of defeat, the thrill of victory. On another level, it is about community. The community that has built itself around eBay's commerce is a community with shared interests and shared passions. That creates the enormous stickiness we have on the site."

With the acquisition of the venerable auction firm Butterfield & Butterfield—best known for its antiques and fine art—for $260 million in stock, eBay signaled the industry that it will invest heavily in building credibility for its brand. The merger hitches an auction house founded in 1865, as a benefactor of the California Gold Rush of 1849, with the leading Internet auctioneer, which struck it rich after going public in 1998. It's a win-win scenario. Butterfield & Butterfield was considering an IPO to raise cash to better compete with the online auction houses. eBay needed an established auction service with a reputation for handling high-ticket merchandise. Now, Butterfield & Butterfield has the funds it needs to grow, while eBay continues to build equity in the eBay brand.

We saw this same dynamic play out when Amazon.com and Sotheby's saw it in their interests to create a partnership in which Amazon.com invested $45 million in world-renowned auctioneer Sotheby's to create an on-line auction service with the 255-year-old company. The ten-year alliance further heats up the battle between Amazon.com and eBay, the Internet's leading online auctioneer, for control of the hugely popular business. The Amazon.com-Sotheby's partnership (www.sothebys.amazon.com) will offer Amazon.com's ten million customers products ranging from collectibles such as coins, stamps, and Hollywood memorabilia to general art and an-tiques. The auction property will be offered by Sotheby's and a network of dealers. The authenticity and condition of all auctioned property will be guaranteed by the sellers—a crucial safeguard for people buying products on the Internet without first seeing them. "In the world of valuable objects, a big problem with online auctions has been authenticity," says Amazon .com CEO Jeff Bezos. "Who better to help solve that problem than Sotheby's?" At the same time, Amazon.com has launched an auction service tightly linked with its traditional retail channel (see "Amazon.com's Entry into the Auction Space," page 213 in chapter 7).

The price for entry into the online auction environment is getting so low that garage-sale fever is taking over. Entities like eBay are close to a pure E-conomy investment, but soon individuals will be able to enable online auctions from their Web sites. Companies such as Webvision (www.webvision.com) are developing software that will power mini-auction capabilities within individual Web sites. Operating as an E-business enabler, Webvision licenses its auction technology to Web sites that want to set up an auction area as a value-added benefit.

Literally hundreds of companies are jumping into the online auction fray. Conceivably, every newspaper site on the Web, every Internet directory, every music and video retailer—even every personal home page—could become a competitor to eBay. The only thing eBay has going for it is its brand, an asset that can depreciate quickly when a bug brings eBay down. If eBay is going to succeed, it will have to move its service up the value chain. The trick is to use the proceeds from its IPO to build a brand and auction infrastructure as unassailable as that of Yahoo! and America Online.

eBay understands the value of migrating to new spaces and taking on new roles, both in E-business as well as in more traditional realms. As *Net Ready* went to press, eBay announced its first steps into the offline world with the launch of a magazine and two books dedicated to the subject it knows best: online bargaining. In an attempt to build brand and commu-nity, the company is publishing *eBay Magazine,* a lifestyle publication geared toward—who else?—collectors, pack rats, and the assorted deni-zens of its growing community. The magazine brings eBay people together in discussions of the latest collecting trends, E-commerce news, and tips on how to buy, sell, and trade over the Web. The auctioneer is also targeting online collectors offline with the publication of two books: *eBay for Dummies* and *The Official eBay Guide to Buying, Selling, and Collecting Just About Anything*. eBay doesn't necessarily expect to lure new users to its Web site through the publications. Rather, its goal is to improve a user's experience with the site through the publications.

Net Ready Strategy

- *What:* Virtual flea market with auction format

- *Company:* eBay (www.eBay.com)

- *Offering:* Personalized, transformative buying experience; digital classifieds listing in which potential buyers bid against each other

- *Net Ready Strategy:* Move the auction service up the food chain

---

Separate the Function from the Form

The traditional economy entangles function and form so thoroughly that it is difficult to calculate where the real value is. In most cases, the value is really rooted in the function. Entrepreneurs who can figure out how to deliver the function using the unique attributes of the E-conomy will often create enormous value by shedding the baggage of the physical container in which the function was formerly moored. Under our discussion of digitization (see "Digitization: Separation of Function and Form," page 61 in chapter 2), we described how Computer Associates International separated the function (professional implementation services) from the form (on-site consultants) to deliver consulting services on a remote basis. Let's briefly consider five other examples of enterprises that created advantage by strategically applying the principles of separating form from function.

Remote Presentations over the Web

Why should people gather together in a conference center to watch a slide presentation that they could more easily watch from any browser? That's the logic of WebSentric (www.websentric.com), a new Web conferencing service that lets professionals deliver slide presentations in real time within any browser. The service, called Presentation.Net, is aimed at companies involved in distance learning, corporate conferencing, and telesales efforts.

WebSentric is betting that it can extract some value by separating the traditional form of a presentation (slide shows in a hotel meeting room) from the function (imparting information). For many years the form and function of these presentations have been inextricably linked. But the Web offers a model for distinguishing between the two. Now, whether the technology is robust enough to give presentation attendees a workable presentation remains to be seen. The company is on the right track by using JavaScript/Dynamic HTML to show slides rather than large GIF files. This decision lowers bandwidth requirements, allowing dial-up attendees to have a reasonable experience over 28-Kbps modems. The company has not yet determined pricing, but says a Web presentation conference will cost less than a teleconference. Beta customers include Sun Microsystems and Federal Express.

The service works with any operating system, hardware, and screen resolution. Conference participants simply log on to a Web site and enter a password to gain full access to presentations with audio, video, shared white boarding, and interactive chat. A companion application, WebPresenter, provides a free alternative for users who don't have presentation software such as Microsoft's PowerPoint.

Net Ready Strategy

- *What:* Remote presentations on the Web
- *Company:* WebSentric (www.websentric.com)
- *Offering:* Eliminating the need for attendees to physically congregate to view a slide show presentation by separating the function and delivering it via the Web
- *Net Ready Strategy:* Separate the function from the form

Home Health Care

An enterprise that has recognized the value of separating function and form is Home Access Health Corporation—a leader in telemedicine as invented by NASA in the 1960s to monitor the health of astronauts on space missions. Today telemedicine is used to exchange medical information from one remote site to another via electronic communications for the health and education of the patient, client, or health care provider.

Much of this concept isn't new. Access to pregnancy test kits eliminated the need for women to go to a doctor's office to determine if they were pregnant. The function (the answer to a question) was successfully separated from the form (a medical procedure). Now that concept is being extended to tests for Hepatitis C and HIV, the virus that causes AIDS. Home Access Health Corporation has petitioned the FDA to allow it to market a home testing kit to detect the HIV virus and to provide a service by which customers can get their test results via the Internet.

In 1992, Home Access Health Corporation invented its proprietary telemedicine platform to extend telemedicine services to the home. The Home Access platform allows clients to access fast and convenient at-home medical testing and consultation. The Home Access telemedicine platform is the technology and service engine that clients use to access medical testing services without the need for a doctor's office visit. It also incorporates home specimen collection kits, professional medical consultation services, laboratory testing services, and information systems for the purpose of delivering counseling, education, and test results by phone.

Let's take another medical example. A cardiograph is a device that monitors the activity of the heart and delivers that data to physicians in some actionable form. Traditionally the function (the delivery of the data) was linked closely to the form, the device itself, in terms of distance and time. The input and output were thought to be inseparable. More recently, medical device manufacturers have created value by separating the function from the form. For instance, Hewlett-Packard's PalmVue is a mobile, pocket-sized system that provides physicians fast, accurate access to vital data needed to assess a patient's condition and consult on diagnosis and treatment options at any remote PC. When security concerns are worked out, the physician will be able to view real-time waveforms and vital signs on any PalmVue-monitored patient from a standard laptop or desktop PC over the Internet.

Net Ready Strategy

- *What:* Remote medical testing
- *Company:* Home Access Health Corporation (www.homeaccess.com)

- *Offering:* User-centric medical testing and result delivery; remote medical testing and virtual delivery of test results at the user's convenience
- *Net Ready Strategy:* Separate the function from the form

Remote Testing of High-End Systems

The more complicated and expensive machines get, the more opportunity there is for manufacturers who can use the E-conomy to separate the testing function from the form. Varian Semiconductor Equipment Associates has created significant value for itself and the customers of its multi-million-dollar ion implanter by following this technique.

The ion implanter is a stand-alone, automated factory the size of a one-car garage that lays tracks of electricity-conducting atoms in silicon. The implanter begins its remarkable work by drawing highly corrosive and poisonous gases—derivatives of boron, arsenic, and phosphorus—from metal bottles in its innards. Then, inside a vacuum chamber glowing with a superheated tungsten filament, it looses mini-thunderbolts of electricity to strip electrons from the gases' atoms, turning them into ions. Electromagnetic fields guide the ions onto the skin of silicon wafers. There they become embedded like bullets and turn back into atoms by stealing electrons from the silicon, giving it properties that make it a semiconductor.

That's the good news. A machine so complex can be very finicky and, for a firm with razor-thin profit margins, very exciting to operate. It reminds us of the NASA astronaut who explained his feelings about being blasted into space: "How would you feel if you were strapped into a machine that has 200,000 parts, each and every one built by the lowest bidder?" Keeping the 8,000 components of the ion implanter in good working order requires a new partnership between manufacturer and customer.

Like most highly complex systems using corrosive gases, the ion implanter needs repairs or routine maintenance every ninety hours. Since it processes hundreds of wafers an hour, each of which can fetch $100 at wholesale, downtime can cost its owner upward of $75,000 per day in lost revenue. Thus anything Varian can do to cut down maintenance and repair time will be very welcome, especially for customers located far from Varian's ion implanter factory in Gloucester, Massachusetts, from which repair teams are dispatched.

The E-conomy solution is to recall that Varian's customers don't really want visits by the repair teams (the form). They really want real-time access to the expertise of the repair teams (the function). Varian couldn't agree more. Repair teams represent costly assets that are squandered through time-consuming visits to far corners of the earth. Far better to have the teams' expertise available on a centralized basis, using the remote management facilities enabled by the E-conomy, to assist customers with maintenance issues.

The response? Remote repair, diagnostics, and maintenance, or simply RRDM. Employing the latest in digital communication, RRDM enables the factory repair teams to remotely diagnose, isolate, and remediate many maintenance issues that confront companies owning ion implanter systems. In operation, customer technicians work in conjunction with factory experts at Varian headquarters to bring a machine back into production. At the machine site, the customer technician puts on a virtual reality helmet incorporating a tiny, digital-TV color camera, a microphone, and earphones, and two display screens that enable the technician to see images being transmitted from the Varian factory via a PC-based videoconferencing system.

The virtual reality helmet brings the customer floor virtually into the Varian factory. The helmet frees the technician's hands while transmitting real-time images of the problem; the microphone and earphones allow the technician to discuss the problem with the factory experts. Thus, the technician can hold up components or lay them on a table to show them to the technicians in Gloucester. The factory experts may circle certain parts in red, indicating that those parts need to be replaced, and the technician can see this highlighting through one of the helmet's display screens. The technician can also see the factory engineers themselves, schematic drawings, and other relevant material. The technician can choose to view any of these images on a large monitor at the work area.

Several trends are spurring the switch to RRDM. Manufacturers now want to run a machine twenty-four hours a day, seven days a week, to get the biggest return on their capital investment. At the same time, the machines are getting faster and faster. In that regime, any method for reducing downtime is welcome. The proliferation of smart factory equipment (see "Informatization: Smart Products Are Proliferating," page 64 in chapter 2), meanwhile, makes remote repair easier than ever. RRDM still has considerable constraints. While it's possible to download a software patch or restart a component, right now it is not possible to send a spare part over the phone. Some day it may be possible to digitize what we call a spare part. The entrepreneur who figures that out will truly be in a good position to create enormous value.

Net Ready Strategy

- *What:* Virtual diagnostic testing for high-end systems
- *Company:* Varian Semiconductor Equipment Associates (www.vsea .com/)
- *Offering:* Virtual, hands-free diagnostic services to empower owners with comprehensive, real-time, incident-specific consulting
- *Net Ready Strategy:* Separate the function from the form

Remote Virtual Quality Assurance

In 1992 Cisco began to build test cells to virtualize the process of testing components. In the past, Cisco people had to be physically present to conduct or supervise the testing. Now, by separating the form from the function, the test can be digitized. The function of testing is preserved while Cisco's Autotest changes the form. The benefits are twofold. First, automation saves time and money with standardized product tests. Second, automated testing compresses delivery cycles. Customers get better quality products faster. Once testing is automated and standardized, Cisco then outsources the process to the suppliers, allowing quality issues to be detected at the source. However, although testing is outsourced, the intelligence behind the testing remains with Cisco.

Net Ready Strategy

- *What:* Virtual testing
- *Company:* Cisco Systems (www.cisco.com)
- *Offering:* Compressing delivery cycle by virtual delivery of standardized test beds
- *Net Ready Strategy:* Separate the function from the form

Music on Demand

Punishment can be swift for those who underestimate the power of digitization. Just ask the recording company executives who were blindsided by MP3, a standard for digitizing and compressing music files that can be easily distributed over the Net. MP3 is quickly becoming an industry that will thoroughly distintermediate the recording industry. MP3 enthusiasts use freely available software to convert CD tracks into music files that they post on the Web for fellow Webheads to enjoy. MP3 sites such as www.mp3.com amount to a virtual and free jukebox stuffed with hundreds of thousands of recordings—legal and illegal—all playable in real time at the click of a mouse. Separating the function from the form gives consumers the exhilarating freedom of being able to listen to exactly what they want at the instant they want to listen. Naturally, the executives at the recording industry are working around the clock to stop the fun using the favored tactics of those who are about to lose: legal challenges. The recording industry seems fixated on account control: the total control over the distribution channel of CDs and music stores. It's too late. If you want to see what gives the executives at Sony, Polygram, and Columbia Records indigestion, just do a search on the keyword mp3. The MP3 technology spawned a whole new E-business that crept up to bite the recording industry before it knew what hit it.

But the logic of the Net won't be denied. CDs, the form that music currently takes, are expensive and rigid. They force people to buy songs they don't want just to hear one or two they do. CDs are organized by companies that have their own agendas. Downloading songs from the Web is overwhelmingly more logical, practical, and cost-effective. What the recording industry should have done is fired the lawyers and put the money into research and development. If they had taken the initiative and developed the infrastructure—the systems, technologies, and standards—to sell songs via the Web, they could have created a landscape in which they would be much better off. They are scrambling to put such a system into place now, but it's too late. MP3 technology and culture will be impossible to dislodge.

MP3 aside, E-business sites such as CDNow (which acquired N2K) and Platinum Entertainment (www.platinumCD.com) are forcing the music industry to look at how it creates value by being able, for the first time, to separate form from function. In the E-conomy, digitization allows function (in this case, music) to be separated from form (CDs) in a way never before possible. Platinum Entertainment, for example, allows consumers to create their own CDs by selecting songs from a 173,000-song pop library. The site blends 13,000 songs from Platinum's library with 160,000 titles from Music Connection Corporation. Customers can elect to have the unique CD downloaded to their hard drives, or Platinum will burn the CD into physical form and mail it.

What if you don't want to bother creating your own CD? After all, there are hundreds of thousands of ready-made CDs out there. No problem. In a further instance of the inbreeding between E-conomy companies, Platinum also has a partnership with Amazon.com in which Platinum will share revenue from sales it refers to the giant online book and music site. What happens to the concept of an album, a series of musical pieces selected by an artist, when every consumer can customize an album from pieces they select? The consumer can choose to keep the resulting album on his or her hard drive or can create a CD by using a programmable CD drive. At CDNow, customers can listen to a sample of a digital CD. If they like the sample, they can immediately buy it. One model is to send the CD the next day, but other models completely isolate form from function. What happens to form when consumers can download a sample of music to their own hard drives?

Digitization of music gives consumers powerful searching capabilities that can drive sales in spectacular ways. For example, say that you are interested in a particular Beethoven sonata. Now, Beethoven wrote dozens of sonatas. If you did not have more information than that it was recently played on the radio, you'd have a hard time describing it to a record store clerk. Moreover, a music store would have a hard time selling it to you if they could not ensure that the sonata they identified is really the particular sonata you wanted.

But digitization makes the process easier. You can be given a sample of the opening notes of each sonata. Moreover, if you have any information at all about the sonata—say that you remember it being used in the soundtrack of a movie—informatization allows the online music source to do an intelligent search to locate the desired music. Finally, once the sonata is found, the music store can give you a choice. You can get the sonata by itself, or in the context of the movie soundtrack, or in a collection of other sonatas. The convergence of broadcast radio and informatization makes it easier to identify the Beethoven sonata in another way. Many radio stations are already transmitting identifying information—selection title, composer, artist, record label, and so on—with each selection they broadcast. All consumers need are smart radio systems to display this information.

Questions on Separation of Function from Form

- What is the function?

- In what form is it encapsulated?

- Is the function and form inextricably linked?

- What will we gain and what will we lose by disentangling them?

- Can we deliver the function, or a subset of it, in a separate form?

- Who besides us is in a good position to deliver that function?

6

Business Process
Transformation

Enterprise focus is the second critical dimension of creating E-conomy value. Deconstructing the infrastructure enabling the business reveals new opportunities for business process transformation.

In this chapter, we shift our emphasis from the product and service components of the transaction to the business processes that enable those products and services. Embedded within those business processes are assumptions, inefficiencies, and redundancies that the E-conomy can redefine, transform, or eliminate. In this chapter we consider four general approaches to identify such opportunities and to exploit them.

As you can see on the E-Business Value Transformation Matrix (figure 6-1), business process transformation comes about through the following strategies: unbundling and outsourcing processes, assuming another role, compressing the value delivery system, and exploding the price/performance ratio.

In Part I, we laid out what we believe is compelling evidence that the world operates under new rules. The most cherished beliefs about business—concepts such as products, customers, scarcity, time, competition, and wealth—are being redefined by the E-conomy. Managers must throw out their old notions about how businesses should be organized. In fact, we believe that managers must question even the concept of notions. As Cybergold CEO Nat Goldhaber explains, "It turns out that everything we know about traditional business is not only inapplicable, but wrong." (For more of Goldhaber's comments, see "Q&A for Nat Goldhaber," page 231 in chapter 7.)

Product and Market Transformation	Business process transformation	Industry Transformation
Reconceive the product/service	Unbundle and outsource processes	Redefine the basis of competition
Redefine the value proposition	Assume another role - E-business storeform - Infomediary - Trust intermediary - E-business enabler - Infrastructure provider	Become the channel enabler
Move the product up the food chain	Compress the value delivery system	Redraw industry boundaries
Separate the function from the form	Explode the the price/performance ratio	Break the unbreakable rules

Figure 6-1. The E-Business Value Transformation Matrix focused on business process transformation. E-conomy opportunities are exposed when a product/service is unbundled or outsourced, when an organization assumes one of five E-business roles, when it compresses the value delivery system, or when it explodes the price/performance ratio.

Challenging your conclusions is tough enough, but questioning your assumptions is the formidable part. For example, you ask, "How can we streamline our inventory operations to make them more efficient?" It's a reasonable question. Too reasonable, as it turns out. The very question assumes that owning inventory is a necessary part of the business. A much better question is, "Is there a value to us in eliminating the need for holding and managing inventory?" Now your organization can start asking some interesting questions about just-in-time methods (the Dell model) and outsourcing of the inventory function altogether (the Onsale model).

It's never easy to distinguish the fundamental from the peripheral, especially if you are in the middle of the action. It takes considerable intellectual power and the perspective of objective observers to ask the most basic questions about companies and how they operate. Questions such as the following are typically the most difficult to answer:

- What is our business?
- Why do we do what we do in the way we do it?

- What are our values?

- What is our goal?

- What rules are unbreakable?

- What is nonnegotiable?

- What are we afraid of?

- What is our corporate culture, and how does it promote and hinder our efforts?

- What are we allowed to take on?

- What is impossible for us to take on?

- What else can we do?

Requiring people in an organization to periodically respond to these fundamental questions is asking a lot. It's hard work and if you do it right, it can be threatening. It forces people to look at the tacit rules and assumptions that underlie the way they conduct their businesses and relationships. Often, these rules and assumptions turn out to be obsolete, unworkable, and counterproductive.

Before reaching a consensus on what is fundamental, organizations should start with a blank slate. Everything must be negotiable, because invariably the areas that are off-limits to consideration contain the greatest opportunities. It is often useful to map out the processes that inform how the organization actually works. Examine work flow by actually walking an order through every step of the fulfillment process from start to delivery. Forget how the process is supposed to work; attend to the steps that people actually take. Map the walk, not the talk.

Look especially closely at the actual points of encounter between the company and its customers. We call these encounters "moments of truth." Without exception, each of these encounters should support the fundamental goals of the organization, or they are distractions. For example, the credit-checking process must have embedded within it the core customer service values of the organization. Of course, by now the company should have challenged the assumption that customer credit is something that must be checked in the first place. In many instances, the cost of checking may, in fact, exceed the bad-debt losses that the checking is intended to avoid. But assuming a credit check supports a fundamental goal, let it be done with a minimum of disruption to the customer and a maximum of integrity for the company.

Eventually, the organization will reach a consensus about the fundamental nature of the organization. Only after participants name it can they claim it. And only after they claim it can they move the enterprise to new destinies in the E-conomy.

Most organizations, when they can muster up enthusiasm for change at all, content themselves with superficial changes. To create value in the E-conomy requires changes of a much more radical nature. The root of the word *radical* derives from the Latin *radix,* which means "root" itself. Radical transformation means getting to the root of the processes to be transformed. "In reengineering, radical redesign means disregarding all existing structures and procedures and inventing completely new ways of accomplishing work," Michael Hammer and James Champy write in Reengineering the Corporation (New York: Harper Business, 1997, p. 33). In the E-conomy, radical transformation is about innovative ways of creating value that exploit the unique attributes of the E-conomy itself: one-on-one personalization, the death of distance, real time all the time, perfect information, and so on.

E-conomy value creation isn't about incremental improvement. It's about knock-your-socks-off achievement. Value creation comes only with dramatic innovation, the kind that takes people's breath away. Think Federal Express when it was new. Remember IBM's ThinkPad notebook computer. "Incrementalism is innovation's worst enemy," observes Nicholas Negroponte, head of MIT's Media Lab.

Hotmail and the value it created is a good example of how tenuous dramatic innovation can be. Hotmail and Juno pioneered the concept of free Web-based E-mail services (see "Free E-Mail," page 162 in chapter 5). But even though Juno had first mover advantage, it got the innovation only 96 percent right. Hotmail got it 100 percent right, and that 4 percent difference resulted in Hotmail's success and its subsequent acquisition by Microsoft.

Juno, which helped pioneer the freemail concept, has been left in the dust by Hotmail because of Juno's decision to relax its reliance on Internet access. In this case, first mover advantage yielded to the power of aligning with standards, or accepting the role of a rule taker. Hotmail can be accessed from any Internet-connected, browser-equipped PC (or kiosk), but Juno made a different decision about access. Juno believes it to be an advantage that Juno account holders do not need Internet access to access their E-mail. However, they do need to install Juno client software on their PCs. We believe this decision is flawed, and the market agrees. Browser access is the accepted model for E-conomy communications, and no advantage accrues to a company offering an alternative platform. Any service that proposes to redefine a value proposition by challenging a de facto standard must have a very sound reason if it is to succeed. We don't believe Juno meets that high standard, and it has paid a penalty for disregarding one of the rules of the E-conomy.

One of the legacies of the traditional economy is a focus on tasks and transactions. The E-conomy rewards enterprises that take a more process-oriented approach. Processes in the E-conomy are not dissimilar from those in the traditional economy: a collection of activities that takes one or more kinds of input and creates an output that is of value to the customer. What is different is the simultaneity and time compression that the E-conomy brings to the input-output equation and the way it redefines concepts such as value and customer.

The process of generating and delivering an airline ticket for a customer illustrates what we mean. For many years, the airlines spent considerable resources in streamlining this extremely complicated, sequential process, integrating activities such as determining availability of seats, checking credit, making reservations, and generating and delivering tickets. But by applying the concepts of business process transformation, the airlines introduced E-tickets. Now, much of the process is concurrent (availability, credit, reservations, confirmation) and the most time-consuming, costly, and risky part of the process (generating and delivering hard copy tickets) is completely eliminated.

As we pointed out in our discussion of telemedicine, Home Access Health Corporation (see "Home Health Care," page 173 in chapter 5) dramatically changed the process of medical testing at home. The company, which got its start selling home testing kits that allow people to send in blood samples via mail and retrieve results over the phone, has asked the FDA for permission to release test results, including HIV test results, over the Net. The advantages to anxious, privacy-conscious customers are enormous. As dramatic as this service is, we believe it can be even more radical. Right now, the weak link in the process is the delay and uncertainty of sending blood samples through the mail to be tested. What if the company could offer an inexpensive measuring device that can attach to the customer's PC? The customer merely inserts a drop of a bodily fluid, and the device then measures the sample and transmits the data to the corporate testing center where it is put through a rigorous testing process. The results are posted to the Web, where they are retrieved through the use of a user name and password held only by the customer. At no time is a name associated with a sample.

Questions on Transforming Business Processes

- What are my key processes?
- Can I assume another E-conomy role?
- Can I compress my key value delivery systems?
- How is the existing price/performance ratio vulnerable to explosion?
- Who, besides me, is a logical candidate for recognizing and exploiting these opportunities?
- What do I have to bring to the table to exploit these opportunities?

Unbundle and Outsource Processes

Destruction is cool. The E-conomy rewards companies that are bold enough to pull apart their most workable processes and reinvent them in harmony with the attributes of the Internet. That means emphasizing speed, parallelism of processes, decentralization, customization, personalization, and the other attributes we mentioned in this book.

McKesson, the largest health care supply management company in North America, is an exception to the rule that the leaders in any particular industry generally do not take a leadership role in leveraging E-conomy opportunities. McKesson has done a remarkable job in redefining its value proposition and thereby further solidifying its market share and leadership position.

Tentatively at first, McKesson took the initiatives expected of large organizations. It started putting its catalogs and product specification sheets online. It managed to launch a Web site before most of its competitors did and made it immediately more than just a site for brochureware. But then the company made a leap of faith in realizing the enormous possibilities offered by integrating its customers and partners in a comprehensive intranet. McKesson integrated elements of decision support systems and other analytical tools into the site. Together, these tools and a new mind-set converted salespeople who had a more or less antagonistic relationship with their customers into sales consultants who are on the customer's side.

In the traditional pharmaceutical sales environment, a salesperson goes to a pharmacy and pitches the benefits of a set of products. Today, McKesson ties the pharmacy's database into the Intranet. By doing so, the sales rep can now demonstrate that if the pharmacy uses drug A, pharmacologically equivalent to drug B, the pharmacy would save $25,000 per year. Naturally, drug A is a product of McKesson. But the pharmacist is happy because he or she can deliver equal functionality at less cost. The Intranet, by virtue of integrating the inventory and sales databases of McKesson and its customers, redefines McKesson's value proposition from that of supplier to partner. The company is no longer just pushing products; it is a-13,000-employee company whose interests arc aligned with the pharmacy.

As customers commit themselves to McKesson's Intranet, they become an inexorable part of an integrated value chain. This value chain provides inestimable benefits to the customers, but it comes at a cost. Should they ever consider moving to one of McKesson's competitors, they will find their switching costs to be in the stratosphere. By redefining its value proposition, McKesson is delivering to customers more value-added information services. These services solidify McKesson's relationships with its customers and amplify the magnitude of their switching costs.

The concept of customer lock-in is a central technique in the creation of sustainable competitive advantage in the E-conomy. McKesson's experience is a perfect example. Traditionally, the pharmaceutical drug wholesaling business entailed ordering pharmaceutical drugs from manufacturers, warehousing them, and delivering them to customers such as drugstores and hospitals. McKesson now offers sophisticated reporting services to its customers. To further entrench these customers, McKesson has developed its own proprietary automated dispensing and reporting systems along with consulting services.

McKesson continues to transform all its key processes by Net-enabling them via a combination of Internet-based and Intranet-based initiatives to improve performance at each point of the health care delivery system. The company focuses on delivering value-added logistical services, materials management, third-party reimbursement support, scheduling, clinical data capture/analysis, billing/cost accountability, and decision support. This breadth of capabilities, coupled with the largest customer base in the health care industry, uniquely positions McKesson to help reduce costs and improve quality for its customers.

McKesson systems and programs rationalize and support every aspect of health care processes. These capabilities are achieved primarily through networks that pool information from various E-business storefronts in the health care industry—including manufacturers, hospitals, pharmacies, and managed care providers. This reach, spanning the entire information technology and supply management structure across the full continuum of care, has enabled McKesson to establish market-leading positions in pharmaceutical and medical-surgical supply management, health care information systems for providers, information services for payors, and health care information outsourcing.

Net Ready Strategy

- *What:* Health care value chain services on a business-to-business (btb) model

- *Company:* McKesson (www.mckesson.com)

- *Offering:* Consolidating customers, distributors, and partners using Web-enabled processes to transform key processes

- *Net Ready Strategy:* Unbundling key purchasing and distribution processes by Web-enabling them through Internet and Intranet technologies with the goal of extending the company's reach to consumers

---

Assume Another Role

As we discussed in chapter 4, five emerging business models are being enabled by E-business technologies:

1. E-business storefront
2. Infomediary
3. Trust intermediary
4. E-business enabler
5. Infrastructure provider

The E-conomy values migration. Organizations create value when they take on new roles. Successful companies in the E-conomy often migrate from one business model to another and are able to manage that migration well. To get the best sense of the power of these business models when they are integrated with a clear value proposition and ruthless execution, we examine here at some length the case of E-Loan (www.eloan.com). This young company serves as a good example of how companies can and do take on multiple roles.

E-Loan

E-Loan, the leading online mortgage company, provides a clear example of how value can be created by taking on a number of E-business models. E-Loan launched its online mortgage operations in June 1997. In the following summary of the company, how many E-business roles can you identify?

E-Loan offers consumers the ability to search more than 50,000 products from more than 70 lenders at substantially lower transaction costs than brick-and-mortar financing alternatives. Borrowers can analyze and compare various products to find the best loan that fits their criteria. By aggregating sources of funds, borrowers can compare, apply for, and obtain home loans from many nationally recognized lenders. E-Loan's efficiency offers borrowers origination cost savings of more than 50 percent compared to mortgages obtained through most traditional mortgage brokers and single-source lenders. After closing a loan, E-Loan can, at the customer's request, continue to send customized information about new products that become available, helping consumers turn a mortgage into a working financial asset. E-Loan has established co-branded loan centers for mortgages on many leading Web sites.

Before we describe the company, let's list the multiple E-business strategies that E-Loan has taken on since its inception:

- Reconceive product or service
- Redefine value proposition
- Move the product up the food chain
- Separate function from form
- Transform key processes
- Embrace an E-business storefront
- Take on infomediary role

- Become E-business enabler
- Aspire to COIN status
- Compress the value delivery system
- Redefine the basis of competition
- Become the channel master
- Redraw industry boundaries

E-Loan delivers value to consumers by acting as an infomediary and aggregating information on more than 50,000 loan products that can easily be viewed and compared online. E-Loan also acts as a business service provider for loan processing, loan tracking, and loan analysis. Most of all, it succeeds by transforming an unwieldy, slow, and error-prone process in which consumers are treated poorly into an informated, integrated process that empowers consumers to take on ownership of the system.

E-Loan offers first- and second-mortgage customers the ability to quickly and efficiently search a database of more than 35,000 loan products. Rates are updated daily. Customers can go online to search for rates, compare loans, project out payment schedules, and apply for and lock in the desired loan online. Unlike other competitors—online or offline—E-Loan displays customized product quotes and comparisons, recommending the best product available that day to the borrower based on his or her responses to qualifying questions regarding debt objectives, risk profile, hold period, and other financial criteria. E-Loan also offers performance forecasts on loans so customers can plan for the future.

As a multilender service, E-Loan seeks to provide a one-stop experience for consumers as they shop for the best rates for mortgage loans. At the center of E-Loan's service is a program called E-Track, which allows users to follow a loan's paperwork process and to compare the lowest daily rates. Consumers can also obtain information about loans that match specific financial needs. The E-Loan site contains all the tools necessary for obtaining home financing.

Americans currently owe more than $4 trillion in outstanding mortgage debt, with 1998 total residential loan origination volume at $750 billion. The Internet is changing the way mortgages are bought and sold, and online mortgage lending is growing at a rate of 200 percent annually. Online sites were generating more than $800 million a month in mortgages by the end of 1998, ten times the amount of online mortgage originations at the beginning of the year, estimates Deutsche Bank analyst James Marks. Using the rapid success of online stock trading as a guide, Marks sees the fledgling online mortgage industry as an area with a very steep growth curve. Online mortgages could swell to about 25 percent of the overall market, or $250 billion, in five years, he predicts.

Ripe for Disintermediation

The traditional home mortgage loan origination business model is ripe for disintermediation. There are five stages in the home financing process: origination, banking, guarantor, service, and capital market. Each of these intermediate stages typically involves a different company or organization, and each extracts a percentage of the value of the loan as a service fee (figure 6-2).

E-Loan entered the market as an alternative to the existing mortgage brokers for loan origination services. The company's E-conomy business model has lower overhead than traditional origination companies and charges consumers only 0.5 percent to originate a loan. This difference saves consumers an average of $1,500 per loan over traditional brokers and represents a significant competitive edge to E-Loan.

But while cost savings are critical, they would not be sufficient without a high level of customer service. E-Loan also delivers value to its customers by making the loan process easier, more consistent, and more predictable. Many consumers are unhappy and frustrated with the long and arduous process of getting or refinancing a home loan. E-Loan makes a portion of

Figure 6.2. Inefficiencies in the traditional loan origination model make this process ripe for disintermediation by a Net Ready enterprise.

Stage	Description	Typical Margin	E-Loan Margin
Origination	Traditional mortgage broker role; connects individual consumers with lending banks	1.25%	0.5%
Banking	The lender of the funds	.75%	.75%
Guarantee	Underwrites the loan; Freddie Mac and Fannie Mae are the most notable	1.125%	N/A
Service	Services the loan and acts as an interface with the capital markets	1.25%	N/A

the process easier by allowing consumers to shop online for mortgages and easily compare mortgage rates for different types of loans.

Part of consumers' frustration with the traditional loan process is the inability to determine their loan's progress without directly speaking with their loan agents. Even in the age of cellular phones and voicemail, this contact can be extremely difficult. In addition to offering loan agents that can be contacted during business hours, E-Loan allows their customers to obtain an update on their loan over the Internet twenty-four hours a day, seven days a week. Users can view the status of their loans through a secure area of E-Loan's Web page that is updated by E-Loan's loan agents at each milestone of the loan process.

E-Loan's core business model is to act as an infomediary that compresses the value delivery cycle of securing new or refinancing existing mortgage loans. Consumers can go to E-Loan's Web page and enter a few parameters to begin comparing loans. In most cases, the loan rates are updated daily, and consumers can even bookmark their loan parameters to investigate how loan rates change over time. These features greatly reduce the time it takes for consumers to investigate and compare loan prices.

A typical traditional loan broker requires consumers to fill out an extensive array of paperwork before a loan quote is given. Loan brokers use this method to weed out consumers who are less than totally committed. It protects the loan brokers, but it imposes a serious burden on customers. Net Ready loan brokers recognize this paperwork as a major weakness of the traditional process and exploit it. The E-Loan business model encourages even casual consumers to frequently browse and investigate loan rates. Why not? There are almost no incremental costs involved. Once consumers find a loan that meets their requirements, they can complete the loan application online. These loan forms are checked by an E-Loan loan agent and mailed to the consumers. The consumer then signs the completed forms and the process follows the traditional mortgage route from this point.

Each consumer is assigned a personal loan agent who assists the loan through the process. This loan agent is available during business hours, which is the same level of customer service that is offered by traditional mortgage brokers. In addition, E-Loan's continuous loan tracking service should enable the company to deliver a higher level of customer service than traditional mortgage brokers.

The vast majority of E-Loan's employees are loan agents, which is the fastest area of E-Loan's personnel growth. Each loan agent can process approximately six loans per day using E-Loan's current back-end loan processing system. The company is in the process of upgrading its back-end loan processing systems so as to allow its agents to process fifteen loans per day without sacrificing its level of customer service.

The banking portion of E-Loan's business model involves two different banking relationships. The first relationship is with E-Loan's own banking arm. This portion of E-Loan acts as a traditional bank and competes with the other banks in E-Loan's portfolio. On the surface it would appear that E-Loan's decision to create its own bank would serve to alienate its existing partner banks. However, this practice is accepted, because most large mortgage brokers have their own in-house banks while still working with a number of external banks. E-Loan avoids conflict with partner banks by not giving its in-house bank any special preferences. In fact, E-Loan pledges to its customers that it will be unbiased with respect to lenders. The same claim cannot be made by E-Loan's competitors that work on a referral mortgage model.

All of E-Loan's partner banks provide E-Loan with an electronic mortgage rate sheet on a daily basis. These rate sheets are loaded into the E-Loan database and posted on the Web site. Users are then able to access and compare all the loans in E-Loan's database directly through the Web site.

E-Loan has a number of online relationships to promote its site and generate Internet traffic, the most significant of which is with Yahoo!. Consumers can use Yahoo! to enter basic loan parameters in the Yahoo! finance Web page to see and compare loan rates. Yahoo! uses E-Loan's engine for this section of its Web site. Although there is no direct link from Yahoo! to E-Loan, a small tag line on the Yahoo! page states that the loan rates search is "powered by E-Loan." E-Loan also has relationships with online stock brokerage companies that provide direct links to E-Loan's site.

E-Loan's online business model offers several benefits, including better customer service and ease of finding a home loan. Beyond the customer benefits are a variety of benefits to E-Loan itself. E-Loan's business model requires less hands-on intervention during the loan origination process and requires fewer overheads per loan. Even while charging about $1,500 less per loan than traditional mortgage brokerage firms do, E-Loan is able to maintain 65 percent to 75 percent margins compared to the 30 percent margin typically maintained by traditional brokers. This difference translates to about $1,200 to $1,400 profit per loan completed by E-Loan. Loans that are funded by E-Loan's in-house bank generate an additional $2,400 per loan.

Compressing the Moments of Truth

Moments of truth represent the actual interactions or encounters between the consumer and a company's representative. Whether the interactions are in person, by telephone, or by correspondence, consumers judge the effectiveness of a service by the professionalism and competency of each of these moments. Inevitably, the weakest or sloppiest encounter defines the relationship. Moreover, consumers generally prefer a smaller rather than larger number of encounters to get the transaction done. In any event, for the organization, encounters are expensive, so it behooves an organization to reduce the number of encounters in general and minimize the opportunities for sloppiness.

By squeezing the inefficiency out of its delivery cycle and giving consumers direct access to much of the information they need, E-Loan has automated many of the operations that formerly required a human interaction. By doing so, it has not only squeezed out costs, it has speeded up the process to the satisfaction of customers. Most important, by encouraging customers to take a self-help approach for most of their information requirements, E-Loan frees up resources for the most meaningful and value-added steps. By reducing the number of moments of truth and by emphasizing customer service for these occasions, E-Loan has succeeded in compressing a key component of the value delivery system.

E-Loan is revolutionizing the mortgage industry by changing the way consumers shop for a mortgage (see figure 6-3). Its goal is to simplify and shorten the lengthy and often inefficient lending process by empowering consumers with timely and accurate mortgage rate information. The unfulfilled gap between consumers and brokers and between brokers and lenders is electronically bridged by E-Loan. Its E-business initiatives have helped transform the traditional mortgage industry and have created a tremendous amount of value to mortgage shoppers who are willing to take advantage of the Internet.

Mortgage Value Chains

E-Loan implemented a mortgage lending process that is speedy and cost-effective. Consumers can fill out an application, qualify for a loan, and shop among numerous lenders by simply logging onto E-Loan's Web site. The mortgage rate information is instant and interactive through direct feed from hundreds of lenders and is updated several times a day. More important, the savings achieved through E-Loan's scale and efficiency are

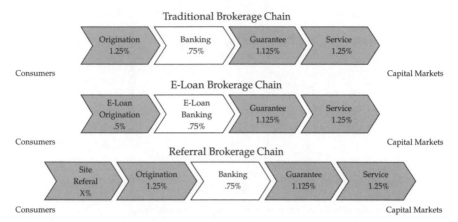

Figure 6-3. Of the three mortgage value chains, the E-Loan brokerage chain is the most efficient and least vulnerable to disintermediation.

passed directly to consumers. E-Loan's packages are extremely price competitive because of reduced commissions and loans based on wholesale rather than retail rates. These features make E-Loan an ideal choice for consumers who are willing to take a more proactive role in selecting their own mortgage. Let's consider a few of the E-Loan's initiatives, how they contribute to compressing various elements of the value delivery system, and how sustainable they are as incremental to E-Loan's competitive edge (figure 6-4).

Interactive and instant multilender quotes. The ability to offer consumers interactive and instant rate quotes from multiple lenders is a major differentiating factor between online lenders/brokers and their traditional counterparts. Mortgage rates fluctuate every day and often make surprising moves. Because consumers' ability to borrow is tightly coupled to interest rates, consumers need to follow rate information in more detail than traditional lenders/brokers are able to offer. By providing timely and accurate information from various sources, E-Loan is empowering consumers to make their best mortgage decisions. This initiative is relatively easy to implement but the potential return is high. It is highly innovative as well as critical to E-Loan's business. Because there are few technological barriers preventing competitors from offering this service, it is likely to become a commodity in the online mortgage lending industry.

E-track. E-track provides E-Loan's customers secure, anytime access to information on the status of their loan application. Customers can review

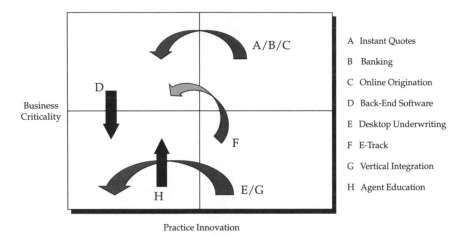

Business
Criticality

Practice Innovation

A Instant Quotes

B Banking

C Online Origination

D Back-End Software

E Desktop Underwriting

F E-Track

G Vertical Integration

H Agent Education

Figure 6-4. E-Loan's E-Business Initiatives. E-Loan's Net Ready initiatives are mapped against the dimensions of criticality and innovation.

the loan product that they have selected, obtain precise closing cost details, or check on the locked interest rate instantly without having to work directly with a loan officer. E-track is a powerful tool for customers to stay abreast of their loans once the loan is submitted for approval. The E-track benefit is highly innovative but not a sustainable differentiating factor because it is a relatively easy technology to duplicate. It offers many of the benefits high on customers' priority list and is of moderate criticality to E-Loan.

Origination of all loans. E-Loan originates all loan applications it receives. It profits from loan originations as well as lending. Some of E-Loan's competitors have a different business model, in which profits are made by aggregating loan applications online and then referring applications to their lending partners. Consumers see little benefit from the "referral" model because of the extra unnecessary step created in the value chain. Referral-type online mortgage companies also offer fewer loan products than does E-Loan, so comparison shopping opportunities are limited. The referral companies become new infomediaries that extract a piece of value. We believe this initiative offers high initial criticality, but is also relatively easy to implement. Over time, competitors are likely to follow suit and the perception of innovation would slowly diminish.

Addition of banking arm. E-Loan created its own banking arm to increase profit and to streamline the lending process. E-Loan's bank offers competitive but more flexible loan packages for individuals with special needs. For example, E-Loan is considering custom loan packages for people who wish to keep their stock options or other financial assets (which could realize significant gain in the near future) when purchasing a home. The initiative requires a core competency that most online mortgage brokers lack and is therefore more difficult to implement compared to online loan comparison and origination. On an absolute scale, however, providing a banking arm is still considered a relatively easy implementation with great potential benefits. It is an innovative move for an online broker striving to streamline its business and boost profits. The strategic criticality is high because banking margins are higher than for mortgage loan originations. If so, the question becomes, is E-Loan in the wrong business?

Core Competencies

E-Loan wisely resists treating online mortgages as a commodity and avoids competing only on price. Its strategy is to differentiate on the quality of customer service. All employees are offered company stock options in their compensation benefits to encourage a sense of ownership. Even though stock options are common among engineers and programmers in the Silicon Valley, this benefit is an unusual one for loan processing agents in the mortgage industry. More critically, E-Loan rejects the advertising model so common to the Net. Unlike other competitors such as Home-Shark (www.homeshark.com) or LendingTree (www.lendingtree.com), E-Loan has no immediate plan to become a content provider on topics of interest to home buyers, such as neighborhood information or listings of homes for sale. E-Loan's Web site has a fairly simple design and will continue to drive traffic as a transaction site. E-Loan will try to expand its loan offerings to include innovative loan products such as a mortgage backed by stocks as collateral and services such as E-track to sustain its competitive advantage.

The success of E-Loan has invited new entrants as well as competition from traditional lenders. As one of the first movers in the online mortgage market, E-Loan has achieved a dominant position in the fledgling market but is seeing its lead diminish as imitators and competitors emerge (figure 6-5). Competition will intensify for two principal reasons. First, capacity is less of an issue for many Internet-based firms that have taken the time to construct a scalable business model and are ready to take over a large

Web Site	Site Launch Date	Loans Closed per Month	Avg. Savings over Traditional Channels	Avg. Size per Loan	Unique Site Visits per Month
www.loanshop.com	June 1994	300	$1,500	$170,000	250,000
www.eloan.com	June 1997	285	$2,000	$190,000	270,000
www.qucken.com	Nov 1997	N/A	N/A	$180,000	500,000

Figure 6-5. E-Loan and its principal competitors.

market share. Second, differentiation is inherently difficult over the Net, and some of the new entrants are likely to choose to compete on the basis of price only, eroding the profit margin across the industry. Such competition will take three forms: true online lenders capable of originating loans, the referral model E-business storefronts, and traditional lenders going online to gain market share.

To maintain its lead, E-Loan has added the capability of rate monitoring and application tracking (E-track) to its site. The company also continues to emphasize customer service to prevent the market from following the path taken by online stock trading markets and becoming a commodity. E-Loan still believes that lower rates made possible through its efficient lending process will be the key differential, but many competitors have since moved to emphasize content, hoping aggregated information will attract and retain traffic to their sites. Traffic is indisputably the driving force behind the profit engine for online mortgage firms. The more traffic an online lender is able to draw to its site, the more applications it is likely to receive and the more revenue it is likely to generate. Increased traffic also opens up the possibility of a new revenue stream from advertising dollars, which could boost the bottom line of the company.

Traditional lenders who are considering jumping on the Internet bandwagon must make several important decisions that will determine whether they should launch a stand-alone site, join an aggregator mortgage site, or do both. Because a marketplace that enables comparison shopping is likely to draw more traffic than does an independent site that offers a limited selection, lenders will benefit most if they partner with a trusted on-line discount mortgage broker such as E-Loan. This is especially true for smaller lenders. Though the partnership is not likely to be exclusive, meaning E-Loan will be offering products from more than one lender, banks are likely to benefit as the overall volume of applications increases. Other lenders are taking extreme precautions before launching their E-business initiatives, fearing their existing retail business could be canni-balized by the discount online brokers. The issue of channel conflict does exist for these lenders but can be best minimized by not revealing lenders' identities before the application is approved.

We have come to some other conclusions as well. First, online lenders that are able to streamline the lending process and pass on savings to con-sumers will likely thrive in an increasingly competitive environment. Refer-ral model E-business storefronts that are incapable of originating loans are likely to fall out of favor if they do not offer competitive mortgage products.

Second, content is the key to driving online traffic, and online lenders should either create or aggregate content to attract and retain traffic. This observation can be validated by the number of unique visits drawn to the Quicken Mortgage site, which contains a comprehensive coverage of home-buying related material, from home listings to neighborhood infor-mation to real estate news. Because proprietary content is costly, licensing material from a third party is an attractive way to jump-start a site's con-tent.

Third, online brokers with multilender affiliation that enable comparison shopping will likely dominate the competitive landscape. Single-lender sites with limited offerings will be forced to partner with a well-established online broker to compete.

E-Loan Exposure

Almost by definition, Net Ready organizations are exposed to a constella-tion of risks. The rapidly changing conditions in which they operate, the temporary nature of their competitive advantages, the low cost of entry into their marketspaces all contribute to a sense of justified paranoia. E-Loan is no exception. Time will tell if the E-Loan leadership and gover-nance models are equal to the task of navigating the company through the following challenges:

Economic downturns. Existing online lenders are extremely vulnerable to unexpected economy downturns. Most of the online lenders are heavily dependent on mortgage refinancing. Refinancing is extremely sensitive to the mortgage interest rate. A sustained high interest rate will greatly reduce refinancing activities among homeowners, and many online lenders are likely to see their revenue plunge. Equally damaging is an unexpected economy downturn, which is likely to drive down consumer confidence levels and slow down the housing market.

Competition. Fierce competition forces online brokers and lenders to innovate and streamline their businesses. Economies of scale become a critical factor of success. Because differentiation over the Internet is difficult, many E-business storefronts are likely to resort to competing on price rather than service. The result is plunging profit margins across the industry, and firms with the best chance of weathering such a hardship are firms with the lowest cost structure and the highest efficiency. Dominant storefronts with economies of scale are likely to become even more dominant, and weak E-business storefronts will be weeded out of the market. To prepare for such a scenario, E-Loan must aggressively grow its market share to become a formidable force before the consolidation begins. New entrants into the market are expected to continue, but E-Loan must streamline its business process to compete more efficiently and effectively. In particular, back-end software automation and desktop underwriting should be high on E-Loan's business improvement agenda.

Also high on its agenda should be content building and strategic alliances. E-Loan should invest heavily in content building to attract and retain traffic. The current transaction-oriented design of E-Loan's Web site leaves little for consumers to associate with the firm beyond low transaction cost. E-Loan should avoid being perceived as a pure price competitor.

Fragmented markets. Fragmentation of the online mortgage market threatens to lose E-Loan in the crowd. The key to E-Loan's success in a fragmented market is to rise above the noise of the thousands of online mortgage sites and differentiate its offerings. It is rather simple to compare quotes from different banks for different types of loans on a single Web site. However, it is very difficult to compare loans from different Web sites. The challenge of price shopping is further compounded by rapidly changing interest rates. The Web site that offers the lowest rates today may not necessarily offer the lowest rates tomorrow.

Net Ready Strategies for E-Loan

As the Net Ready leader in the online mortgage space, E-Loan is in an excellent position to capitalize on the growing number of loans that will be initiated over the Internet. However, the company cannot rest on its laurels. It must initiate a number of experiments aligned with its strategic goal of compressing even further the mortgage value delivery cycle. These initiatives include driving traffic to its Web through compelling content, and partnerships with high-traffic sites. Other initiatives should include:

- Networking with real estate agents
- Back-end software efficiency improvement
- Vertical integration
- Online brand-building partnerships

Net Ready Strategy

- *What:* Online mortgage origination and refinancing
- *Company:* E-Loan (www.eloan.com)
- *Offering:* Reducing complexity for consumers
- *Net Ready Strategy:* Multiple strategies

Compress the Value Delivery System

The Web, by virtue of its ability to bring buyers and sellers together, is a perfect medium for compressing aspects of the value delivery system such as purchasing, global sourcing, help desks, and E-commerce. This strategy is especially pertinent for business-to-business models. Let's look at an E-business initiative from Ford Motor Company.

Ford Supplier Network

Ford Motor Company has compressed the value delivery system with an extranet business portal to make it easier for its thousands of partner companies to automate their interactions with the $145 billion car maker. Using the Ford Supplier Network (FSN), suppliers can access customized views of their business activities to track bids, engineering changes, shop-floor status, and assembly reject rates. FSN is part of Ford's ongoing effort to reduce cycle time and inventory requirements by sharing data about business processes with suppliers, dealers, and consumers. The goal is to build an online community that will consist of about one million partners who regularly interface with the manufacturer.

FSN serves as a focal point for data residing in Ford's many client/server and mainframe applications that manage activities ranging from product design and quality control to sales and aftermarket services. Under Ford's pre-Web infrastructure, a supplier who wanted to check the status of a bid, for example, would have to know which application managed the bid process and drill down several layers to the right project and part number. Today, partners from around the world can create "My FSN" personalized pages, similar to those offered by Yahoo! or Netscape Netcenter, that extract that same data from the source application and present it on the customized home page, alongside pending projects managed by different applications. It is a much more coherent and customized view of all of Ford's repositories.

FSN launched in June 1999 with more than 14,000 individual accounts at 1,500 companies, 400 of which sell nonproduction supplies to Ford. The ultimate goal is to build a community with more than one million accounts representing more than 16,000 companies. The biggest push is to reduce inventory, a key requirement if Ford is to transform itself into a build-to-order business. That goal will require the extranet to integrate suppliers' back ends with Ford's to automate the flow of data in the supply chain.

Net Ready Strategy

- *What:* Global sourcing initiative in which Ford business units across the world make partnering with Ford easier and more efficient
- *Company:* Ford Motor Company (www.fsn.ford.com)
- *Offering:* Reducing information inefficiencies; permanent online information and transaction connections between a company and its key suppliers
- *Net Ready Strategy:* Compress the value delivery cycle

Explode Price/Performance Ratio

"Buy low and sell high" remains a bedrock principle of all economic activity. But Buy.com (www.buy.com) is chipping away at this certainty and, in so doing, is changing the price/performance ratio of retailing. Buy.com is determined to compete by offering the lowest retail price on every possible kind of product, at cost or even below cost if necessary. The company will profit through the ad sales and partnerships that follow all the traffic to its site. In this way, Buy.com explodes the price/performance ratio by recognizing that the information about a transaction is often more valuable than the transaction itself. In a Net Ready world, the information that Buy.com generates from the sale of a digital camera can be much more lucrative than the spread between its cost and the sales price for a product.

The company is ruthlessly committed to becoming the price leader in E-tailing—even if this means losing money on every sale. We've seen companies offer loss leaders in the hopes of getting traffic into stores, but what Buy.com is doing is fundamentally different. Every product becomes a loss leader. Buy.com has developed software agents that crawl the Net, polling competitor's Web sites, and aggregating prices to ensure that Buy.com's prices are indisputably the lowest. The company's tag line, "The lowest prices on Earth," may be the most precise brand positioning statement ever.

Buy.com is a paradox in the Net Ready world. The company is betting that its brand of lowest prices will make it a logical destination for any shopper and that advertising dollars will follow those shoppers wherever they go. So even if Buy.com loses a few cents on each E-conomy transaction, it will more than make up that loss with ad sales. We have noted that as the Net eliminates information inefficiencies and rationalizes prices, competition on the basis of price alone cannot be sustained. Now here comes Buy.com to challenge that conclusion. Is it possible to build a brand completely on price? Will a value discipline predicated on low prices alone be sufficient to ensure Buy.com's success? Will consumers put up with the ad serving and privacy issues inherent in the Buy.com business model? Can Buy.com execute its customer service and fulfillment promises as well as it executes its pricing strategies? These are open questions that will determine the company's success. In the meantime, let's take a closer look at Buy.com's business model and what it can teach Net Ready companies.

The company was founded as Buycomp.com in October 1996, and its first emphasis was on selling computer products at cut-rate prices on an Amazon.com infomediary model. In the very familiar model we have come to see, Buy.com did not take possession of inventory; rather, its wholesalers shipped products directly to customers. Renamed Buy.com in 1998, the company started an aggressive portal and branding strategy by acquiring more than 3,000 domain names, all incorporating the common theme of "buy" in them.

The Buy.com business model combines equal parts of E-conomy and aggregating eyeballs for advertisers. The company's portal strategy aggregates the attention of millions of customers. It uses this audience to sell ad space to supplement its low or nonexistent margins. Is the ad space on a product order form as valuable as the product being ordered? It's premature to say for sure.

Buy.com's governance model is impressive in that it keeps all its business critical processes in-house rather than outsourcing them. It also relies on a number of proprietary software systems instead of using off-the-shelf components. For example, Buy.com develops its own software to troll the Net for product prices. It does its own ad serving as well. The company recognizes that the innovative software infrastructure it creates represents its best chance for success. It doesn't take any brains for a competitor to lower prices. But a real competitive advantage is possible with a proprietary infrastructure that is not available to your competitors.

We are not alone in being skeptical of this model, but are nevertheless fascinated by it. Predictably, competitors who believe in the standard notion of selling goods at a profit criticize Buy.com. Many companies, as well as Buy.com's dissatisfied customers, argue that retailing is about more than just pricing and that Buy.com is substandard on other important qualities, particularly customer service, ease of use, and overall customer experience.

How about the members of Buy.com's value chain? Will the manufacturers and distributors balk at this model? It appears not. Manufacturers like it when their wares are used as a loss leader because it increases the market share of those products. Wholesalers and distributors, likewise, retain their standard markup, whether or not the virtual reseller loses money. The biggest downside for distributors is that Buy.com and other virtual resellers may circumvent distributors entirely and have the manufacturer ship products directly to the customers. This outcome would first require that manufacturers create an infrastructure to disintermediate the distributors, which is not likely.

Buy.com has aimed its sights squarely on Amazon.com and a number of sites offering books, software, videos, and computers. How should competitors respond to Buy.com's threat? Should they match Buy.com's prices or even try to get them lower? Should they concede the price wars to

Buy.com and put energy into building the best customer service experience? Should they throw in the towel and quit peddling commodity products? Or should they copy Buy.com's rule breaking model and change to an advertising-driven environment in which the ad space on an order form is valuable enough to pass the order on at cost? The answers to these questions will be played out in the next few months.

Net Ready Strategy

- *What:* Retailing at cost or even below cost

- *Company:* Buy.com (www.buy.com)

- *Offering:* Becoming a category killer by offering products at cut-rate prices; building brand as a low-price leader that attracts riches from advertisers

- *Net Ready Strategy:* Explode the price/performance ratio

7

Industry Transformation

Industry focus is the third critical dimension of creating E-conomy value. Sometimes the best strategy is to redefine the industry in which you operate or, better yet, start a new industry.

This chapter examines four E-business strategies that look beyond the boundaries of the product and even the business (figure 7-1). The strategies described here (redefining the basis of competition, becoming the channel enabler, redrawing industry boundaries, and breaking the unbreakable rules) attempt to redefine the very industry in which the enterprise operates. It is not as difficult as it may first appear. Industries, especially in the E-conomy, respond quickly to "space invaders." Space invaders are players who redefine the competition by introducing new products, services, or technologies. They also transform the industry when they offer a new infrastructure so compelling that even their competitors find value in hitching their wagons to it. Finally, whenever space invaders break one of the unbreakable rules that govern an industry, they effectively transform it. By understanding the strategies that enterprises such as Charles Schwab, Amazon.com, LoopNet, and DoubleClick have used to transform the industries in which they operate, you are in a better position to evaluate whether similar opportunities are available in the industry in which you operate.

You'll see the same names over and over again, testimony to the fact that the most successful E-conomy storefronts have activity in a number of areas of the E-conomy. Aggressive participation on many levels—some strategies will bear fruit, others will fail—determines sustainable competitive advantage over the long haul.

Product and Market Transformation	Business process transformation	Industry Transformation
Reconceive the product/service	Unbundle and outsource processes	Redefine the basis of competition
Redefine the value proposition	Assume another role - E-business storeform - Infomediary - Trust intermediary - E-business enabler - Infrastructure provider	Become the channel enabler
Move the product up the food chain	Compress the value delivery system	Redraw industry boundaries
Separate the function from the form	Explode the the price/performance ratio	Break the unbreakable rules

Figure 7-1. The E-Business Value Transformation Matrix focused on industry transformation. E-conomy opportunities are exposed when organizations have the boldness to question the very foundations of the industries in which they operate, including breaking the unbreakable rules in which they have prospered.

Redefine the Basis of Competition

The most celebrated instances of leadership in the E-conomy happen in the strategic space of redefining the basis of competition. There is no stronger strategy than rewriting the rules organized around your individual competencies and making your competitors play catch-up. While the upside to this strategy can be phenomenal, the investment necessary to make it happen is considerable and a cast iron stomach is often necessary to swallow the risks.

The poster organization for this strategy is, without dispute, Dell Computer. We have discussed the Dell model in chapter 3 and a number of excellent case histories exist elsewhere, so we do not propose to rehash what has become a very well-known story. Let us just note that Dell has been able to leverage its first mover advantage. It is now the dominant storefront in the online distribution of PCs and, at its present rate of growth, is likely to become the number one storefront in the industry, passing both Compaq and IBM in sales.

But first mover advantage, even in this most strategic of spaces, is not sufficient to guarantee long-term success. E*Trade pioneered the discount, Internet brokerage industry by using the attributes of cyberspace to permanently redefine the basis of competition. In the beginning, it made full-service firms such as Merrill Lynch and even discount brokers such as Charles Schwab squirm, forcing a general decrease in prices and eroding margins across the board. Unfortunately for E*Trade, Schwab accepted the challenge of playing in a new space, even one it did not create. By betting the farm on low-cost Web trading and leveraging its existing channels, Schwab redefined and took the lead in the industry that E*Trade had pioneered. It accepted the role of rule taker and is now acting as the rule maker.

Charles Schwab

Schwab had a number of things going for it. First, it has always been a technology-driven institution. Second, it has a culture of taking huge risks, often on emerging technologies. Third, it is capable of breathtaking speed in making decisions and implementing them. And finally, it has built a number of channels—bustling branch offices and call centers staffed by the most efficient phone reps in the business—on which it could build a staggeringly effective Web presence. And that it did. In 1995, Schwab's exposure to the Web was zero. Today, more than half of Schwab's trading volume goes through its Web site. Of its 5.5 million customers, more than two million are active Web customers, who collectively account for approximately a third of Schwab's $435 billion in customer assets. That makes Schwab the number one Internet brokerage; its 30 percent share of daily trading volume equals that of its next three online competitors (E*Trade, Waterhouse Securities, and Fidelity).

Schwab's success is somewhat counterintuitive in view of how price-sensitive a commodity service that executes securities transactions has become. Yet Schwab, at $29.95 per trade for most online transactions, is by no means the low price provider. Both E*Trade ($15 per trade) and Ameritrade ($8 per trade) beat Schwab in discounts. Schwab's strategy is to build up the value of its relationships with its clients. Thus, the transformative event is not price but value in the form of personalization, integration of people and technology, advice, and total relationship management. Although Schwab must compete with its low-cost competitors in the Internet trading space, the company is much more of a threat to its traditional foes, the full-serve brokers.

Net Ready Strategy

- *What:* Financial services on the Web

- *Company:* Charles Schwab (www.schwab.com)

- *Offering:* A self-service application that allows two million Schwab investors to research and control their investments online; value is created through customer relationships by providing advice, counsel, and commerce

- *Net Ready Strategy:* Redefine basis of competition

Amazon.com

Like Dell, Amazon.com belongs to that rarefied group of E-conomy storefronts that have captured the public's imagination. At this point, we offer Amazon.com as an example of a company that has not only created a new industry by redefining the basis of competition, but continues to redefine that industry, placing itself at the forefront at every turn.

Amazon.com created its virtual bookstore by leveraging the power of the Net to streamline distribution, avoid inventory, and build community. Amazon.com is a perfect example of creative use of Web technology. Readers who like a certain author can use Amazon.com to find out what other books the author has written as well as other authors who write in the same genre. Customers can see what Amazon.com's in-house reviewers say about a book and what other customers have written. Readers can be notified whenever a new book by a particular author appears. In real-world terms, Amazon.com is not an online bookstore as much as it is an online service that sells books and, now, lots of other things. The real value of Amazon.com resides in the company's databases, that is to say, in the information itself. As Amazon.com evolves, the value of information about its transactions may well become more valuable than the transactions themselves.

The investment community finds Amazon.com's business model so compelling that it rewarded the company with its best endorsement. Although Amazon.com has not yet turned a profit—and won't even predict when it will—its shares are trading at more than twenty times its May 1997 IPO value, making its market capitalization, $11 billion, greater than that of Mattel or Delta Airlines.

From a strategic sense, what Amazon.com has done is create an infinitely flexible infrastructure for electronic commerce and erect a highly prestigious brand in the bargain. So from one perspective, Amazon.com—competing as it does in a world of commodity items such as books and videos—is at risk for losing customers to lower-priced rivals. On the other hand, Amazon.com's brand inspires considerable customer loyalty. A brand, as we have noted, is something customers will pay extra for even if it's on a product or service identical to a competitor's. The $64 billion question (perhaps literally) is, will the Amazon.com brand command the customer loyalty it hopes for? Wall Street is betting it will.

Amazon.com continues to reinvent itself around the strategic theme of redefining the basis of competition. The company moves at a breakneck pace to transform itself from its original business as an online bookstore into something closer to an electronic department store. It started selling music in mid-1998. By late in the year, it had introduced videos and a gift section with toys, consumer electronics, and games.

How can competitors such as Borders Books and Music or Barnes and Noble, with roots deep in the terrestrial world, hope to compete in the E-conomy environment to which Amazon.com has the considerable advantage of being born? The war will be won by brand and customer loyalty. And what are customers loyal to? That's just it. No one knows. Amazon.com has created and must maintain a brand and an information infrastructure, but there is absolutely no guarantee that either will ensure customer loyalty. A cut-rate competitor site such as Buy.com (see "Explode Price/Performance Ratio," page 202 in chapter 6) can come in with nothing more than the ability to pick books off any particular best-seller list and offer them at a cheaper price. Amazon.com now benefits from customers who browse at Borders and then order books from Amazon.com. What's to stop customers from browsing on Amazon.com's richer infrastructure and then clicking over to Buy.com to save a few bucks?

The question then becomes, will online consumers be willing to pay something extra for a trusted, branded service provider? In terrestrial economics, many local stores have been put out of business by bigger chains offering deep discounts, a pattern that could be repeated online. Or consumers may develop a loyalty to sites/brands that they feel are providing them with more objective and trusted information (or, as is very likely, superior privacy protection).

In its most recent departure from its roots, Amazon.com introduced a service through which it will refer its customers to other Internet merchants selling goods that it does not stock. This service is different from the one offered by Macy's in the film *Miracle on 34th Street,* in which Macy's clerks told customers where they could find goods that Macy's was out of or did not carry. There is nothing altruistic about Amazon.com's strategy as it places links marked "Shop the Web" throughout its Web site. Clicking these links allows shoppers to search for items in a number of categories, including apparel, toys, computers, and travel. Amazon.com receives revenue from the resulting transactions because online merchants pay Amazon.com a linking fee or a percentage of sales.

When Amazon.com customers search for items, the company invokes software from its acquisition of Junglee. Junglee creates software that enables Internet users to compare the prices and features of products for sale on any number of sites spread across the E-conomy. Notice how this strategy is moving Amazon.com from its role as a *product magnet* up the food chain to the role of a *category destination* and then, finally, *customer magnet.* Amazon.com has already branded itself to be synonymous with book retailing on the Web. But as the company establishes direct links to its customers and to a large set of prestigious retailer partners, it is well on its way to becoming the E-conomy analogue of today's category-killer stores, such as Toys "R" Us and Wal-Mart.

As *Net Ready* went to press, Amazon.com announced a program of rational experimentation that calls on all of its Net Readiness competencies. With its zShops E-business initiative, Amazon.com leverages its brand with its E-commerce, infrastructure, shopping portal, and customer relationship management experience. The zShops program lets any business, from major manufacturers to small-fry retailers, add their wares to Amazon.com's Web site and its 12 million customers.

Let's say you sell luggage from a storefront in a strip mall in Omaha. You can set up a presence on zShop and immediately expand your reach to untold numbers of people who will never set foot in Nebraska. Amazon.com handles the whole thing, including the credit card transactions, and lets its blue-chip customers use its 1-Click ordering feature, which allows customers who have ordered from Amazon.com before to purchase additional items without reentering their credit card information. Amazon.com will handle the credit card processing and make a direct deposit into the seller's checking account. Sellers will also be instantly notified when the deposit has been handled, which eliminates the need for a seller to wait for checks to clear before shipping goods. In exchange for the value generated by its brand and 1-Click infrastructure, Amazon gets $10 per month and 5 percent of every sale. It's a hefty fee, but we predict merchants will be glad to be allied with a proven Net Ready partner. For its part, Amazon.com will not only generate new revenues from previously unserved markets but will also enrich the value of its own brand by aggregating even more content for all its customers.

Amazon.com's Entry into the Auction Space

What does it take for a Net Ready company that is successful in one E-business to enter another? Amazon.com's recent entry into the hyper-competitive online auction space is an opportunity to see best-of-breed Net Readiness navigate some tricky waters.

First, let's provide a little background. In early 1999, Amazon.com launched an auction service to compete primarily with eBay (www.eBay .com). Although eBay has first mover advantage and has enlisted some three million users, Amazon.com is trying to leverage its own customer base of twelve million customers by preregistering them to bid in any of 1,000 categories. Several features make participation even more enticing: Amazon.com cross-sells auction items from its E-commerce area (for instance, a person looking for a book about guitars will be alerted about the current guitar selection up for auction); customers can request E-mail notice on auction items in which they have an interest; and Amazon.com provides a $10 gift certificate for first-time auction users. In addition, Amazon.com has taken another step to differentiate itself from eBay and other auction sites by offering no-cost fraud protection up to $250. It can offer such protection because Amazon.com already has exquisite credit histories for its registered customers. Note that Amazon.com's auction venture is not based on leveraging its book, CD, or video business at all. Rather, it is designed to leverage Amazon.com's current customer base.

Now let's consider what options Amazon.com had as it started formulating its strategy for integrating an auction service into its array of services. The company had at least six ways to enter the market:

1. Acquire an auction site such as eBay outright and integrate it with the rest of the Amazon.com storefront.

2. Buy off-the-shelf auction software and integrate it with the rest of the site.

3. Partner with an online auction company like Fair Market—which hosts sites that can be integrated into the company's Web site—and maintain the site's brand name.

4. Partner with a site such as AuctionUniverse to create a co-branded auction site.

5. Partner with an auction E-business enabler such as OpenSite that would service Amazon.com-generated auction traffic.

6. Form a relationship with a brick-and-mortar auction house such as Sotheby's.

At the same time, Amazon.com did enter into a partnership with Sotheby's—perhaps the most respected name in the business—in a bid to transfer some of the trust that the venerable auction house has established over the centuries. What's interesting is to look at what strategies Amazon.com didn't follow. Most conspicuously, it did not acquire eBay or another auction company to fold into its array of services. Nor did it buy an off-the-shelf package solution. Nor did it partner with anyone. Rather, the company invested up to twelve months and more than $12 million to build a custom solution. Why would Amazon.com invest a year of opportunity and millions of dollars to build a solution that it could have acquired either much quicker, if it elected to buy a competitor, or much cheaper, if it elected to use an off-the-shelf template or form a partnership?

Here's where Amazon.com's Net Readiness—leadership, governance, competencies, and technology—came into play. Its decision to develop an end-to-end auction experience is evidence of its desire to maintain its role of rule breaker, to retain control over its brand, and to keep tight reins on customer experience. The company had invested in an infrastructure that allows for seamless integration of rapidly developed technologies. Amazon.com has the leadership and management experience to execute flawlessly. And it has the patience and the deep pockets to do it right.

Amazon.com's governance model puts a premium on brand and on total customer experience. Perhaps the easiest solution would have been to buy an existing auction site outright, giving Amazon.com an instant presence in the market and control over that presence. But aside from the enormous expense of buying an eBay, whose market capitalization is hovering around $18 billion, Amazon.com would have found it difficult to mesh its site with an existing auction site and maintain the quality of its back-end systems. One governance value is that responsibility for managing the customer experience—a common look and feel across all Amazon.com services—cannot be diluted.

Nor would the company's governance model find much comfort in tweaking an existing auction site to fit with the rest of the Amazon.com site. First, such a move might not really be faster or cheaper than developing a site in-house. But more important, partnering with an existing site would diminish Amazon.com's brand and divert eyeballs elsewhere, perhaps permanently. Finally, Amazon.com's Net Ready technology values place a premium on controlling technology so that its ability to differentiate itself from its competitors is not hampered. In a world in which everyone seems to be offering online auctions, Amazon.com's ability to quickly introduce rule-breaking wrinkles may spell the difference between leadership and accepting a me-too role.

Net Ready Strategy

- *What:* Book, music, and video retailing on the Web with integrated services such as online auctions

- *Company:* Amazon.com (www.Amazon.com)

- *Offering:* Virtual sales experience centered around books, music, and video, but branching out to all corners of the Net, driven by the Amazon.com brand and a combination of ruthlessly executed convenience, personalization, and customer obsession

- *Net Ready Strategy:* Redefine basis of competition

Amazon.com as a Rule Breaker, Rule Maker, and Rule Taker

Amazon.com, the poster child for the possibilities of creating an online brand in the E-conomy, participates in the E-conomy, as appropriate, as a rule breaker, rule maker, and rule taker (see chapter 9 for a description of these roles).

Amazon.com's moniker, chosen for its alphabetical advantage as well as its image of strength and size, has become one of the best-known brands on the Net. Despite forays into online selling by megachain brick-and-mortar competitors such as Borders Books and Music and Barnes and Noble. Amazon.com, launched in 1994, has continued to lead the market. More recently, it has expanded into selling music online, and it has plans to start a giant video store as well. Amazon.com is gearing up to be the Wal-Mart for customer value on the Web.

Amazon.com's success stems from an old-fashioned concept—exquisite attention to customers—coupled with ruthless execution exploiting the advantages of an online channel. The company appreciates the online power of word of mouth. "If you do a great job of servicing your customers and providing them with the best possible service, you'll turn these people into evangelists, and they will help you grow the business," says founder Jeff Bezos. "So, that's what we've focused on. We've focused on just having a better store, [where] it's easier to shop, where you can learn more about the products, where you have a bigger selection, and [where] you have the lowest prices. And you combine all of that stuff together and people say, "Hey, these guys really get it."

Amazon.com has been well rewarded for taking on the risks of being a rule breaker. Though it has yet to turn a profit, the company is far and away the greatest commercial success in cyberspace. It's the only electronic retailer among the top twenty most popular sites on the Web in terms of daily visitors. Both consumers and Wall Street love the brand.

As a rule maker, Amazon.com has defined the playing field for its competitors Barnes and Noble and Borders Books and Music, both of which must be content with accepting the role of rule takers. Borders (www.borders.com), for example, watched Amazon.com and Barnes and Noble (www.barnesandnoble.com) slug it out and expend lots of blood and sweat (not to mention capital) to build the ultimate bookselling sites. Meanwhile, Borders was quietly honing its rule-taking strategy. Its plan: compete as a "Johnny come lately" by offering the best selection, service, community, and pricing on the Web. The $2.2 billion retailer finally got into the E-conomy a full four years after Amazon.com did (although it's had brochureware on the Web since 1996) and presents its site as the first integrated book-, music- and video-selling Web commerce site with dedicated back-end fulfillment. Borders is betting that it can leverage the hundreds of millions of dollars that its competitors have spent building the concept of online book buying. Borders' strategy is to minimize its investment and to learn from the many mistakes its competitors have made and thereby avoid the heavy losses that continue to plague them.

For its part, Amazon.com is not embarrassed to be a rule taker on occasion. When it began selling books, it was first to the market. In selling CDs, it's not even second. With its acquisition of the movie database IMDB (www.imdb.com), Amazon.com is just now positioning itself for a presence in the E-conomy video industry. That's okay. Amazon.com recognizes that its bread is buttered on three sides: rule breaker, rule maker, and, on occasion, rule taker.

Become the Channel Enabler

The Sabre Group first demonstrated the power of what appeared to be a paradox. An outgrowth of American Airlines's reservation system, Sabre at first represented American Airlines's flights exclusively. As such it operated squarely in the tradition of what was called proprietary lock-in. The strategy was to earn market share by making it cheaper and easier to book American flights than the flights of competitors. But as the Sabre system expanded its coverage to partners and then found favor among travel agents, pressure grew to open up the system to a greater number of partners and travel providers. Some American Airlines managers were afraid that their own flights would take a hit if competitors' flights were offered on equal terms. But a curious thing happened. The value of Sabre grew exponentially as it became more open and less biased. The number of participants grew, commanding higher licensing fees. The Sabre system gradually became a standard and then suddenly a brand. Today, in a spectacular display of informatization, The Sabre Group is an independent company whose value actually transcends the airline operations of its parent company. Former American Airlines CEO Robert Crandall has been quoted as saying he'd sooner sell the airline than the technologies developed by Sabre.

Today, whenever an E-business storefront consolidates its position by creating an infrastructure sufficiently open to invite a great spectrum of the industry in which it operates, we say that that business has become a channel enabler, or has "Sabre-ized" its marketspace. Although every attempt at Sabre-ization must necessarily be unique to meet the requirements of the industry in which it operates, a number of common initiatives appear. A Sabre-ized organization will generally

- Build and own an infrastructure or platform that serves as a transaction engine
- Invite the broadest participation from every corner of the industry
- Provide a secure, stable, standard environment for all members of that community to interact
- Promote an unbiased E-conomy environment that is trusted
- Maintain the network on behalf of its members
- Derive revenues from a mix of subscription, advertising, and transaction fees

Channel enablers universally want to own the playing field. When they do, their performance on the field relative to their competitors suddenly becomes less important because now they take a percentage of every transaction. Companies who set out to become channel enablers should ask themselves the following questions:

- Who are my customers?
- Who are my partners?
- Who are my competitors?
- What are the common challenges of each?
- What information needs to be shared?
- What benefits will accrue to the agent who reduces duplication of function?
- What benefits will accrue to the agent who provides a frictionless transaction environment?
- Can I build and own a platform that they will have to play on in order to do well?

In chapter 2, we spoke of the relationship between content and container. As we noted, products in the E-conomy employ attributes of both content and container in original ways to create new value. An infrastructure provider, then, builds an infrastructure around a collection of relationships, enabling a set of transactions to occur. It tightly integrates advertising, E-conomy, and fulfillment. Leveraging the new opportunities enabled by E-conomy channel enablers, organizations can establish new relationships with previously underserved constituencies, forge tighter links with business partners and customers, and achieve stronger strategic alliances across the board.

If the company's business model is sound and, in a disciplined fashion over time, succeeds in building and owning a platform on which a critical mass of the industry participates, it has become a channel enabler and has Sabre-ized its industry. Ask the Sabre Group. Ask Fruit Of The Loom. When you succeed in becoming a channel enabler and can protect your turf from inevitable encroachment, the rewards can be significant.

LoopNet

Since its founding in 1995, LoopNet has grown into the largest commercial real estate listing service on the Internet by virtue of its strategy of becoming a channel enabler. LoopNet has aggregated more than 60,000 real estate agents in its participating organizations and an additional 20,000 individual agents and owners. It ties buyers and sellers together with a value-added infrastructure called PLS—Personal Listing Service. The result is a community so dependent on LoopNet that switching costs become prohibitive.

Many of the largest commercial real estate firms—RE/MAX International, Coldwell Banker Commercial, Trammell Crow Company, Grubb and Ellis—belong to the LoopNet network. LoopNet has become the preferred listing service of almost every large commercial real estate organization currently utilizing the Internet. LoopNet receives more than $200 million in new properties for sale and more than 3.6 million square feet in new properties for lease every day. It currently receives more than 400,000 page impressions and more than 2.5 million hits per month.

LoopNet offers the power of Internet networking and unparalleled exposure for commercial real estate listings. LoopNet allows interested parties to list and search its database of commercial real estate listings for free via its Web site (www.loopnet.com). User-friendly search screens allow for searches based on many parameters, such as location, property type, square footage, price, and so on. LoopNet is free for professionals to use. Agents can add listings and search available inventory at no cost. Listings are generated interactively by users and are comprised of site, financial, and operating information as well as photos and area maps. The flexibility of the search, the timeliness, and the richness of the information offered with each listing make LoopNet an indispensable tool.

LoopNet competes against a number of good regional systems, but so far it has the biggest Web-based national presence. According to founder Neil Aronson, LoopNet's biggest challenge is innovating fast enough to maintain its leadership position. That effort takes the form of governance and leadership initiatives as well as technology, such as offering new analytical tools to advertisers. A simple example is a view counter that lets advertisers know how many times a specific property has been viewed. "This provides them with real-time feedback as to the effectiveness of their marketing campaigns," Aronson says.

LoopNet derives revenues from four sources. First, by virtue of aggregating a very focused niche audience and creating a sticky Web site, LoopNet offers advertisers a compelling environment for ads and banners. Second, LoopNet sells information products such as demographic databases, tax roles, environment data, and other information needed by agents for due diligence. Third, it offers a variety of information services such as escrow, title, and lending services. Fourth, it licenses the PLS software. Web sites such as RE/MAX use the PLS engine for their own sites. From the LoopNet site, all of RE/MAX's listings are branded with a link to the RE/MAX home page.

By taking on the strategy of channel enabler for the commercial real estate industry, LoopNet benefits its partners in a number of ways. The infrastructure it provides for listing and searching properties, the demographic data it bundles with the searches, and the ancillary products and services represent enormous value. Most individual sites would find it prohibitive to duplicate them. The interconnection that allows secure, stable, real-time communication adds value for the buyers, sellers, and agents.

Net Ready Strategy

- *What:* Virtual community for commercial real estate
- *Company:* LoopNet (www.loopnet.com)
- *Offering:* Aggregating commercial real estate buyers and sellers using technology, infrastructure, governance, and services to add value to every transaction
- *Net Ready Strategy:* Become the channel enabler

Redraw Industry Boundaries

Ingram Micro, a $16.5 billion computer products distributor, is redrawing industry boundaries by tying together a series of high-tech initiatives to create a competence in channel assembly, an emerging expression of creating value in the E-conomy. Channel assembly is the practice of collecting computer components from various manufacturers and putting them together in response to a customer's shifting requirements. It's the ultimate extension of one-to-one channel logistics in the E-conomy because it enables customers to use interactive Internet applications to specify exactly what they want rather than to buy cookie-cutter products pumped into a channel by manufacturers. Ingram is one of the first E-conomy storefronts to execute channel assembly via the Internet.

Ingram is responding to competitive pressures from its computer-maker customers who need to tie distributors more intimately into their channels. Manufacturers such as Dell, Compaq, and Hewlett-Packard consider channel assembly as their insulation from ever-changing microprocessor and memory chip prices—the two most expensive pieces of any personal computer.

By taking on channel assembly responsibilities, Ingram assumes the most critical risk that its customers want to outsource: holding inventory. Although this risk is nothing new for a distributor such as Ingram—it has managed inventory for years—transforming this process to the E-conomy gives the company the unique flexibility to anticipate fluctuations in prices and allocate inventory more precisely. In other words, inventory data can be accessed over the Internet from Ingram's online sales applications to better calculate inventory requirements, which reduces the possibility that the company will need to store costly parts and accessories that aren't in demand. The ability to match real-time data to inventory demand is the key competence: if the flow of real-time information breaks down, inventories could pile up or run dry, eliminating profits for Ingram.

Channel assembly is causing Ingram to transform specific business practices as well. Manufacturers increasingly send Ingram half-built computers and assembled components. Server farms at the distribution centers automatically match demand taken from interactive Internet applications to inventory in stock. The company expects that its foray into channel assembly will pay off by collapsing production cycles, reducing inventories, and fine-tuning production. As it better manages the fundamental question of all inventory managers—the balance between supply and demand—the company builds relationships with its customers and partners. At the same time, the company is deploying intranets to let salespeople and customers compare products, obtain accurate pricing that reflects their purchase agreements, check whether the item is in stock, and post an order.

In redrawing industry boundaries, Ingram has also embarked on a comprehensive extranet strategy to tie together its best customers into a value-added infrastructure. The company's goal is to host and partially fund a collection of branded transaction sites on behalf of its computer reseller customers. This value migration technique redraws industry boundaries by reframing Ingram, the leader in the space, as an enterprise server provider (ESP), says Esther Dyson, chairman of EDventure Holdings and editor of *Release 1.0.* The effort is aimed at keeping otherwise fickle resellers, who will aggressively shop multiple distributors for the best price, in the Ingram fold by making it easier for them to conduct business in the low-cost Internet environment. At the same time, it imposes higher switching costs for those resellers who might want to defect from the fold that Ingram has so carefully constructed.

Ingram is deploying a packaged Internet electronic commerce application that it is making available to its more than 10,000 value-added resellers around the world. The management, transaction, and communication services offered by this intranet are designed to enable resellers to offer their customers real-time inventory, sales-tax calculation, transaction processing, shipping, and personalization on their own branded Web sites. The reseller will have the option to host all or only part of its site on Ingram's existing extranet, and those links would be completely invisible to the user. The more resellers that participate in the intranet, the more successful it will be and the more attractive it will be for other resellers to come aboard. Eventually, Ingram expects that this infrastructure will dominate electronic commerce in its industry segment, becoming the de facto standard.

When that happens, Ingram will be in a position to Sabre-ize by inviting competitors to offer their wares on the site. Resellers will then have a central, unbiased repository of information and sources to go to whenever they need or can offer inventory. Ingram hopes that its prices and customer service will continue to keep it a leader in its industry. But even if it does lose a deal now and then to its competitors, the company will take a piece of the action on those deals it loses by having all the transactions take place on the infrastructure it controls. Eventually, if Ingram's experience parallels that of American Airlines, the company will derive more value from the information and infrastructure services it offers than from the electronic components it distributes. Thus is value created in the E-conomy by redrawing industry boundaries.

We believe the Ingram model will prove to be very attractive as an architecture for distributors in other industries. To the extent that the company is perceived as being successful, Ingram's ability to empower the indirect channel will be an important breeding ground for other industries. Ingram is using a broad channel strategy to collapse cycles. If Ingram proves it can compete with Dell and others, distributors with strong indirect channels in other industries will want to copy it.

It took a lot of analysis for Ingram to make the decision to pursue the ESP strategy. Although the company was one of the first to provide private-label catalogs to its customers, the idea of its IT department building custom applications for inventory, order management, and transaction processing was deemed too costly. The turnaround came when the company realized that it didn't have to build everything from scratch. The maturity of packaged intranet and database applications was such that the company could readily assemble the components of a world-class system. "Our development lies in the integration of various packages put together in newer, innovative ways," says David Carlson, Ingram's senior vice president and chief technology officer. "When history is written on this era, we want Ingram Micro to be categorized as helping move the industry from vendor push to customer pull."

Net Ready Strategy

- *What:* Channel assembly services for the electronics industry
- *Company:* Ingram Micro (www.new.ingrammicro.com)
- *Offering:* Better use of information that minimizes the risk to its clients of holding inventory; cycle-time compression that hedges manufacturers' risk of obsolescence
- *Net Ready Strategy:* Redraw industry boundaries

Break Unbreakable Rules

The first step in breaking unbreakable rules is to understand the rules you are not supposed to break. This first step is not as easy as it sounds, because the shackles most difficult to break are precisely those you least acknowledge to be chains. Outsiders to your industry are the key to completing this step. Use their insight to articulate the rules as you understand them. Without doing so, you can't break those rules. Your mind will at first be bound by old rules of economic growth and productivity. The lesson is clear: in the network economy, don't respect rules, break them. Here are a few rules from the traditional economy and their possible replacements (table 7-1). Now go out and break the replacements.

DoubleClick

It's just been five years or so since the Net emerged as a viable advertising medium. In all that time, none of the traditional advertising agencies that rule the broadcast or print media environments has emerged as a Net Ready advertising presence. The roles of rule breaker and rule maker have gone to a born-on-the-Web company that has—by virtue of its governance model, leadership vision, and superior technology—redrawn industry boundaries. DoubleClick has succeeded by breaking the industry's un-

Table 7-1. Net Readiness Means the Willingness to Break Rules

Different is not always better, but better is always different. Net Ready companies relish the opportunity to break rules and challenge conventions.

Net Averse: Mistakes must be avoided; get it right the first time.
Net Ready: Mistakes must be welcome; experiment.
Net Averse: Attract new customers.
Net Ready: Retain and grow profitable ones.
Net Averse: Delegate tasks.
Net Ready: Delegate process.
Net Averse: One size fits all.
Net Ready: Markets of one.
Net Averse: Fear competitors.
Net Ready: Embrace competitors.
Net Averse: Vertically integrate for permanent advantage.
Net Ready: Virtually integrate for flexibility.
Net Averse: Work toward the bottom line; reduce total cost of ownership.
Net Ready: Work toward the top line; enhance revenue creation.
Net Averse: Strategies must be revised periodically.
Net Ready: Strategies must be revised continuously.
Net Averse: Scarcity reigns; prices get higher.
Net Ready: Embrace plenitude; inverse pricing anticipates lower prices.

breakable rules to exploit the exquisite measurability and interactivity of the Net as an advertising vehicle.

When DoubleClick was launched, there was still a huge question mark to as whether the Internet was a fad, a niche, or a mass market. What the Internet "economy" was going to look like was still up in the air. The value proposition for the Web was completely untested. Would sites charge a subscription or would advertising pay the bills? Kevin O'Connor, CEO and cofounder of DoubleClick, saw that the wealth of all successful media companies derived from ad sales. All DoubleClick had to do was build the technology to tame the anarchic culture of the Web so that executives would invest their media dollars.

"We believed that technology was going to be the key in redefining the way marketing was going to be done on the Internet," O'Connor says. "People from traditional media dragged in all the limitations of their media into the Internet space. We sat back and studied what an advertiser wanted to accomplish and then created a system to solve their problems."

The company did so by becoming a rule breaker. Says O'Conner: "We broke many assumptions about targeting and feedback. The online ad model is a completely new way of looking at advertising. The medium has the potential to give advertisers their highest return on investment. In fact, for many companies it already is. The targeting, reach, and real-time reports on the status of their campaign all create a higher efficiency. Having the ability to check on the status of a campaign allows advertisers to modify creative campaigns that are performing badly or adjust targeting. It breaks all the rules of traditional advertising." (For more of O'Connor's comments, see "Q&A for Kevin O'Connor.") Let's look at some of the unbreakable rules DoubleClick has broken.

- *No distinction between the ad and the transaction.* DoubleClick understood that the unique interactivity of the Net results in an environment in which a purchase can be made seamlessly from the ad itself. In all other advertising media, the purchaser must take an extra step—go to a store, make a phone call, mail a letter—to buy something.
- *Broadcast or direct response? Both.* DoubleClick marries the virtues of brand advertising with the measurable efficiencies and effectiveness of direct response advertising. Its infrastructure serves both.
- *Just in time for just-in-time ad serving.* DoubleClick's technology quests for perfect information—serving up just the right ad targeted for just the right consumer and then watching what happens on a real-time basis.

- *It's the metrics, stupid.* It's a truism in advertising that 50 percent of all advertising dollars are wasted, but no one knows which 50 percent. DoubleClick created the metrics to answer this question. Who saw the advertising message? Exactly where and when? How often? And what, if anything, was their reaction? If they didn't accept the offer, did they invite more information?

- *Infrastructure first.* DoubleClick is an example of the integrated Internet media company that is fundamentally an infrastructure provider. Like the post-Netscape America Online, DoubleClick is a vertical Internet company with holdings on all sides of the business—from ad repping to outsourcing to Web publishing to E-commerce.

DoubleClick is a born-on-the-Net company. It morphs nimbly as the Net advertising environment twitches and buckles. It serves up more than 10 billion banner ads every month, but to DoubleClick, banners are a very low bandwidth form of advertising. Look for ads in the form of interactive audio, video, and animation. Go to the Dilbert Web site (www.dilbert.com), with which DoubleClick is an integrated sponsorship partner. DoubleClick serves and fulfills all the Dilbert promotions. As for banner programs, DoubleClick is responsible for a fair share of them. By managing the entire process of selling Internet advertising inventory (selling, serving, and reporting) for content sites that want to outsource these tasks, DoubleClick creates value by matching content sites with the advertisers that want to reach them. This value, in turn, is then split between DoubleClick and the sites that DoubleClick represents. The resulting advertising network represents some of the strongest branded sites on the Internet and serves more ad impressions to more unique users than any other Internet network. When coupled with its ad-serving product, DART, DoubleClick is responsible for more than 50 billion advertising impressions on the Internet in recent months.

DoubleClick has positioned itself as a rule maker. Its infrastructures and architectures for Internet advertising are the leading contenders for standards. It has tapped into and leveraged the nascent trends that are shaping this turbulent marketplace. DoubleClick understood early on that Internet advertising may look like it follows a broadcast model (deliver a certain size of audience for a certain fee) and that it also has attributes of a direct marketing medium. But it is more than just an integration of the two processes. They are entirely separate channels in one environment, and DoubleClick created an infrastructure to exploit both.

The foundation of all DoubleClick's efforts is its DART ad serving infrastructure management technology. DART utilizes the industry's largest database of Internet users and companies and offers advertisers a portfolio of products and services, twenty-four-hour customer support, and real-time upgrades as well as the ability to target users. By virtue of DoubleClick's global expansion, DART has been internationalized to meet the complex challenges of managing Internet ad sales across multiple countries operating in different languages and currencies. International advertisers are able to manage a highly targeted global buy and achieve a localized campaign in any market.

More than 7,400 DoubleClick partner sites worldwide use DART technology to support their advertising initiatives. DoubleClick also licenses the technology to companies who prefer to do their own ad serving. As DART emerges as an industry standard, it becomes of greater and greater value to DoubleClick's partners even as it builds the DoubleClick brand and locks them in to the network. For competitors, DART represents an almost insurmountable entry barrier.

DoubleClick's technological challenge is daunting. It is responsible for serving ads on more than 4,200 sites around the world. And behind every one of the 10 billion ads it serves each month is a user who is in a hurry. Any delay means the user moves on and a selling opportunity is lost. It's as simple as that. In response, DoubleClick has evolved a decentralized architecture, with twelve data centers around the world. The reality is that the best response times demand servers as close to users as possible. Since more than half the ads DoubleClick serves are in the United States, the domestic data centers are much larger than those abroad. Each of the three U.S. data centers have about thirty ad servers running, while the nine data centers abroad each have about three ad servers.

DoubleClick rides nimbly on top of one of the most amazing developments of the Net. DoubleClick is perfectly positioned to exploit the insatiable desire of organizations to harness traffic and to reach and gain loyalty that can be redeemed later for, presumably, consumers who are willing to fork over cold cash for something. In the meantime, DoubleClick is a facilitator of a business model radical enough to make even recent business school graduates feel reactionary, or at least rude, for actually charging customers.

DoubleClick at a Glance

DoubleClick (www.doubleclick.net) combines technology and media expertise to centralize planning, execution, control, tracking, and reporting for online media campaigns. DoubleClick has U.S. headquarters in New York City, international headquarters in Dublin, and maintains offices in Paris, London, Oslo, Helsinki, Barcelona, Copenhagen, Tokyo, Madrid, Milan, Sydney, Hamburg, Stockholm, Toronto, Montreal, Atlanta, Boston, Chicago, Detroit, Dallas, Los Angeles, and San Francisco.

DoubleClick leverages technology and media expertise to create solutions that help advertisers and publishers unleash the power of the Web for branding, selling products, and building relationships with customers. The DoubleClick Network, the company's flagship product, is a collection of highly trafficked and branded Web sites, including AltaVista, Dilbert, Macromedia, and over 1,500 others. This network of sites is coupled with the company's proprietary DART targeting technology that allows advertisers to target their best prospects based on precise profiling criteria. DoubleClick then places the ad in front of the advertising partner's best prospects.

DoubleClick began licensing DART to partners in 1996. DART is a comprehensive Web-based service that allows a site (or network of sites) to manage all its ad serving and reporting functions through DoubleClick's central servers. DART partners include The Wall Street Journal Interactive Edition, NBC, Excite Europe, Reader's Digest, and Real Network's Real Audio.

In a bid to create the world's leading online advertising and database marketing company, DoubleClick merged with Abacus Direct Corporation. Abacus is the leading information and research provider to the direct marketing industry and manages the nation's largest proprietary database of consumer catalog buying behavior. If you have ever bought anything from a catalog, chances are better than even that Abacus Direct knows all about it and has a pretty good guess what you'll buy next. DoubleClick's goal is to leverage Abacus's data-driven targeted marketing with DART. DART technology lets DoubleClick target banner ads to surfers who visit sites on the network. Until now, though, it has been able to target based only on general information gleaned from a surfer's online behavior.

DoubleClick plans to connect surfers with their profiles in Abacus's offline database so that DoubleClick can serve up an exquisitely tailored ad in real time. The possibilities for customization are as limitless as are the possibilities for loss of privacy, which is why privacy advocates are asking regulators to reject the merger.

How DoubleClick Serves a Banner

You click to *USA Today,* your favorite Web site, and up pops an ad for a scuba diving vacation in the Caymans. "Escape the blizzard. Dive Cancun," the ad beckons. Is it a coincidence, or did they know you are freezing your snorkel off in Vermont and have been considering a diving holiday in the Caribbean?

No coincidence, and who are "they" who know so much? The omniscient "they" is probably an advertising broker such as DoubleClick that serves both companies with Web sites and advertisers looking to reach Webheads. Dozens of sites, including those of USA Today, Intuit, General Electric, AltaVista, The Wall Street Journal, CBS Sportsline, and eBay, rely on DART to manage their ad inventory. DoubleClick has also inked deals with advertisers such as IBM, BankAmerica, and Nissan.

How does it work? Let's say that the last time you went online you clicked on pages about travel packages, scuba gear, and the Caymans. These sites create software files called cookies that are stored on your computer. DoubleClick's software notes that those packets of data went to your Internet address. Just like that, DoubleClick starts to build a profile of you and your interests. Sometimes DoubleClick uses those databases to create lists of user categories—scuba divers, car enthusiasts, wine drinkers, and so on—that represent targets for ad banners on member sites. DoubleClick manages the entire process, taking a 30 percent to 50 percent cut of revenues.

So, chances are that during the last online search for the perfect diving vacation, you gave DoubleClick enough clues to guess that you might be interested in a scuba excursion in the Caymans. The next time you log on to one of the thousands of sites on the DoubleClick network, its software notes your E-mail address, checks out your user profile, and uploads an ad customized for you—within milliseconds of your signing on.

Net Ready Strategy

- *What:* Integrated Internet advertising
- *Company:* DoubleClick (www.doubleclick.net)

- *Offering:* Delivering the right ad message to the right consumer at the right time
- *Net Ready Strategy:* Breaking the unbreakable rules of traditional advertising

Q&A for Kevin O'Connor, CEO & Cofounder, DoubleClick

If E-commerce depends on buyers and sellers finding each other in the most efficient way, firms that lubricate the process will be rewarded. Those that add friction will be eliminated. Both DoubleClick and Cybergold (see "Q&A for Nat Goldhaber") are committed to reducing friction. Both DoubleClick's O'Connor and Cybergold's Goldhaber agree that technology is the key to sustaining a frictionless, zero latency marketspace.

Net Ready: In our book, we argue that technological advantage cannot be sustained in the E-conomy because technology is so easy for competitors to duplicate. Do you agree?

O'Connor: No. Technology is our "secret sauce." It takes a lot of smart engineers and a huge investment in equipment, and most important, it takes time to develop. Our technology is consistently winning us clients because our competition is not able to provide a reliable and scalable technology solution. However, you are correct that technology could become less of an issue over time and market share will become the dominant factor. We are very focused on market share.

Net Ready: DoubleClick has attributes of a media company and a technology company. Given the assumption of the past question, is it fair to say that DoubleClick has a more assured future as a media company than a technology company?

O'Connor: I don't think it's an either/or answer. We are both. This is what makes us unique. We create technology for a vertical market that happens to involve media.

Net Ready: How has the industry responded to DoubleClick's initiatives? Our book shows that market leaders often create new rules that are then embraced by the industry. Can you point to instances of how a DoubleClick initiative has become a new rule or "standard"?

O'Connor: Outsourcing has become a new rule or standard. Because the online business is growing so rapidly, sites need to outsource their ad sales (and other back-end business) so that they can focus on their core business, whether it's generating revenue from E-commerce, building compelling content, or maintaining traditional ad sales. We created the concept of an ad network. Ad networks are now commonplace—even the portals have positioned themselves to be ad networks. Using technology is a key part of advertising. Traditional advertisers were not used to targeting, frequency controls, real-time reporting. Now, thanks in large part to DoubleClick initiatives, advertisers know how to use technology to their advantage.

Q&A for Nat Goldhaber, CEO, Cybergold

If it's cold, hard cash you want for the value of your attention, you will have to wait awhile. There is no mechanism yet for your browser to spit out quarters in exchange for your sitting through a pitch on the Web. But Cybergold (www.cybergold.com) offers the next best thing. It pays you for your attention in increments of 50 cents to one dollar. As you accumulate your credits, you can transfer them to select credit card accounts, exchange them for Cybergold credits that can be used for merchandise at participating sites, or donate to a charity of your choice from a list of charities affiliated with Cybergold.

By paying Web surfers to read ads, Cybergold has essentially quantified the value of an individual's attention and has broken some cherished rules of advertising. CEO Nat Goldhaber reflects on the nature of advertising and how the E-conomy changes the balance of power between advertisers and consumers.

Net Ready: What very unbreakable rules of advertising and marketing did Cybergold break?

Goldhaber: The key insight we had was, there were alternative methods for delivering value in the normal consumer-publisher-advertiser relationship that had not been tried in any digital environment. We believed that the traditional methods of supplying advertiser-supported content, while applicable in the E-conomy, could be supplemented by alternative models.

Net Ready: What about the E-conomy made you think that?

Seiff: The remarkable frictionlessness of the environment for the distribution of content. Anyone with no more than a computer and a scanner can suddenly be a publisher. This extraordinary fact led to great flowering of human creativity. But the existing infrastructure model of advertising-supported content for publishers does not lend itself to that New World vision. So to create an environment in which publication can occur and the relationship between publisher, author, and consumer can be more intimate—in which the author talks directly to consumer—requires an alternative view of the value and methods of doing advertising and marketing.

Net Ready: Can you describe the traditional model?

Goldhaber: In the traditional publishing structure, advertisers are solicited by publishers to pay them to support content that they in turn are going to deliver to consumers. The publishers then insert, either by physical proximity or temporal juxtaposition, the advertising messages. So the flow of dollars is from advertiser to publisher and then from publisher to author; and the flow of content is from author to publisher and from publisher to consumer. The advertisers ultimately derive value when the consumer is willing to make a connection directly back to the advertiser or one of their retail outlets.

Net Ready: How can Net Readiness streamline this process?

Goldhaber: What the Net provides is the ability for the author to speak directly to the consumer: the consumer can consume the wares of the author directly from the author's own publication site.

Net Ready: But is there room in this model for the infomediary, the advertiser?

Goldhaber: We wouldn't need the advertiser if consumers were prepared to pay to have that content be delivered to them. But we are accustomed—I would say even addicted—to having content paid for by advertisers.

Net Ready: Your model shifts power to the consumers and puts them at the center of the action, right?

Goldhaber: The consumer, not the advertiser, becomes the locus of the business of publications. The consumers are at the center of the economic exchange, and then they can turn around and use the proceeds of that economic exchange for the purchase of intellectual property and content.

Net Ready: What have you learned from your mistakes?

Goldhaber: I really thought that "if we build it, they would come." Maybe a year earlier that would have been true, but by the time we got to the market, it wasn't. Today, if you want to get mind share you need to spend a lot of money or be unbelievably clever in ways nobody thought of. Time to market is not everything, but it sure is a lot. It's also not enough to get it almost right; you need to get it exactly right before it takes off.

PART

III

Net Readiness Realities

There's likely to be a measurable disconnect between what you know is the right approach to building the E-conomy and the haphazard way you will most likely muddle through. Don't feel too bad about it. Muddling through is par for the course for even the most Net Ready companies. The important thing is to get your leadership, governance, competencies, and technology lined up. Then take on a lot of E-business initiatives, make many mistakes, learn a lot, and by sheer assertiveness or luck, find something that makes a high impact on the enterprise.

In the first two parts of *Net Ready,* we introduced the concept of Net Readiness, identified business models that work, reviewed many E-business dos and don'ts, and evaluated some of the strategies that have charted many companies to success. In chapter 8, we present, in a case history format, a discussion of how powerful and transformative this work can be. We selected Cisco Systems to be the subject of this chapter because this company so compellingly demonstrates how an organization can apply the principles of Net Readiness to create unprecedented levels of service for its customers and extraordinary value for its investors.

We could have selected many other organizations to be a poster child for the evolving concept of Net Readiness. In some areas, other companies have exceeded Cisco's accomplishments. But on balance, we could not find another company that has so thoroughly incorporated the lessons of Net Readiness into the very fabric of its organization. Moreover, Cisco is not a born-on-the-Web company. We agree that it's somewhat easier to embrace the principles of Net Readiness when you can create everything from scratch. But the reality is that most of us represent existing organizations that have to contend with legacy systems and various levels of industrial age baggage. Cisco Systems serves as a role model for a company that matured before the Internet explosion yet has successfully navigated the shock waves on the way to Net Readiness.

As you study Cisco's experience, keep in mind the issues of leadership, governance, competencies, and technology. See how Cisco juggled these dimensions one by one while maintaining a level of ruthless execution in all four. Realize that Cisco's fabulous journey, which in hindsight looks effortless and inevitable, was in fact arduous and filled with potholes and false starts, and it continues to be so. There are no guarantees in this journey. Although we don't dwell on its mistakes, rest assured that Cisco has made its share of errors and miscalculations, just as you will. No matter. Mistakes are a part of the road to Net Readiness. What's important is creating a culture of learning within your organization. One of Cisco's strengths as an organization is that it is forgiving of mistakes and has evolved the ability to identify mistakes quickly, kill them, and propagate the lessons learned swiftly throughout the enterprise. We offer the Cisco case as an object lesson of what is possible through a focused application of the principles of Net Readiness.

We close the book with a chapter designed to guide you on your road to Net Readiness. Chapter 9, "Finding Order in Chaos," lays out eleven guiding principles in a prescriptive manner to help you with your E-business initiatives. The appendices—the "Net Readiness E-Business Planning Audit" and the "Comprehensive Net Readiness Scorecard"—offer comprehensive audits to test how well prepared you and your organization are for Net Readiness.

8

Net Readiness at Cisco Systems

Cisco's success in the E-conomy derives from its Net Readiness, exhibited by seizing control of the Net's infrastructure, setting the rules, and then executing ruthlessly.

Cisco Systems of San Jose, California, is a company that has truly transformed itself through Internet business solutions into an end-to-end Internet corporation that embodies many of the Net Readiness lessons prescribed by this book.

The company has staked its future on providing the infrastructure for the E-conomy. What makes the Cisco story so revolutionary is not what it sells, but the process by which it enables anyone doing business with the company—customers, partners, vendors, and suppliers—to create value with the Net. Cisco is at the forefront of challenging a world of three independent proprietary networks: phone networks for voice; local area and wide area networks for data; and broadcast networks for video. More than most organizations, Cisco has seized on the drivers of Net Readiness— leadership, governance, competencies, technology—and integrated them so seamlessly within the processes of the company that it cannot be separated from the Net culture in which it operates. Today, Cisco is a market leader. It sets the standards for both end users and competitors. As an organization, it has no trouble recruiting capital or talent. It occupies either the number one or number two positions in fourteen of the fifteen market segments in which it participates. Our up-close investigation of Cisco Systems along with other best-of-breed companies in E-business has led us to believe that Cisco is a exemplary model of the Net Ready company. How did Cisco attain this enviable record of Net Readiness?

Cisco at a Glance

Cisco Systems is the worldwide leader in networking for the Internet. Cisco's networking solutions connect people, computing devices, and computer networks, allowing people to access or transfer information without regard to differences in time, place, or type of computer system.

Cisco provides end-to-end networking solutions that customers use to build a unified information infrastructure of their own or to connect to someone else's network. An end-to-end networking solution is one that provides a common architecture that delivers consistent network services to all users. The broader the range of network services, the more capabilities a network can provide to users connected to it.

Cisco sells its products in 115 countries through a direct sales force, distributors, value-added resellers, and system integrators. Cisco has headquarters in San Jose, California. It also has major operations in Research Triangle Park, North Carolina, and Chelmsford, England. Cisco serves customers in four target markets:

- *Enterprises:* Large organizations with complex networking needs, usually spanning multiple locations and types of computer systems. Enterprise customers include corporations, government agencies, utilities, and educational institutions.

- *Service providers:* Companies that provide information services, including telecommunication carriers, ISPs, cable companies, and wireless communication providers.

- *Small/medium businesses:* Companies with a need for data networks of their own as well as connection to the Internet and/or to business partners.

- *Consumer market:* Consumers who want seamless access to voice, data, and multimedia applications.

Up-to-date information can be found at Cisco Connection Online: www.cisco.com

A Networked Solution

Earlier than most companies, Cisco determined that the Internet should shape substantially every encounter with its customers and partners. As a result, the company has built an intricate network that links its customers, prospects, business partners, suppliers, and employees together in a seamless value chain. Cisco people live, eat, and breathe the Net. As this chapter points out, the Web is the glue for the internal workings of the company. It swiftly connects Cisco with its web of partners, making the community of suppliers, contract manufacturers, and assemblers look like one brand to the outside world. Cisco's network is a classic example of a COIN in action. Via the company's intranet, outside contractors directly monitor orders from Cisco customers and ship the assembled hardware to buyers—often without Cisco having its fingerprints on an order. By outsourcing production of 70 percent of its products, Cisco has quadrupled output without building new plants and has cut the time it takes to get a new product to market by one fiscal quarter. This accomplishment, in an industry in which obsolescence is a greater issue than in most industries, is a critical advantage.

The benefits of Cisco's Net Readiness go on and on. Eight out of ten customer requests for technical support are filled electronically—at satisfaction rates that eclipse those involving human interaction. Using the network for tech support allows Cisco to save more money than its nearest competitor spends on research and development.

We believe the Cisco story reveals the impact that a sustained dedication to the principles of Net Readiness can bring to an organization willing to accept its disciplines. But Cisco's success was not inevitable. It would be a mistake to assume that the seamless electronic processes that enable Cisco emerged out of a well-ordered, analytical process. What really happened is that a lot of dedicated Cisco people responded to a clarity of leadership vision with a large number of initiatives, many of which proved to be quite effective. More important, Cisco's evolvement didn't happen overnight. In fact, the Cisco story is the product of five years of effort, millions of dollars in investment, and hundreds of projects, not all of which proved sustainable. This kind of effort is often overlooked by executives and is certainly exacerbated by the hyperbole of the "easy-to-become-a-millionaire-on-the-Web" press. Success in E-business is not easy and certainly not cheap.

To its credit, Cisco has been willing to make itself more transparent in this process than many other companies do. To a remarkable degree,

Cisco people have let go of the addiction to hoarding information. Cisco people, by and large, may be stewards of knowledge, but they don't pretend to own it. The company encourages risk taking and provides its people with impressive degrees of authority if they are willing to accept equal doses of accountability. It turns out that a culture of transparency, openness, and sharing of information is absolutely critical to any organization that wants to advance on the road to Net Readiness. It's a paradox of the E-conomy that companies that hold their cards close to the vest may win the hands, but they nevertheless lose the game. Bluffing doesn't work in the E-conomy because it doesn't cost much to force players to show their hands. Playing with an open hand may be the best way to demonstrate commitment.

Cisco Net Readiness

In its quest for Net Readiness, Cisco pushes the envelope in each of the four dimensions we have described: leadership, governance, competencies, and technology. The company balances its efforts, moving its strategic agenda forward on all four fronts without overemphasizing one dimension at the expense of another. There may be companies that are more mature than Cisco on one or two dimensions, but we can't think of many that are more prepared along all four. That's not to say there isn't room for improvement. Cisco is relentlessly trying to perfect its E-conomy culture and vision, fine–tune its governance model, and more closely align its IT investments with business objectives. Cisco has taken on the four dimensions of Net Readiness in ways that can barely be described, but in the rest of this chapter we present some highlights.

Cisco's Net Readiness stems from its roots as a quintessential technology company. Cisco's founders, out of Stanford University, understood the power of the Net in a way that few people in 1984 comprehended. We know that because Cisco's founders registered the Internet domain name before they registered Cisco as the name of the company! It was in the company's genes to service customers electronically. The World Wide Web merely builds on that legacy. The success of Cisco's initial foray into Net Readiness was phenomenal. Today, almost all non-value-added interaction with customers is handled via the Net, and customer satisfaction with Cisco's E-business tools is up more than 25 percent. That success has led Cisco's internal business units to seek IT solutions to their customer-facing and internal business problems.

In the following sections, we take a closer look at Cisco's performance on the four dimensions of Net Readiness: leadership, governance, competencies, and technology.

Leadership: Redefining the Networked Economy

Cisco constantly redefines what a networked economy company looks like. Over the last five years, Cisco has driven networks and the uses of them through every aspect of the company. On the inside, all job candidates apply over the Internet or on internal networks. CEO John Chambers says he can look up any applicant and sort applications by skills or by which competitors they're coming from. Accounting uses the network to gather instantaneous financial data from Cisco outposts worldwide. Cisco can use that data, says Chambers, to close its books in one day. Most global companies need two weeks for that task. In the same spirit, training at Cisco is done over the network using Web-based courses. Most customer service requests are dealt with over the network.

Cisco leadership has promoted strategic fit between most parts of its value chain, from customer service to relationships with suppliers and other partners. In the absence of that kind of fit, strategies get reduced to tactics, and the possibility of gaining a long-term competitive edge vanishes. Barnes and Noble failed to become Amazon.com when it announced that it, too, sold books online, because the legacy of brick-and-mortar retailing is not easy to transcend. An established value chain cannot be moved on a dime. By the same token, Compaq did not become Dell when it started selling computers direct, because Dell's entire value chain is structured by its direct selling whereas Compaq's is not. These contradictions are not impossible to work out, but they do have to be worked out and pain is usually involved. The process does not just happen. One of the tenets of leadership in the E-conomy is not only to know *when* to change, but to actually *commit* to change, and then ruthlessly execute the new direction.

Like most Net Ready companies, Cisco is so talent hungry that it puts recruitment on the top burner. For example, Cisco measures the success of every acquisition first by employee retention, then by new product development, and only then by return on investment. The company has been phenomenally successful at holding on to the intellectual assets it buys: overall turnover among acquired employees is just 6 percent per year, two percentage points lower than Cisco's overall employee churn, which, in turn, is lower than the industry average.

However, it is the clarity of focus around the requirement to do E-business that is the force behind this leadership component and the core reason for Cisco's success as a Net Ready company. First, E-business is understood to be a top priority of every Cisco employee, most specifically including top management. Not only does this understanding empower each business unit to take on E-business measures on behalf of its customers, but it is also a very clear mandate. Let's look at a small artifact of the Cisco culture: the plastic cards listing Cisco's top yearly priorities that all 24,000 Cisco employees carry around with them. On these cards are listed Cisco's top ten objectives for each year. Having "Leadership in Internet capabilities in all functions" as one of the top ten makes the import of E-business very clear. Just as important, however, lest you think that carrying around a cute little card does the trick, each business unit gets evaluated based on how successful it was in reaching that goal.

The way Cisco functions, both internally and externally, is to make sure all employees are on the same page, that is, that they understand the importance of beefing up E-business measures to create value. These E-business practices and the benefits they have spawned have created an E-culture that encourages even more E-business experimentation. By empowering and encouraging employees to take risks, Cisco has engendered an E-culture up and down the organization. Such an E-culture is vitally important to E-business success, and it is certainly not easy to create. Cisco's development of an E-culture has taken more than five years. Born-on-the-Web companies obviously have less of a problem developing E-culture, because E-business is at the core of their organization. E-culture is more problematic for industrial age companies. We study specific instances of the E-culture problem when we look at how Cisco has transformed its very approach to customer service and managing its value chain.

Governance: Funding Information Technology to Create Business Value

Cisco Systems has had an enviable track record with its IT spending thanks to its free-market fulfillment formula called the Client Funded Project (CFP) model. By following the CFP formula, laying a robust enterprise-wide network foundation, and creating a truly interdependent partnership between its IT department and business units, Cisco has achieved impressive results. Over the last five years, investments in IT have helped Cisco improve annual profits by more than $550 million, raise customer satisfaction by 25 percent, and grow revenues at almost twice the rate of the industry. Cisco's IT management philosophy is built around four major ideas:

- Cisco's business units drive the applications to be deployed. This strategy enables the company to make optimum business decisions.

- Business units within Cisco consider the cost of deploying applications as a cost of doing business. The costs of deploying an application are assigned to the cost center of the "client" that gains the benefit from the application. Only when the benefit from a project cannot be directly attributed to a functional unit, for example, a corporate-wide data warehouse, is the expense treated as corporate general and administrative (G&A).

- Business and IT teams implement applications together to achieve desired project objectives. Both business and IT have the same MBOs and are evaluated on the same set of criteria.

- Standards are strictly enforced through a central chief information officer (CIO) function. This enforcement ensures that little duplication or unnecessary spending is incurred by business units deploying their own unique technologies or implementing standards that are incompatible with the rest of Cisco.

By 1992, Cisco was growing at more than 100 percent per year through a combination of organic growth and an aggressive acquisitions strategy. Sometimes, the company was hiring engineers at a rate of 1,000 every quarter. As Cisco grew, the company experienced a number of growing pains, not least of which was the realization that its IT governance severely limited the organization. Cisco regarded IT as little more than an overhead line item. Two implications were especially troubling:

- Cisco could not differentiate itself from the competition and sustain its growth objectives by hiring people; it would have to overhaul its technology.

- Unless Cisco could find a scalable way to serve customers, for example, through self-service technical support, it could never meet its customer satisfaction targets.

Cisco also saw the incredible opportunity it faced. If it could move key systems (such as the order status data) closer to the customer, it could solve a number of problems at once: customer support could scale more effectively because customers would be able to service themselves without Cisco assistance, and the company could differentiate itself from its competitors by being easier to do business with. In order to make IT more customer-facing and to achieve the required business impact, however, two things had to happen. First, business functions would need to be responsible for deciding on and paying for the projects they wanted to implement. At the same time, these functions would be measured on customer satisfaction goals. Second, given the lack of existing infrastructure, Cisco would have to fund the underlying infrastructure to allow the business to build applications—desktops, connectivity, bandwidth—because the business units' own budgets would never be able to absorb the cost of replacing legacy systems.

To become so customer-facing, Cisco took on three strategic commitments:

First, IT would become focused on customers rather than on operations and support. Cisco moved IT from the chief financial officer (CFO) organization to a new entity called Customer Advocacy, a business unit that is responsible for any activity that touches the customer from a service and support standpoint. Thus Cisco made a structural change, emphasized a customer focus above every other consideration, and adopted a value that projects simply would not be funded if they were not designed to raise customer satisfaction levels.

Second, Cisco would require general managers of operating business units to make the decision on which applications to fund. These functional heads could trade off IT spending against head counts in deciding how they wanted to change the way they do business. They would decide "what" to build; IT would decide "how."

Third, the network would play a strategic role in providing the connectivity necessary for business units to creatively build applications. Cisco would build an open, standards-based, enterprise-wide highway, and business units would not have to justify infrastructure investments application by application.

Under this structure, IT costs moved out of G&A overhead and became a component of cost-of-goods-sold. New development projects and associated ongoing maintenance and support costs would be funded by the requesting business unit's profit and loss. Only costs not associated with a specific decision maker—for example, data center operations, centralized planning, and support—would be held in a central funding pool. G&A

such as network infrastructure cost would be allocated by head count—no complex usage tracking would be required. Only direct billable costs would be charged back to business functions, while common infrastructure would not be allocated.

The Cisco Funding Model

What is a "funding model," and why is it important in our discussion of Net Readiness? In our context, funding model refers to the process by which the IT budget is developed. Peripheral issues in the funding model specify how a company determines return on investment (ROI) for IT projects, who within the organization is responsible for initiating and developing the ROI for a proposed project, and who in the organization is ultimately responsible for IT as a business unit. Although numerous activities and processes are involved in any funding model, the three just listed tend to be the most critical as well as most problematic.

Over the last several years, many companies have experimented with a variety of funding models. These models depended to a large degree on to whom IT reported within the organization. Traditionally, IT reported to the CFO of the company, and therefore IT was viewed as a cost center. That is, the objective was to raise the level of service while lowering the cost of IT to the organization. In this environment, industry norms were established for judging the effectiveness and, to a degree, the efficiency of IT. For example, the industry norm for a manufacturing company would suggest that the IT budget should be no more than 1 percent to 2 percent of the gross revenues of the company. Using this rule, the IT organization was constrained by the growth of the company. Projects were evaluated and selected based on reduction in the cost of doing business or reduction in head count. The ROI model was based on a three-to-five-year return, and the IT organization assumed total responsibility for the development and implementation of the project. Through the years, organizations attempted numerous permutations of this model with varying degrees of success. Although some companies believed that IT could be used for establishing competitive advantage, the basic premise in most companies was that IT was a bottom-line expense that should be minimized rather than a top-line contributor that should be optimized.

In the early 1990s, Cisco was no different from most manufacturing organizations. IT reported to the CFO, and it was considered a cost center rather than a profit center. When Pete Solvik became the CIO of Cisco, he adopted the CFP model. One of the driving forces of Cisco is its passion on customer focus. The company would do anything to satisfy the needs of the customer, and all energies were directed toward solving customer-facing problems.

Solvik initiated a spectrum of significant changes to how IT was structured; to whom it reported; and, given the customer-focused driving force, how projects were funded. Only then did Cisco get into the particulars of developing the E-business budgets. One of the significant changes made was to have the costs of the infrastructure be allocated to G&A—in essence, the cost of the infrastructure was part of the cost of doing business. For many companies, the cost of any required infrastructure was part of the ROI calculations for a single project. Allocation of infrastructure into an ROI model implied that a single project had to absorb the cost of any incremental additions to the infrastructure although the infrastructure could be used by many different business units within the company. By taking out the cost of the infrastructure (on average the infrastructure cost was approximately 25 percent of the total cost of the proposed project), the ROI hurdle rate was significantly reduced. In addition, the business unit making the request was responsible for funding the project. If the business unit had the funds and the project met the internal ROI criteria, the project would be implemented. In essence, the IT budget was the sum of all requests for E-business projects. The IT function was allocated a budget only for normal increases in the growth of the infrastructure.

As part of its governance model, Cisco established some additional policies:

- Projects had to show a return in six to nine months
- Projects could last no longer than one year
- IT personnel assigned to the project reported to both the IT organization and the requesting business unit

The funding of E-business initiatives is an area in which most companies, Net Ready or not, continue to struggle. Net Ready companies at least have a framework for testing their funding decisions. The reality is that few organizations have evolved reliable baselines for funding and then for justifying the costs of E-business ventures. One thing is clear, however. The funding models that have been employed to bring traditional initiatives to market are not sufficient to handle the compressed time cycles and cross-functional properties of most E-business processes. Because funding models in the E-conomy are so tightly linked with infrastructure, the obvious solution of giving each business unit unlimited latitude in this area results in unacceptable costs. Enterprises demand a high degree of consistency in processes and linkages across business units. Such consistency can only result from giving business units well-considered funding models and enforcing their usage. Organizations can select from an array of local, global, collaborative, and other configurations. Each organization needs to determine this area of the governance model for itself.

The CFP Model at Work

Cisco's philosophy regarding ROI is unique. While Cisco rightfully insists on serious and accountable metrics, it does not require that Cisco managers justify every investment *if* that investment is aligned with Cisco's stated strategic objectives. For example, a strategic Cisco objective—perhaps the fundamental objective—is raising the level of customer satisfaction. Cisco allows its managers to deploy systems or processes designed to reach that end without requiring them to state a dollar amount to be returned. On the other hand, Cisco does expect managers to measure the improvement in customer satisfaction. That measurement is justification enough for the investment. The result is that managers have a great deal of latitude in experimenting with initiatives that move the company's agenda broadly forward.

The CFP model has created a very strong partnership between Cisco IT and the business units. It has greatly reduced unnecessary activity related to developing an appropriate budget plan, and it keeps employees focused on the areas in which they can be most creative and effective. Functional and general management, accountable for achieving business objectives—customer satisfaction targets and revenue/cost objectives—decides what role technology plays in achieving these goals and approves or prioritizes spending plans for technology. Because the CIO does not determine or approve overall technology spending, his or her team can focus on delivery while the rest of management is engaged in creative use of technology as well as in setting appropriate spending priorities to achieve customer satisfaction and financial objectives. CFP roles—aligning accountability for results with the organizational competencies—require that all Cisco constituents accept responsibility for specific policies. The following lists describe the roles and responsibilities under the CFP model.

Business Functions

- Create a clear business vision and strategy that includes the role of automation in achieving the objectives
- Determine return on investment
- Identify automation opportunities to improve customer satisfaction, reduce expense, increase revenue, or increase customer, distributor, and supplier loyalty (maintain revenue)
- Evaluate and reengineer business processes to exploit automation investment
- Balance investment between automation efforts and head count increases
- Create a culture of data responsibility in which data is meant to be shared, not owned; business units may have responsibility for data integrity or audibility, but they don't own the data

Executive Management Team

- Determine financial objectives that emphasize aggressive productivity goals
- Create corporate vision and reward program that reinforces taking prudent technical risk to increase shareholder value
- Ensure cross-functional and global oversight to minimize duplicate or overlapping initiatives and to monitor business risk
- Establish and maintain a culture of teamwork and cross-functional cooperation
- Sponsor continuous process improvement and reengineering to exploit technological advancements

Application Development Team

- Educate clients on new technologies and potential use in business processes
- Assess technical costs and risks in the calculation of ROI
- Bridge technical infrastructure capabilities and business requirements
- Participate in establishing technology standards

- Drive automation process standards (project management and system design) to maximize cross-functional application integration, scalability, and globalization
- Partner in business process reengineering efforts through automation

The CFP model created a strong partnership between Cisco's IT organization and its individual business units. It also changed several traditional practices and roles. For example, under the CFP model the business objectives of Cisco's IT department and business units are aligned. Business units decide which applications to build and IT decides how to build them.

The project collaboration process between the IT departments and business units at Cisco involves several stages. In the planning and budgeting stage, business units develop an ROI for their own projects and meet periodically with their IT groups to discuss the relative priorities of each application and the impact it will have on the network infrastructure. The major factors that the business units consider are:

- Can the project be completed quickly, in three to six months?
- What are the benefits? For instance, can additional head count be avoided with the application?
- What's the cost of not doing the project?

In addition, Cisco also attempts to calculate market share, productivity gains, and long-range impacts, such as improved competitive position. These metrics are all used to develop an ROI. A key point about the planning stage is that the business units can make their own informed, timely decisions based on their objectives and budgets instead of having a centralized corporate process prioritizing investments for them.

Moreover, once the priorities are set, small cross-functional teams including business and IT members prototype, develop, review, and implement projects. Because of the short duration of the projects, those that appear unlikely to be successful are quickly dropped in favor of other priorities. Project teams typically employ both a business and a technical lead. These individuals, operating as partners, are responsible for the overall success of the project. The rest of their team is selected from among other key constituents impacted by the project.

At Cisco, business and technology people work as a team to deliver applications that achieve business goals. This alignment ensures a win-win partnership between the business and IT groups—each project implementation team has the right incentives to ensure that the applications are technically sound and provide the functionality that the business function wants. Of course, for such a structure to be successful and cost-effective, a strong, central CIO function that enforces enterprise-wide standards is clearly required.

Competencies: Executing Ruthlessly

At the core of Cisco's Net Readiness is a commitment to a small number of principles that Cisco stakeholders have agreed are the drivers of success. Individually and as a team, stakeholders have agreed to measure themselves against these drivers and to hold themselves accountable for meeting the targets. Four fundamental principles and approaches guide Cisco in deploying these solutions.

First, Cisco is committed to raising customer satisfaction by solving customer-facing problems first. Cisco started with customer care as its first solution. Second, Cisco leverages its relationships with partners. The company enables each partner in the value chain to manufacture high-quality product at low costs. Third, Cisco is committed to organizing business and IT units to work together as closely as possible. To that end, Cisco's IT organization reports both to individual functional areas and to the CIO. This dual reporting structure enables a very strong partnership between the business and IT sides of the company. Fourth, Cisco created a robust, standards-based network that serves as a collaborative platform and foundation for the deployment of new applications. Laying such a foundation up front has allowed Cisco to continue to build its suite of networked applications without repeatedly having to invest in new infrastructure.

In summary, Cisco transformed itself into an E-business over the last five years through a number of key competencies informed by a strong leadership vision and principles of governance. Cisco's competencies include:

- *Putting customers first.* Cisco's fundamental yardstick in funding E-business initiatives is to the extent they will advance customer satisfaction.

- *Intense customer focus.* Cisco raises customer satisfaction by addressing customer-facing problems first.

- *Leveraging partner relationships.* Cisco partners with its suppliers in the manufacturing chain to enable them to manufacture high-quality product at low costs (i.e., build a strong E-cosystem).

- *Ability to identify and prioritize opportunities and projects.* Cisco understands that it can't do everything. So it makes priorities, insists that everyone's priorities are aligned, and bases everyone's evaluation on his or her contribution to the priorities.

- *Ability to execute ruthlessly (three months or less).* Cisco believes, as we do, that there is no such thing as long-term success in the E-conomy.

- *Ability to change quickly.* Cisco has learned how to build up competencies quickly to capitalize on emerging opportunities. Just as important, it has learned to kill underperforming initiatives quickly so it can redeploy resources to more value-added projects.

- *Hiring the best.* Cisco's core competency may be recruitment. Its target: smart people who are fired up about customer service.

Technology: Standardization Is Key to Streamlined E-Business Processes

Early on its path to Net Readiness, Cisco spent in excess of $100 million on a complete overhaul of internal systems, laying a robust end-to-end network and providing employees high-speed Ethernet connectivity to every desktop. Only truly strategic, enterprise-wide applications like Oracle's Enterprise Resource Planning (ERP) package have been deployed centrally. Today, close to half of Cisco's IT budget is spent on new applications and maintenance; less than 30 percent goes to general administrative overhead. As a result, Cisco has been able to reengineer all its key business relationships across its extended business system—with customers, partners, suppliers, and employees.

Cisco's IT platform architecture is standardized throughout the company: 100 percent UNIX at the server level, 100 percent Windows NT at the LAN level, Oracle at the database level, and 100 percent TCP/IP for the worldwide network. Voice mail, E-mail, meeting schedule software, desktop and server operating systems, and office productivity suites are all standardized. Virtually all business functions utilize single applications packages worldwide.

Being standardized to this degree has given the company a high level of flexibility. For example, when Cisco recently reorganized its research and development department and its marketing department from multiple business units to three lines of business, it completed all the changes required across all applications in less than 60 days for a cost of less than $1 million.

According to Solvik, "without the IP- and open systems-based IT architecture and standards, we would never have been able to accomplish such a feat in the short time that we did, and at an incredibly low cost." Although standardization means flexibility, from a scalability perspective, distributing the company's systems and yet keeping a single system image remains a daunting task. Solvik explains that the biggest and most challenging projects for the company involve distributing its centralized core systems. "We have very big UNIX servers with huge databases that just don't have the inherent reliability and scalability that the same size DB2 database would have on a mainframe. A tremendous amount of our effort goes into designing our systems to be reliable and scaleable. The whole UNIX platform has a much lower cost than mainframes so we're able to spend that money to have plenty of server capability," he says.

A very high percentage of Cisco customer-, partner-, and supplier-interaction with the company is network based and begins at Cisco's Web site (figure 8-1). From Cisco Manufacturing Connection Online, the user navigates to the information needed for the interaction, or "publishes and subscribes"—that is, the user directly contributes information required to do business with Cisco or enriches Cisco's intellectual asset base. This direct connection allows other constituencies (both internal and external) to do business more efficiently and effectively with Cisco. Cisco has built its business processes on its own global intranet, and Cisco people deployed around the world interact on this intranet to address business issues and customer needs. Links to strategic vendors and customers allow Cisco to collaborate more efficiently with partners outside the company. The intranet also provides a proving ground for new Cisco technologies and products, ensuring that they are ready for mission-critical applications before they are offered to customers.

In deploying its internet business solutions, Cisco realized the importance of laying a robust, standards-based network architecture. Cisco has established standards at all levels of its infrastructure: at foundation technologies, at enabling technologies, and at information repositories. The key principles of such an architecture are threefold:

- *Strategic, not tactical.* A strategic, enterprise-wide framework doesn't change each time Cisco deploys a new application.

Business Goals

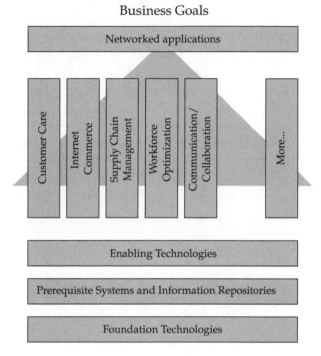

Figure 8-1. Cisco's Standards-Based Network Architecture. Only after Cisco addressed the foundation layer did it begin to build the value-added information repositories and applications that make it so Net Ready. The enabling technology layer is the tool kit that bridges the gap between the foundation and the network applications such as work management, collaboration, legacy data to transform and access, or intersystem communication. Cisco standards ensure that for any application deployment, the early phases of the project are used to implement standards for each layer of the architecture as it emerges as an enterprise-wide solution. This standard also ensures that future projects and phases can leverage these technologies without duplicating effort.

- *Standards-based at every level.* Standardization throughout the enterprise ensures future reusability and lower costs. Whenever a business unit or a functional area wants to deploy an application, it adheres strictly to established standards for each of the three layers of the architecture.
- *Iterative, not fixed.* Standards are in place but are always thoughtfully evolving as projects are executed.

Three E-Business Initiatives

The four elements of Net Readiness (leadership, governance, competencies, technology) have been key enablers for driving the transformation of

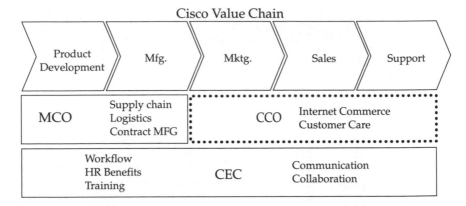

Figure 8-2. Cisco's E-Business Solutions. Cisco's three strategic E-business solutions span the value chain of manufacturing, marketing, sales, and support.

Cisco to a compelling example of E-culture in action. Hundreds of E-business initiatives across Cisco's many programs can be segmented into three broad categories (figure 8-2). First, Cisco Connection Online deals with customer-facing issues, including using the Net as a collaborative platform to better serve customers around the world. Second, through Cisco Manufacturing Connection Online, Cisco has created an Extranet application that increases productivity and efficiency in the manufacturing, supply, and logistics functions among globally networked partners. Third, Cisco Employee Connection deals with the class of E-business initiatives that facilitate employee services and thereby empower some of the most productive and committed workers in the industry.

Cisco's determination to embrace Net Readiness up and down the organization—to exploit tactical and strategic E-business initiatives along the company's core disciplines—accounts for much of the company's success. The following sections lay out some of the specific initiatives that Cisco has developed to make its mark on the E-conomy.

Cisco Connection Online

The centerpiece of Cisco's Internet commerce initiative is Cisco Connection Online (CCO). Cisco's Web site (www.cisco.com) represents just the front door to this comprehensive and ever-shifting resource. With about 150,000 active registered users from around the world, CCO is accessed approximately 1.5 million times each month, making it the primary vehicle for delivering responsive, around-the-clock customer support. Customers rely on CCO to answer questions, diagnose network problems, and provide solutions and expert assistance worldwide. In fact, more than 80 percent of Cisco's technical support for customers and resellers is delivered electronically, saving Cisco more than $200 million annually and improving customer satisfaction. For its international customers, portions of CCO have been translated into multiple languages with nearly fifty different country pages.

Cisco is committed to a self-service model for customer satisfaction. The company understands that no one is better motivated to help the customer than the customers themselves. It knows that most customers are agreeable to helping themselves if they are given the tools. Given Cisco's rapid growth in the early 1990s and the scarcity of skilled engineers to provide technical assistance, the goal of automating customer care was to scale Cisco's support operations to meet customer needs while improving customer satisfaction and reducing support costs. Cisco started by building a Web site to automate the dissemination of technical information and upgrades. Customers responded enthusiastically to a self-service model for this information, and it saved Cisco millions of dollars.

Perhaps the best known of Cisco's Internet business solutions is its suite of networked commerce agents that enables users to configure, price, route, and submit electronic orders directly to Cisco. Cisco started small with this initiative, as it did with customer care, by first deploying a subset of the overall commerce solution—in this case, the Order Status Agent—and then adding pieces to its commerce suite. Today, Cisco has a full suite of Internet commerce applications in place. The Pricing and Configuration agents allow more than 10,000 authorized representatives of direct customers and partners to configure and price Cisco products online. Customers walk through an intuitive series of steps to pick the product they want and all the related accessories for that product, such as memory, power supply, and cable. Customers are prompted to modify orders until they specify a workable configuration. Once the product is configured, customers can obtain pricing information for their selection using the Pricing agent.

In the same way, Order Placement allows customers to drop their selections into a "shopping cart" in Cisco's virtual marketplace. Order Status lets users check on an order using a purchase order or sales order number. This application even connects users directly to Federal Express's tracking services to determine in real time exactly where their order is in the shipping process. Service Order Agent lets users find information about specific service orders, including case and contact numbers, process date, ship dates, and carrier and tracking numbers. Invoice Agent provides controllers, finance officers, and accounts payable staff with rapid, easy, online access to track their invoices with Cisco. The company is also working with its best customers to place a Cisco server directly on those customers' premises as part of their own intranet. This server then interfaces directly with the customer's legacy systems and links back to CCO, creating a more seamless partnership.

CCO is Cisco's Internet storefront. It is the company's comprehensive resource for customers, suppliers, resellers, and business partners. CCO is essentially a portal to information stored in Cisco's ERP databases, legacy systems, and client-server systems around the world, a storehouse of more than 1.5 million Web pages. CCO has five key components.

1. *MarketPlace* is a virtual shopping center in which customers can purchase items online including networking products, software, training materials, and Cisco-branded promotional items such as T-shirts and coffee mugs. It uses a shopping cart model so familiar to consumers on the Web. It also offers users tools for configuration pricing and purchase requisition.

2. *Technical Assistance and Software Library and Open Forum* enables customers and business partners to get online answers to technical questions and download software updates and utilities for Cisco hardware. Technical assistance consists of tools to identify bugs and to take needed preventive or repair measures. The software library enables downloading of software updates on a 24x7 basis. The open forum allows users to pose networking questions, search a database for answers to technical problems, and interact with networking experts from other customers and resellers who participate in the forum and offer their own solutions to problems posted by users. The open forum has created a virtual community of technical experts that reduces Cisco's demand for help and enables its experts to focus on complex or unusual problems.

3. *Customer Service* provides nontechnical assistance on a self-help basis for customer requests such as product status, price lists, latest releases, and service order status. It uses intelligent agents and is available on a 24x7 basis.

4. *Internetworking Product Center* is a suite of applications for order processing to enable users to configure price, route, and submit orders directly to Cisco. This password-protected application is available only to

authorized representatives of direct customers and business partners. Orders placed through this application are entered into the distribution database and are immediately queued for shipping. The application connects directly to the tracking site (enabled by Federal Express) to determine exactly where an order is in fulfillment. (As you recall, we explored the tight integration of Federal Express and its customers as an example of an E-business enabler; see "Federal Express Enables Omaha Steaks and National Semiconductor," page 134 in chapter 4.) These kinds of linkages and those between the order processing applications and Cisco's IT infrastructure are most impressive. Order processing links the company's order management system to its scheduling system, which looks at product availability to determine a priority time slot for each order. The component data are then translated into parts orders for Cisco's contractors and distributors, which in turn have direct links into Cisco's ERP systems. This tight linkage enables the Cisco team to forecast demand and react quickly, essentially acting as extensions of Cisco's own internal management systems.

5. *Status Agent* gives Cisco's sales force, as well as direct customers and sales partners, immediate access to critical information about the status of customers' orders. Specifically, it is used to monitor expected shipment dates, generate complete backlog status reports for all Cisco orders, view line-item details for each product on order, verify bill-to/ship-to addresses and shipment methods, and track shipment status with direct hyperlinks to Federal Express and UPS Web-based tracking systems. Status Agent is a member of the commerce agent suite of Web applications that also includes Configuration Agent, for configuring the entire line of Cisco enterprise products online, and Pricing Agent, an intelligent pricing application that provides convenient access to Cisco's online price list. Status Agent provides real-time access to order and shipment status and gives the sales force more timely information, greater control of orders, and increased success with installations. The sales force can be more proactive in tracking orders and can prevent possible billing or shipment problems by accessing order information. The Status Agent has also transformed the role of the sales force. Instead of spending up to eight hours a week on clerical tasks such as tracking order status, the sales force is now devoting that time and energy to building relationships with clients and seeking new business opportunities.

To make Net Readiness a common element of its entire value chain, Cisco is making it possible for its largest customers and resellers to integrate their enterprise applications directly into Cisco's own back-end systems, using the Web as the bridge. The new strategy takes hold just as the staggering success and bottom-line benefits of CCO are beginning to sink in. The site, which automates product ordering and customer support activities, is on track to save the company a little more than $350 million per year in operating expenses. Cisco dedicates most of its efforts to making better customers out of its existing customers, but it also has its sights set on customers who have not yet purchased products online because of the lack of back-end integration. Taking the strategy a step further, Cisco is encouraging its suppliers to Webify their supply-chain processes to further integrate the value chain on behalf of Cisco's customers.

Cisco's response is to recognize that building strong customer relationships is the key driver to sustainable profitability. The first step is to retain existing customers because the costs of acquiring new customers are so high that repeat business is essential. The next step is to acquire new customers on a profitable basis. Cisco knows that the best way to do that is by giving customers tools for self-configuration and turning its back office into the customer's front office.

One of CCO's biggest accomplishments may be the way it has taken Cisco's channel partners along for the ride. Seventy percent of Cisco's overall business is funneled through third parties; similarly, resellers and integrators make up the same proportion of CCO business. The Net is also a way for Cisco to tap the small-business market that once eluded the company. Specifically, the Web gives Cisco both a vehicle through which customers can find out about products and buy them and an automated support system that can reach a larger audience.

In addition to these capabilities, Cisco also allows customers to track case status online whenever they want to. Today, a majority of Cisco's support is performed online, and the company employs only 1,000 engineers in four technical assistance centers worldwide to handle the most difficult support issues. The bottom line? Cisco's self-service model has driven adoption rates up and increased customer satisfaction substantially. Surveys indicate that customers prefer to use CCO for technical support (60 percent) and for general product and marketing questions (80 percent). The use of CCO has resulted in 98 percent accurate, on-time repair shipments and an increase in customer satisfaction by 25 percent since 1995.

CCO was not created fully formed overnight. It evolved slowly, sometimes fitfully, over many years. Figure 8-3 shows the migration of CCO over time.

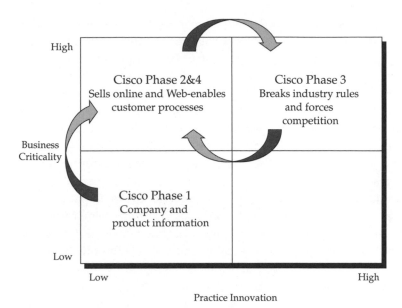

Figure 8-3. CCO continues to evolve. Cisco Connection Online started with low critical company and product information (phase 1). As CCO facilitated more and more of Cisco's commerce, from product orders to fulfillment, its business criticality rose (phase 2). At this point, the innovation driven by CCO became a competitive force (phase 3), driving competitors to either keep up or be left behind. As much of the industry also started doing business in this fashion, CCO moved back to operational excellence.

Cisco Manufacturing Connection Online

That the foundation of Cisco's Internet commerce initiative is its Manufacturing Connection Online (MCO) is as it should be because Cisco's ambition is to create nothing less than a globally networked manufacturing environment. Employees, suppliers, and other authorized logistics partners access MCO as a central point of access to manufacturing applications, reports, tools, and information. Although MCO cuts costs, compresses cycle times, and promotes scalability, it adds most value by enabling unprecedented levels of customer service. MCO is designed less to save Cisco staff time in serving customers than to expose the possibilities of additional revenue streams. MCO enables new classes of customers to imagine new ways of applying Cisco solutions to new classes of requirements. Ultimately, by virtualizing much of the manufacturing logistics process, MCO will provide the infrastructure for identifying and exploiting new business opportunities.

We can best view MCO as a supply chain portal or COIN that seamlessly connects Cisco to its contract manufacturers, suppliers, distributors, and logistics partners. First deployed in June 1999, MCO provides simple and secure access to real-time manufacturing information for both Cisco employees and suppliers. The biggest challenge in deploying MCO was consolidating the access points of numerous manufacturing information systems into a single user interface. Through a required user profile, the graphically driven user interface of the MCO site displays dynamically generated pages containing links to a wealth of manufacturing information. Forecast data, inventory, purchase orders, and other critical data can be viewed through the secure site. As a highlight, the main page immediately brings to the user's attention all approvals and alerts mined from a host of individual manufacturing systems, including the Oracle ERP database. Such integration was made possible by a strategic relationship with Oracle to team up in developing this data-extraction solution.

Partnerships are indispensable in the E-conomy, requiring every networked organization to develop competencies in building, maintaining, and renewing a variety of relationships. Relationships with suppliers are especially critical in the E-conomy. Through MCO, Cisco has created an Extranet application that leverages productivity and efficiency in the supply function. For example, Jabil Circuit, a contract manufacturer of Cisco products, uses MCO to streamline the order fulfillment cycle. Through a direct link to Cisco's manufacturing resource planning system, Jabil can "see" orders almost as soon as Cisco customers place them. Jabil assembles the parts from stock and ships directly to the customer. After the assembly is completed, the system prompts Cisco to pay for the parts used. Through MCO, Cisco has

- Gained real-time access to supplier information
- Experienced lower business costs in processing orders
- Improved the productivity of its employees involved in purchasing
- Seen order cycles reduced substantially

Cisco has created a virtual factory by tightly integrating its end-to-end value chain with the Net. The challenge Cisco faced in its supply chain in the early 1990s was the ability to swiftly scale up manufacturing operations in times of massive technology and market change. The market was growing very rapidly, and Cisco wanted to move to a build-to-order model for customers. In response, Cisco implemented a five-part strategy to scale its supply chain in a cost-effective manner.

Automating Cisco's supply chain involved five initiatives:

1. *Single Enterprise.* The creation of the single-enterprise concept has been instrumental in the company's ability to deliver customer services across its constituencies. In effect, it has created an infrastructure that enables key suppliers to add value, manage, and operate major portions of Cisco's supply chain. A major advantage is that a single enterprise ensures that the entire supply chain works off the same demand signal. Cisco furthers the single-enterprise concept by empowering its key suppliers in three ways. First, Cisco extended ERP systems to suppliers. By using networked applications, Cisco has integrated key suppliers into its production systems. The electronic links across the single enterprise allow Cisco and these suppliers to respond to customer demand in real time. Any change in one node of the supply chain is propagated throughout the supply chain almost instantaneously. Second, Cisco has automated routing data transfer using electronic data interchange (EDI) transactions. Third, Cisco has developed cross-organizational processes and business models that automate redundant or repetitive processes. For example, it has eliminated the need for purchase orders and invoices to be sent back and forth and has reduced the cost of issuing such documentation to less than $5 each. Prior to this initiative, each PO and invoice cost Cisco upwards of $125 to issue.

2. *New Product Introduction (NPI).* A Cisco study revealed that as many as four to five iterations of prototype building are required, with each iteration taking, on average, one to two weeks. One of the biggest drivers of costs and time delays in the prototype phase was the labor-intensive process for gathering and disseminating information. In response to this problem, Cisco automated the process for gathering product data information, thereby reducing the amount of time required from as much as one day to less than 15 minutes. The use of networked applications in NPI has reduced time to volume by three months and reduced total cost of NPI by $21.5 million in 1997.

3. *Autotest.* Cisco realized that it could never scale its own manufacturing operations at a rate compatible with its growth goals. For example, Cisco's manual testing procedures in the early 1990s compromised the integrity of product testing, given engineer-specific testing methods. At the

same time, Cisco wanted to focus on its core competence—new product design and introduction. As a result, Cisco outsourced almost all its manufacturing to selected suppliers. To resolve the testing problem, Cisco undertook a three-step process: First, it created test cells on its supplier's line that embodied Cisco's standard test procedures. Second, it ensured that the test cells automatically configure test procedures when an order arrives. Third, it developed strong supplier partnerships so that suppliers shoulder greater responsibility for quality. Testing processes were made routine and were embodied in the software test programs that ran the test cells. Once testing had been automated and standardized, it was outsourced entirely to the suppliers, allowing quality issues to be detected at the source. However, although Cisco outsourced much of the physical testing, the company retained the intelligence behind the testing.

4. *Direct Fulfillment.* Until recently, Cisco's fulfillment model followed the industrial age mode. Products configured by partners would have to go through two shipping legs: first from the partner to Cisco and then from Cisco to its customer. Each of these legs put Cisco fingerprints on the process and added approximately three days to the cycle. But in 1997, Cisco successfully launched a global direct fulfillment model under which most of the company's manufacturing partners can now ship directly to customers. The bottom line? Cisco can now build to ship within three days.

5. *Dynamic Replenishment.* Prior to supply chain automation, Cisco manufacturers and suppliers lacked real-time demand and supply information, resulting in delays and errors. To compensate for uncertainty, Cisco managers had to hold inventory levels higher than necessary. The uncertainty resulted in higher overhead. The dynamic replenishment model allows the market demand signal to flow through directly to the contract manufacturers without any distortion or delays. It also allows contract manufacturers to track Cisco's inventory levels in real time.

Supply chain management at Cisco has become, by virtue of the Net Readiness of the company and its partners, a massively parallel process. Traditionally, a new product introduction had been a sequential process in which various activities were performed by engineering, procurement, manufacturing, and marketing in a time-consuming series of steps. Cisco has networked these functions in order to extract real benefits by compressing cycle times and exchanging real-time information with its partners. Engineers can now gather information to build and simulate designs in a matter of minutes—a process that used to take weeks. Cisco has thereby reduced both the number of iterations required to design and build a prototype as well as the number of such iterations required to pro- totype and deliver a new product. Overall time-to-market for new products is down significantly while quality and yields of new products have risen.

Cisco Employee Connection

Cisco's Net Readiness looks inward as well as outward. Whereas CCO ad- dresses the needs of Cisco customers, partners, suppliers, and employees, Cisco Employee Connection (CEC) is limited to information and services that address the unique needs of individual Cisco employees. CEC includes dozens of initiatives designed to make all internal and human resources processes exploit a common self-service model using the Net as a collabo- rative platform. In order to improve employee satisfaction and scale its workforce without incurring unnecessary overhead, Cisco reengineered all its internal and external employee services. Perhaps the most visible em- ployee services application is Metro, the travel expense reporting applica- tion that allows employees to easily report expenses. Expenses charged with a corporate American Express card automatically appear on the indi- vidual's electronic expense account form. Only two auditors are needed to audit expenses for more than 15,000 Metro users per month.

CEC applications, which are created by nearly every department in the organization, provide employees with the following benefits.

Ubiquitous communications. Every one of Cisco's employees around the globe is connected through the Cisco network. CEC adds significant value to that network by affording instant, one-shot communication with each employee. Cisco's marketing department, for example, uses CEC to distrib- ute the latest product and pricing information to employees in offices around the globe, saving tens of thousands of dollars in printing and mail- ing costs and decreasing time to market by as much as a week.

Streamlined business processes. CEC's interactive tools reduce the time that employees spend handling repetitive tasks and streamline routine business processes. For example, an employee using CEC to enroll in an internal training course completes the registration online, anytime, from anywhere, without ever speaking to a training department employee. The intranet application then routes the training class request to the employee's manager for approval, enrolls the employee in the class, and sends the employee E-mail confirming enrollment.

Integrated business systems. The CEC home page serves as the launching pad for dozens of Web-based information sources and services, all of which share the same navigational tools and a common user interface. An employee can check the online floor plan to reserve and locate a meeting room, report a software problem to information services, and glean the details of the latest product promotion.

By aggressively moving all its processes to the Web, Cisco has shortened the time it needs to close its books at the end of each quarter from ten days—still pretty good by most Fortune 500 standards—to two days. Even that's not good enough for CFO Larry Carter. Carter not only insists that the company's final figures be available less than twenty-four hours after the close of the quarter, he is committed to slash spending on finance from 2 percent of sales to 1 percent. This ability to maintain a "virtual close," in turn, supports a governance structure that empowers people to make decisions quickly. The system lets senior managers call up data on the performance of a particular part of the business or of individual salespeople. The following application list highlights the breadth of CEC interactive services.

- *Engineering.* All technical documentation, release notes, software library, and bug navigator

- *Sales.* Pricing, configuration, and order status information

- *Marketing.* Complete technical document library, product catalog, directory of offices and service centers, newsletter, event listings, press releases, advertising, and Packet and CiscoLink publications, sales, and marketing material

- *Training.* Online training registration, training schedules, and synopses

- *Financial.* Annual report, links to Cisco stock prices and volume histories, financial press releases, downloadable income statements, balance sheets in Excel format, and the administration of travel expenses

- *Human resources.* Benefits enrollment and administration, exercising of stock, job listings, insurance plan information, health care provider listings, employee address-change forms, news services, clubs and groups, business-unit definitions, and organizational initiatives

- *Facilities.* Technical Response Center, network and system performance data, work request forms, floor plans, and cafeteria menus

- *Procurement.* Purchasing of capital equipment and other nonproductive goods

A growing number of CEC applications are interactive services that empower employees to take charge of their work environment. We describe a number of these applications here.

Cisco Technical Response Center

Cisco employees use the Intranet's Web page to report problems with their telephone, computer hardware, or software; they can then review the status of their request or alter the request if the problem changes. Forms that are available on the Web lead into a database that feeds requests directly to the appropriate support organization. Since the introduction of the Web page, the number of calls that the Technical Response Center receives has been cut in half. The Web page currently receives between forty and seventy-five inquiries each day. Response time is faster because employees report problems directly to the support organization. As its workforce grows, Cisco can use less costly electronic solutions to scale technical assistance. Employees are more productive because they can track their work requests through the system and avoid telephone calls to the help desk.

Metro

Although initially Cisco used the Intranet primarily as a publishing platform, Metro represents a new wave of applications designed to streamline business processes. Consider, for example, the procedure that employees follow for getting reimbursed for business expenses. In the past, employees recorded business expenses using an Excel spreadsheet. After completing the spreadsheet, the employee printed it, received approval from the appropriate manager, then sent the spreadsheet to Cisco's Travel and Expenses Department for payment.

In contrast, Metro provides employees with a point-and-click interface for recording all expense-related information online. If an employee has used an American Express corporate credit card to charge an expense, Metro displays a copy of the employee's current credit card statement; the employee then will move all relevant charges from the bill into the expense report. Metro has had a significant impact on how quickly employees are reimbursed. In the past, employees received reimbursements in four to five weeks. With Metro, employees' bank accounts or American Express cards are electronically reimbursed within forty-eight to seventy-two hours.

Employee Self-Service: Internal Applications

The majority of Cisco's internal applications have been Web enabled. For example, almost all functions that salespeople perform on the computer are done using a Web browser. Cisco's Executive Information Systems and Decision Support Systems (DSS), training (including distance learning), and self-service human resources are all Web based. CEC supports instant global communications among the thousands of Cisco employees world-wide. Whether an employee wants information about a company event, requires access to health benefits registration, or needs recent expense-tracking reports, CEC streamlines business processes and lowers costs throughout the company. In excess of 1.7 million pages of information are available to employees, who access CEC thousands of times each day. Because of internal applications such as CEC, the need for written memos and printed documents has been sharply reduced.

Communication and Distance Learning

Cisco's network has continued to enhance the ability to communicate with employees and added an important dimension to training. Distance learning modules available to Cisco employees can be activated at the employee's desktop. The use of these distance learning modules—as well as information about their effectiveness—can be easily tracked to determine the extent of use of the various education modules. From tracking information, the quality of the modules can be assessed to ensure high levels of effectiveness as the needs of the organization change.

In 1997, Cisco CEO John Chambers addressed the company's quarterly meeting, which for the first time could be viewed from employees' desktops in real time. Approximately 1,000 employees tuned in to view the address and another 1,000 watched it in a delayed broadcast over the intranet. This streaming of live video provides another capability that strengthens the Cisco culture by making the company seem more intimate to each of the employees. Cisco estimated that the 2,000 employees who viewed the address remotely were equal in number to those who were in attendance at the quarterly meeting. As a result, Chambers doubled the number of employees who participated in his quarterly address.

Also in 1997, Cisco initiated an arrangement with Yahoo! to make available a Cisco-tailored version of My Yahoo! My Yahoo! is a push technology application whereby certain information is specified by the user, and agents search the Internet for the information and then "push" it out to the user's desktop. When the user signs onto the Internet, the information is waiting for him or her. My Yahoo! tracks everything from breaking news reports about competitors to up-to-the-minute information about world-wide financial markets. Coupled with E-mail, My Yahoo! has become a powerful communication tool within Cisco.

CEC Strategic Benefits

The measurable savings that Cisco has realized from the CEC-driven Workforce Optimization Solutions amounts to more than $58 million annually (figure 8–4). Cisco is grateful for the savings, but cost avoidance is not the justification for CEC. The true justification for CEC is customer service. CEC is justified by giving Cisco employees better access to information and to each other. These applications have allowed Cisco to scale its infrastructure without adding armies of bodies, a fact that keeps Cisco nimble and responsive to customers. The result is more responsive employees, the

Total Savings	58,000,000
Employee Directory	3,000,000
Expense Submission	3,000,000
Benefit Enrollment	1,000,000
Employee Communication	16,000,000
Recruitment and Staffing	3,000,000
Training Delivery	25,000,000
Compensation Management	3,000,000
Stock Administration	1,000,000
Procurement	3,000,000

Figure 8-4. Savings Attributed to CEC. Although its primary focus is on optimization of employee services rather than cost reductions, Cisco nevertheless enjoys considerable savings from CEC. Here is how CEC saved Cisco money in the following areas: *Employee directory*—eliminated directory print/distribution costs and reduced the time it takes to look up information; *Expense submission*—reduced time to process expense report from twenty-five days to three; *Benefits enrollment*—reduced head count needed to administer benefits by 50 percent; *Employee communication*—reduced time required for processing communications (five minutes per employee); *Recruiting and hiring*—reduced cost per hire applied to the 17 percent of hires received directly via the Web; *Training delivery*—reduced travel costs for training (both live video broadcasts and the virtual classroom training); *Compensation management*—reduced management time by 25 percent for doing compensation administration; *Stock administration*—avoided hiring administrative head count; *Procurement*—avoided hiring more buyers, clerks, or managers.

measure of which is revenues per employee. The average Cisco employee drives more than $668,000 in revenue. Additionally, the productivity gains from better information flow (estimated conservatively at 1 percent per employee, or thirty minutes per week) add more than $100 million in savings. Because of the three core initiatives (CCO, MCO, CEC), Cisco has been able to avoid costs in excess of $800 million across the organization.

Outside-In Company

We emphasized throughout Part I of *Net Ready* that the most successful organizations engage the E-conomy in the top half of the E-Business Value Matrix. It is the top half of the matrix that returns the most value. Enterprises that participate in the top two quadrants accept the highest risk but in return are rewarded with the kind of high-impact returns that define markets and redraw industry boundaries. Cisco has consistently sought out and implemented initiatives in the upper half of the E-Business Value Matrix. At the same time, Cisco participates in every one of the quadrants (figure 8-5).

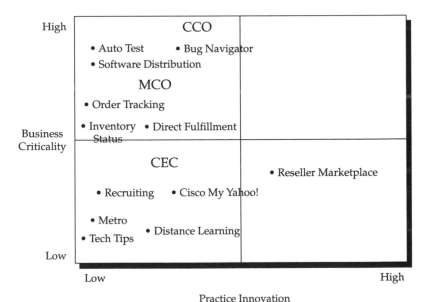

Figure 8-5. Mapping Cisco E-Business Initiatives. Snapshot of Cisco's portfolio of business initiatives. The company's portfolio displays experimentation in different quadrants. This figure maps a few of Cisco's strategic E-business initiatives as they are today.

Mighty corporations look invincible, but the once-unthinkable decline of many of the world's largest companies reveals them to be far more fragile than they appear. Fully one-third of the firms listed on the Fortune 500 in 1990 disappeared by 1995. Much of the disappearance, of course, was due to mergers and acquisitions, but value migration took its toll as well. Blunders and oversights by management have pulled down some of the most celebrated companies. Some of these blunders can be laid at the doors of marketing errors, technological arrogance, organizational rigidity, or even bad luck. But most of them are the result of lack of vision and other limitations of leadership. That's why we place leadership first among the core disciplines of Net Readiness.

Cisco may look invulnerable, but Cisco's management team knows better. As we have seen, Cisco has navigated an enviable record for a new model of management. Partly because it makes the tools to build the powerful networks that link businesses to their customers and suppliers, Cisco has combined all the attributes of Net Readiness to transform management practices.

More than its innovative use of technology, Cisco has developed an E-cosystem that makes itself as transparent as possible. Cisco is an outside-in company. Its E-culture results in its passionate focus on the customer, its commitment to driving value through E-business, and its willingness to empower Cisco people to take risks. The transparency encourages Cisco people to share knowledge, not hoard it. It inspires the company to team up with outsiders to acquire and retain intellectual assets.

Finally, Cisco vindicates the notion that you do not have to be a born-on-the-Web company—you don't have to have a "dot com" at the end of your name—to make it in the E-conomy. Although Cisco is by no means a refugee from the industrial revolution, many companies of Cisco's vintage have been steamrollered by the E-conomy. At the same time, others, like Cisco, are well on their way to transforming themselves into thorough Net Ready E-businesses.

9

Finding Order in Chaos

The Net may well become the primary space in which we all do business, but it is still a hostile environment for organizations unprepared for the uncertainties and risks. Luckily, Net success has been shown to be a function of Net Readiness. Is your organization prepared?

If you have read this far, you know what Net Readiness is and what your organization must do to get there. The central lesson of Net Readiness is that you don't take on any E-business initiatives until your organization is prepared along the dimensions of leadership, governance, technology, and competencies. The way success is supposed to happen is that rational experimentation leads to breakthrough strategies and operational excellence through the use of careful strategizing, flawless execution, and exquisite measurement. You know what the real world is like, too. Business units disagree among themselves about priorities, goals, and resources. They hide what they actually require and demand things they'll never use. The organization responds opportunistically and blindly, desperate to keep up, but not sure of what it is chasing.

Yes, the E-conomy appears chaotic and thwarts every attempt to impose order on it. But that doesn't mean this space is lawless. Although the distinct rules and opportunities may not yet be fully understood, we can articulate some of the rules that govern the orbits of economic entities in the emerging E-conomy. Based on our accumulated experience, we can confidently make a number of observations. The outlines of the E-conomy have been observable for many years. As far back as 1969, management guru Peter Drucker distinguished the formation of a knowledge economy, driven by information and operated by a new breed of people he called knowledge workers. More recently, the impacts of the PC revolution on productivity, organization, and every segment of our society from education to medical care have been well documented.

Almost all the rules that we describe in this chapter are the consequence of the Net's single most significant impact: its ability to cut the incremental costs of interaction—the searching, coordinating, and monitoring that customers and organizations take on when they exchange goods, services, or ideas. The cost of searching for a mortgage, executing a bank transaction, or obtaining customer support, for example, drops by as much as 90 percent or more when these activities are handled electronically. In some cases, the transaction costs drop so radically that it becomes possible to give the services away. At that point, collaboration between the service provider and the service consumer, not costs, becomes the paramount issue and services turn into experiences, the highest value-added form of commerce.

The New Realities: Eleven Rules of the E-conomy

A not-so-silent revolution is stirring up the rules of business, challenging every assumption and turning many conclusions on their heads. It is nothing less than a revolution in the way organizations create value. The new economy is breaking long-held axioms and conventions concerning interactions with customers, suppliers, and partners. Among the traditional distinctions the E-conomy redefines are many precepts cherished by conventional wisdom. Here, then, is our attempt to articulate eleven new realities and their corollaries for the E-conomy:

1. Decide if you are a rule breaker, rule shaker, rule maker, or rule taker (p. 273).
2. Cannibalize parts of your value chain: Experiment with eating your young or someone else will (p. 282).
3. Be opportunistic: initiatives must be continuously questioned, improved, and explained to the customer (p. 282).
4. Focus on what's in motion rather than on what's standing still (p. 283).
5. No one can go at it alone (p. 285).
6. Upside down: suppliers and customers must cooperate as never before (p. 286).
7. Run, don't walk (p. 287).
8. It's the network, stupid (p. 288).

9. Smart-size the offer (p. 289).

10. Think brand equity and channel equity (p. 290).

11. Planning is critical. Don't do it (p. 291).

Decide if You Are a Rule Breaker, Rule Shaker, Rule Maker, or Rule Taker

Challenge the rules. Inspect your own rules. Fall out of love with your own rules and ideas. Think frivolously. Make jokes about the problem you are working on.

—ROGER VAN OECH

These labels—rule breaker, rule shaker, rule maker, rule taker—reflect attitudes to risk. They are strategies or postures that you and your organization take on to define your relationships to the E-conomy and to deliver value to your chosen customers. E-conomy leaders choose one of these strategies and then build their organization's intellectual contribution around it for a time. One of the ironies of the E-conomy is that as your vision becomes ever more expansive, your company focus must become narrower and narrower. One formula for failure is to spread yourself too thin. Seemingly limitless market opportunities and roles abound. Pinpointing the unexploited opportunity that could develop into a large market is the first challenge for any leader. But the second is just as critical: deciding on the best path to the opportunity and then sticking with it, relying on your focus to keep you from being distracted by the myriad other paths calling out to you.

Choosing one discipline to master does not mean abandoning the other three. Indeed, most companies will have initiatives falling under all four disciplines at any one time. Nevertheless, to achieve success over the long term you must stake your reputation within a particular channel—and focus your energy and assets—on a single discipline. There is no moral weight to any of these disciplines, no right or wrong. Each one can represent the most valid course for your organization at a point in time. Generally, each discipline can be evaluated in terms of the level of risk that your organization is willing to take on as well as the level of reward it hopes to secure.

Rule Breakers

Rule breakers explode business models. They bust an industry up by offering a new paradigm so compelling in its benefits that it simply cannot be ignored. By virtue of the insanely great value proposition of their offers (think Apple in 1985, Amazon.com in 1996), they quickly redefine their industries and instantly change the norm (more recently, think Autobytel.com for automobiles and E*Trade for online securities). Rule breakers often cause a shift that carries organizations to new, unexplored territories.

If they get lucky, rule breakers can dictate the rules of the industry to such an extent that they essentially create a new market and dominate it. In such a case, the rules offered by the rule breaker become the standard, de facto or otherwise. When this happens, the rule breaker shifts to being a rule maker (see the next section). Rule breakers often enjoy early mover advantages that translate into significant economic value. Rule breakers usually have first and preferred access to:

- Customers and markets
- The best talent in the market
- Funding and venture capital
- The most influential partners

At the same time, as rule breakers create relationships with customers, they have unprecedented opportunities to lock customers in by imposing high switching costs.

Rule breakers also take on disadvantages. The downsides for rule breakers include

- Business models that are readily replaceable
- Profit margins that are thin
- Technology changes that create obstacles
- High risk

If you think about who the rule breakers are, you start to notice a curious thing. Rule breakers rarely emerge from the set of dominant players in the markets they serve. Rule breakers are more commonly the second- or third-tier participants or even come from entirely outside the industry. A moment's reflection offers the reason. There is generally no incentive for the dominant players in an industry to be rule breakers because they already own the industry. It's a very rare executive who questions the practices that made the organization rich. That's why rule-breaking activity usually comes from without.

Not all rule breakers succeed, and for those who fail, the penalties can be high. Jim Manzi, the creator of the fabulously successful Lotus 1-2-3, founded Nets Inc. to create a category-killer virtual mall for industrial and business-to business applications. Had Manzi succeeded, a number of industries would have found the rules by which they operated not only broken but forever shattered. Alas, Nets Inc. went for a proprietary, lock-in business model when the world was moving to open standards. As it turned out, various parts of the company's value proposition were assumed by entities such as VerticalNet and Netbuy.

Dell Computer's phenomenal success stems from its rule-breaking realization that combining sophisticated logistics software with the mass customization opportunities of the E-conomy would give it a direct relationship with customers and allow it to build only PCs that have actually been ordered. The paradigm is so superior to the established model of building systems and inventorying them in anticipation of orders that competitors immediately struggled to copy Dell's model.

The position of rule breakers is perilous, however, because they are completely exposed to every competitor. Netscape broke the rules in the browser space and for a while completely dominated the industry with an almost 100 percent share. But first mover advantage cannot be sustained in the E-conomy. As we have noted (see "Advantage Is Becoming More Temporary," page 72 in chapter 2), temporary advantage is the only advantage in the E-conomy, and in Netscape's case, its advantage was measured in months.

In the same way, Onsale (see "Move the Product Up the Food Chain," page 163 in chapter 5) didn't intend to be a rule breaker. It started out tentatively, asking itself how the Net can be used to leverage the distribution of surplus computer equipment. The company experimented with a number of auction formats before standardizing on the model it now has. More important, the company is still experimenting, still breaking rules—witness its new experiments with auctions for corporate markets—to see what other channels it can exploit. Through a period of rational experimentation, Onsale's strategy is to move the most successful of these experiments through the upper half of the E-Business Value Matrix, where they can have a higher impact on the company's success.

How Linux and Open Source Software Break the Rules

To get a glimpse of how hopeless it looks at the beginning for a rule breaker, check out the passions raging around Linux. An operating system that breaks the rules by making its source code freely available to everyone and owned by no one, Linux breaks the rules of the proprietary operating system market so dominated by Microsoft.

Followers of Linux display a noncommercial fervor that can be best described as religious. Linux is the best example of open source software: software that is owned and modified by its users in a democratic and cooperative model. Linux has always advocated the freedom of developers to mold its product into a tool to fit their needs. Many of Linux's early developers adopted it and contributed to it because it gave them a sense of camaraderie, a meeting ground in which they could mutually contribute to an increasingly robust operating system with a diverse array of applications. Lately, the software has become a darling of the media, the "Microsoft Killer." As more and more mainstream computer companies bundle versions of Linux along with Windows, few analysts dispute that Linux has earned its place in the operating system hierarchy. Whether the rule-breaking promise of Linux will go anywhere is a big question mark. Even now, the relentless forces of commercialization are threatening to collapse the fragile cooperative network that is responsible for its care and feeding.

If Linux is to be commercially accepted, it must deal with an inherent contradiction. Net Ready organizations demand standardization. But the Linux community tends to resist standardization. In the Linux world view, "standard" versions of Linux are incompatible with the open source value. Although some developers feel that a standardized commercial version of Linux is unacceptable, we believe that if Linux is to be anything more than a marginal operating system favored by college students who don't want to add to Bill Gate's bottom line, it must become more like, well, Microsoft Windows.

Rule Shakers

Rule Shakers believe that a good way to obtain fruit is to grab the branches of a tree and start shaking. Not every initiative will bear fruit, but

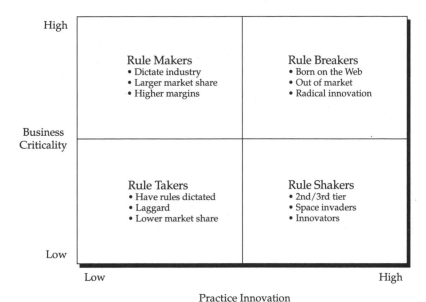

Figure 9-1. Characteristics of Rule Makers, Rule Breakers, Rule Takers, and Rule Shakers. By mapping the roles of rule makers, rule breakers, rule takers, and rule shakers against the E-Business Value Matrix, certain conclusions about the characteristics of these roles are revealed. Market-dominant players tend not to be rule breakers, because they are more risk averse and see no incentive in disturbing a business model that is perceived to work. Rule breakers are usually born on the Web. Rule shakers are second- or third-tier companies or companies in tangential markets. Rule makers, who tend to be early adopters, end up with higher market share and higher margins.

depending on what branch you grab and how you shake it, one or two initiatives will bear fruit. For that reason, Net Ready companies have initiatives in all four quadrants of the E-Business Value Matrix (Figure 9-1). Although the highest impact initiatives often appear to take place in the top half of the matrix, they generally don't start there. Most initiatives, in fact, have their origins in the bottom half, in the new fundamentals and rational experimentation quadrants. Rule shakers distinguish themselves from rule breakers by being content to Web-enable or otherwise jiggle a larger number of noncritical business processes. By experimenting with business processes before they become mission critical, rule shakers hope to build something that clicks in the marketplace. It's a lower-risk approach than the rule breaker model. When a rule-shaking innovation works, rule shakers then migrate the innovation to breakthrough strategies and then operational excellence.

The Williams Company (www.williams.com) is a good example of a rule shaker. Founded ninety years ago in Fort Smith, Arkansas, Williams was an unremarkable construction company until it started assembling its nation-wide system of interstate natural gas pipelines in 1982. By 1992, Williams established itself as the largest volume-transporter of natural gas in the United States. What makes Williams a rule shaker, however, was its realiza-tion that decommissioned pipelines represented an infrastructure that could be used to run fiber-optic cables. Overnight, Williams shook itself into a communications company. Today, Williams is a global leader in en-ergy and communications. Through entrepreneurial-style risk taking and rule shaking, Williams carved out a position for itself in the E-conomy. Priceline (see "Auction Partnerships," page 130 in chapter 4) is another good example of a rule shaker. It did not originate the concepts—buyer aggregation, informatization, auction, customization, and community—on which it is based, but it aligned these concepts around a unique value proposition in such a way that it has shaken up the travel industry.

Rule Makers

Holding a position as a rule maker is a highly desirable state because it is a token of the fact that the company dominates the industry to such an ex-tent that everyone else has little choice but to play follow-the-leader. Mi-crosoft, by virtue of its market share, is a rule maker. It would be a foolish software vendor who decided to test its independence by developing a product that ignored the rules of Windows 98. Rule makers exploit the new dynamics of the E-conomy: customization, digitization, personaliza-tion, just-in-time processes, lack of inventory, and, most of all, perfect alignment between front-end and back-end processes and the entire value chain. Without ruthless execution, even the most compelling vision never matures into rule-making status.

Benefits of being the rule maker include taking on less risk than the rule breaker does. After all, rule makers can exploit the experiences—good and bad—that the rule breakers paid for. Rule makers take the strategy of allowing the other guy to develop a market for them. They give up first mover advantage in exchange for leveraging the other guy's mistakes. If they time it right, rule makers introduce new operational refinements that they hope will ultimately install them as rule makers of the industry and al-low them to enjoy higher margins in a more mature market. Rule makers can also pursue other possible strategies in addition to competing head-on with the rule breaker. For instance, they can buy the rule breaker. Once having purchased them, they can either exploit the technology or, in rare cases, kill it.

A company does not necessarily have to first be a rule breaker to become a rule maker. Nor does it necessarily have to be first in an industry to apply for the role. For example, Netscape was the rule breaker by virtue of its development of the browser, the first killer application for the Internet. But Microsoft exercised its overwhelming credibility in the operating system and desktop space to launch Internet Explorer and quickly usurped the rule maker role. In much the same way, E*Trade was the rule breaker that first established the legitimacy of deeply discounted, online trading. But there is a good argument to be made that Schwab is, in fact, the rule maker of the industry. By reacting swiftly to E*Trade's challenge and by using a combination of its core competencies—strong brand and channel equity supported by a robust dealer network—Schwab has taken on the mantle of the standard setter of the online trading space. Schwab has clearly integrated its existing infrastructure and channels with the E-conomy. Today, Schwab clients enjoy multiple channels for trading—they can trade online, in person at a Schwab office, or by phone with a Schwab trader. Other financial companies desiring to enter the market would be wise to follow Schwab's leadership.

Rule Takers

Companies don't have to be trailblazers to be successful. Rule takers can look at what competitors are doing, measure companies outside their industry, study the track records of what's worked, and then copy. On the other hand, rule takers operate at a distinct disadvantage. Rule takers have to adhere to the rules of the road as dictated by other companies. For example, Gateway, IBM, and the other PC makers have to adhere to the rules that have been established by Dell. Dell is a rule breaker by virtue of its pioneering success in making the Web a successful channel for selling PCs. Dell has been accepted as a rule maker, and now Gateway and the other PC makers have by default, and against their interests, been forced to take on the role of rule taker. They have little choice.

A rule-taking strategy represents the lowest risk of the four disciplines. Rule takers are satisfied with adhering to the rules established by others and identifying a corner of the industry in which they can somehow add value. While risk is low for rule takers, potential returns tend to be low as well. Margins and market share are usually small. It's a perilous strategy, but it can work. Risk aversion is a legitimate tactical consideration for operations that are not strategic. A rule-taking model is usually not useful for a core business or primary play.

In the information technology space, applications developers are the clearest examples of rule takers. Currently, applications must be written for operating systems, which in this context are nothing more than an elaborate set of rules. One of the first strategic decisions a company with a new software product has to make is which operating system it will support. For business software, at least, this question is a no-brainer. Microsoft's Windows controls more than 90 percent of the world's business desktops. Microsoft is the rule maker that these rule takers must follow. Only after the company releases the Microsoft version of the application does it have the luxury to think about porting it to other rule makers, such as Apple's Macintosh or UNIX. In specialized environments, other rule makers prevail. For photography applications, the Macintosh operating system may come first; applications for animating movies are often written for the Silicon Graphics operating system.

In the electronic components distribution space, the dominant E-business storefronts are Arrow Electronics (www.arrow.com) and Avnet (www .avnet.com). Marshall Industries (www.marshall.com), a second-tier storefront, took on the role of rule breaker by establishing a Web site that fundamentally changed the way business is done. Marshall was a pioneer in creating a highly effective mix of process, vision, Web presence, and execution for the electronic components industry. How did Arrow and Avnet respond? They hung back in a deliberate strategy to see how things played out and whether Marshall really had something or would get its wrist slapped. To their credit, Arrow and Avnet have seen the advantages, and now they are also moving to incorporate Internet-related processes and opportunities in their digital value chains. The two companies were not overly concerned by Marshall's attempt at rule breaking. Arrow and Avnet watched Marshall's experiment and made decisions to capitalize on its results and mistakes. They felt comfortable that their dominant positions would allow them to react in time to preserve their dominance. The jury is still out about their decisions.

Incumbents Beware

As a rule, the E-conomy treats incumbents harshly. Incumbents generally have neither the risk tolerance nor the Net Readiness characteristics required to make a successful go of it in the E-conomy. Their inflexibility makes them vulnerable to all manner of new entrants (often infomediaries) that can nimbly exploit electronic channels to circumvent (and in some cases replace) the physical channels that incumbents rely on. New entrants are more visible in some markets than in others, but the pressure is on traditional businesses everywhere to think through the competitive implications. Some organizations will need to adopt radically different leadership styles, governance models, and business practices if they are to compete for the emerging value-added roles being targeted by new entrants. Their key to success will be to leverage their franchise into the electronic marketplace.

This task will not be easy. For most incumbents, the E-conomy will require broad changes in organizational approach and structure as well as in leadership, attitude, mind-set, human resources, and measures of economic success. Many will have to cannibalize existing businesses or channels and risk demotivating the traditional organization while building the new. As is usually the case with dramatic change programs, a small core of people will be critical to the effort. However, they may have to be recruited from outside rather than nurtured as homegrown champions. For most traditional organizations, designing a compensation strategy to appeal to such people will probably entail setting up an independent business unit for the E-conomy or redrawing existing organizational lines. Even companies that succeed in carving out an organization that propels innovation will have to be careful not to stifle the venture by trying to convert it back into a traditional model in the longer term.

An organizational tolerance for risk will be vital. Emphasizing iterative learning will help build the necessary skills and mind-sets quickly. Long-term strategic plans relying on elaborate management processes are unlikely to prevail against nimble new entrants unencumbered by past decisions. AT&T has come to fear how quickly MCI and Sprint can move. Above all, what incumbents need to power the shift toward E-conomy is courage. Success will involve piloting new approaches, mastering new technologies, challenging conventional market definitions, surviving an initial period of low revenues, and perhaps cannibalizing core businesses. But the potential rewards are great: a new platform and set of tools for competing in a new and dynamic marketplace.

Cannibalize Parts of Your Value Chain:
Experiment with Eating Your Young or Someone Else Will

All great truths begin as blasphemies.
—George Bernard Shaw, Irish playwright

The E-conomy demands change and introduction of new technologies and business solutions every six to nine months. The product life cycle is collapsed. No more waiting for models to mature before introducing the next one. These days, new models are being introduced while the previous models are selling briskly and the next generation is ready to ship. Will you have to cannibalize your value chain and risk alienating your established trading partners? If you do it right, you will! You cannot take advantage of new electronic linkages and restructure the foundations of creating new value without destroying old ones.

Columbus, Ohio–based Bank One, for instance, is using this rule as part of its rational experimentation. Despite having an existing online property that it has spent millions developing (www.bankone.com), Bank One launched a stand-alone Net entity called Wingspanbank.com (www.wingspanbank.com). Wingspanbank.com ("If your bank could start over, this is what it would be") competes with Bankone.com. The risk is that the strategy unnecessarily creates channel conflict and sets up existing customers to buy less lucrative banking products than those offered by either the physical bank or its Net channel. We applaud Bank One's gutsy strategy. We believe the Web bank should help Bank One extend its franchise to new customers and opportunities outside its existing profile. Bank One hopes multiple online banking brands will attract more technology-savvy customers even at the risk of cannibalizing some of its base. "If customers have a propensity to bank with a pure online bank with no physical locations, the objective is to still have them bank with us," says George McCane, senior vice president at Wingspanbank.com in Wilmington, Delaware. "The demography of the 'pure online' customer is someone who wants to 'participate and be involved' in cutting-edge technology—someone very different from the individual who likes the cachet of an established physical bank," he adds.

Be Opportunistic: Initiatives Must Be Continuously Questioned, Improved, and Explained to the Customer

If you are not bloodying your nose in today's warp speed economy, we have a name for you. Dead.
—Forbes ASAP

When value propositions shift quickly, you can't wait for customers to figure out what your product or service can offer. In the E-conomy, change is happening so fast that you need to be out in front. You can't wait for the customer to educate you; you have to educate the customer. You need to offer the customer new technology that, maybe, you will be able to customize to meet customer desires as those desires are created.

We have talked about how opportunistic the E-conomy is. Unless you are very opportunistic yourself, you will find lean and hungry new competitors insinuating themselves into your value chain and extracting critical value that you counted on. As recently as 1997, Merrill Lynch dismissed discount brokerages by saying that the full-service brokerage offers "wisdom" that the Internet brokers, who are interested in "opportunistic trading," can't meet. We know that discount brokers E*Trade and Schwab cleaned Merrill Lynch's clock by disaggregating two decisions that Merrill Lynch thought were inextricably linked. It turns out that the steps to decide to buy or sell a security (that's where the wisdom comes in) and the step of actually buying or selling a security are two very different things. Many of its customers recognized the difference, even if Merrill Lynch did not. Clients of full-service brokerages happily accepted their wisdom and even more happily executed the transaction through a discount broker. Merrill Lynch finally smelled the cappuccino and embraced discount trading, cannibalizing parts of its value chain, and causing a mini-revolution among its full-service brokers (see previous rule) who suddenly had to accept that opportunism is what Internet trading is all about.

Focus on What's in Motion Rather Than on What's Standing Still

The art of progress is to preserve order amid change and to preserve change amid order.

—ALFRED NORTH WHITEHEAD, AMERICAN PHILOSOPHER

You need a new mental model to succeed in the E-conomy, and that means that you should focus on what's changing, not on what's standing still. The traditional economy waited for events to slow down. In the E-conomy, you need to focus on individual elements in the revolving door while it is in motion. You need a biological mind-set to replace a physical framework. Physical algorithms treat things as if they were inactive and sequentially dominate the worldview of the traditional economy. A biological mind-set treats data, bits, thoughts, markets, and organizations as if they were inherently capable of change and growth. Here are some other required focus shifts:

- *Focus on the top line, not the bottom line.* The traditional economy emphasized costs and their reduction. The E-conomy focuses on relationships and opportunities for revenue enhancement.

- *Focus on relationships, not things.* What's important is the network, not the nodes. The real value is at the center, not in the little orbit that your business occupies. Although the intelligence does reside in the nodes, that intelligence has no value without the myriad interconnections that nurture relationships and free up the intelligence in a way that creates value.

- *Focus on process, not outcomes.* Business in the E-conomy is short-changed if it is reduced to a single calculation or a simple outcome. Individual transactions become less important than relationships, processes, and histories. Look at the E-conomy as transformational, not transactional. In other words, think big. Chances are, the opportunities you have in mind are way too limited.

- *Focus on optimization, not maximization.* The industrial economy's emphasis on maximization has led to rigidity, short-term thinking, strained relations between workers and management, and a spectrum of ecological and social problems. By regarding organizations as part of an interconnected network whose collective well-being depends on the health of the relationships within it, the E-conomy focuses on optimization. What's the difference between optimum and maximum? Let's put it this way. The optimum body temperature for humans is 98.6 degrees Fahrenheit. The maximum body temperature will kill you every time.

- *Focus on transformation, not equilibrium.* The traditional economy was seen as a machine to be tweaked to reasonable productivity and then maintained against all disruptions. Innovation, unfortunately, was often treated as a disruption. The traditional economy rewarded a strategy of incrementalism, but as they say in Texas, that dog won't hunt anymore. "Incrementalism," Tom Peters notes in *The Circle of Innovation* (New York: Alfred Knopf, 1997), "is an almost inadvertent obsession with polishing yesterday's paradigm." Nicholas Negroponte, head of the MIT Media Lab, agrees when he notes, "Incrementalism is innovation's worst enemy." The E-conomy achieves stability only by welcoming transformation. Strive for a balance between order and chaos, and when in doubt, favor chaos.

No One Can Go At It Alone

Mr. Morgan buys his partners. I grow my own.
—ANDREW CARNEGIE, FINANCIER, COMPARING HIS STYLE OF PARTNERING
WITH THAT OF J. P. MORGAN

It's a paradox. Customers demand best-of-breed products and services and seamless integration of those products and services from the organizations that provide them. At the same time, each customer demands flexibility and the sense that he or she is being treated as an individual. These values are in perpetual tension in the E-conomy. Companies dedicated to giving customers a blanket of options often decide they have to be large and all-encompassing. But that very size creates hierarchies and processes that are inflexible and detract from individual response.

The expanding E-conomy requires that companies form relationships in order to compete effectively. It has no tolerance for the arrogant and will punish the greedy who believe that a single seller can serve customers better than a partnership. There is no way around it—and the evidence is already persuasive—the expanded E-conomy requires enterprises to form relationships to compete. Events and technology change too quickly. No one organization can possibly develop all the core competencies required to perform all the tasks customers expect. Through the application of Web-based networks, companies are building value chains that embrace not only traditional partners such as customers, distributors, and suppliers but also new storefronts, competitors, and regulators. The formation of COINs and other networks helps your organization bring together the core competencies and capabilities necessary to capitalize on opportunities. Moreover, it also reduces the risk normally involved in going after opportunities. Your capability to bring together the necessary E-business storefronts to form these relationships is a required competency in this emerging economy.

The E-conomy's insatiable insistence on partnerships is setting up all sorts of unlikely relationships. Competitors are partnering with competitors; customers with suppliers. Many of these relationships would have been anathema—possibly illegal—a few years ago. Now they are par for the course.

The benefits of partnerships for start-ups are especially pronounced in the area of promoting brand by leveraging the credibility of the more established partners. Start-ups also see other benefits, such as using the partner to build customer traffic, promoting brand by associating it with a partner's name recognition, and leveraging the partnership to acquire critical resources such as capital, systems, talent, information, and markets. Finally, a strong partnership works to discourage other players from entering the space and can thereby preempt competition.

Organizations with well-established brands often benefit from partnerships with emerging players. At the minimum, the partnership extends the brand into new markets and domains. Beyond that, intelligent partnerships give companies access to new customers and more information about existing customers. They provide better understanding of needs (instant market research). The right partners can augment revenue streams and help accumulate essential knowledge. A partnership with a start-up can bring to the established company a renewed sense of entrepreneurial drive and start-up spirit.

Net Ready companies also recognize that establishing and, perhaps more critically, managing partnerships is fraught with peril. Coordination puts tangible value on each partner's contributions and benefits to make them more visible and persistent. This helps maintain or enhance commitment over time. Coordination is essential to assign clear responsibilities to individuals within the organizations and to establish and monitor metrics for success. Differences in objectives, perspectives, and cultures create an array of challenges to partnering. Trust issues often intrude on the seamless coordination required for success. In many cases, a lack of coordination about assigned roles results in declining commitments. Other potential obstacles include different prioritization of activities or different timing issues. For example, tension results when one partner wants to drive E-business while the other wants to build brand. Governance models of the partners often conflict, leading to power struggles that can be difficult to resolve. Finally, other problems may arise if one partner is more committed to the relationship than the other partner is, especially if the very survival of one partner is at stake while, for the other partner, the relationship is only one of many.

Upside Down: Suppliers and Customers Must Cooperate as Never Before

The Web allows you to have an iterative debate with your customers and your prospects. Make a Website where the debate about the soul of the company is going on.

—WATTS WACKER, SRI CONSULTING

The E-conomy is turning conventional wisdom on its head. Imagine: only a few years ago, sharing pricing information between suppliers and customers was grounds for firing. An organization's procurement officer had an almost adversarial relationship with its suppliers. People felt that procurement was a zero-sum game: if they get one more, we get one less. As a result, corporate procurement of commodities was almost a clerical activity, a process driven by the lowest cost. Totally lost was any opportunity to build on the common interests of suppliers and customers for the benefit of both.

The E-conomy makes online procurement possible and, in so doing, changes the rules between companies and their suppliers, elevating the long-overlooked and barely automated purchasing function to a more strategic activity. One of the rules was that a company never, ever shared demand or production information with suppliers, because that information gave suppliers an unfair advantage in negotiations.

Watch the E-conomy kill another stupid rule. Enron, Occidental Chemical, and five other petrochemical companies have established a Web site to coordinate procurement of maintenance, repair, and operations products. The goal is collaboration with materials suppliers rather than an adversarial relationship based solely on price. The fruits of collaboration are a streamlined buying process that improves productivity and delivers better customer service.

Run, Don't Walk

Time is the friend of the great company, the enemy of the mediocre.
—Warren Buffet, CEO, Berkshire Hathaway

Velocity is the dominant dimension of the E-conomy. The metabolism of the E-conomy is characterized by a real-time enterprise that is continuously adjusting to changing business conditions through information immediacy. Just-in-time goods and services are received from suppliers and products and transshipped to customers. Two immediate benefits result. First, companies can reduce or eliminate inventories and the warehousing function. Second, enterprises can shift from mass production to custom, one-to-one production.

In an economy based on bits, immediacy becomes the critical driver, or variable, in creating value. Immediacy is not fixed on location. It's pace, not place. Whatever you do, you have to learn to do it faster until it is virtually instantaneous. In every encounter with your customers, you have to decrease the inefficiency until encounters are frictionless. Revenue streams become as short as product life cycles. The lion's share of revenues for many computer companies today derive from products that didn't exist two years ago. In the traditional economy, a product like the Polaroid camera ensured a revenue stream for decades. Today, consumer electronics products have a typical life span of less than six months.

It's the Network, Stupid

*Somebody has to do something, and it's just incredibly pathetic that it
has to be us.*

—Jerry Garcia of the Grateful Dead

What happens to the members of a system that has no clear center and no clear outer boundaries? What happens is the almost total disintegration of one of the most fundamental distinctions of the traditional economy: the *us* (the self, usually the seller) and the *them* (the nonself, the other, usually the buyer). In the connected E-conomy there is no us versus them but only various permutations of us. Membership becomes the key, and the focus shifts to the plumbing that holds the members together. In other words, it's the links that are important, not the nodes. The appliances on the networks will be replaced—and good riddance to them!—but the conduits persist.

The traditional economy's focus on the nodes led to organization soldiers who were conformist and fiercely loyal to institutions that rewarded conformity and loyalty. The E-conomy pummels conformity, and as for loyalty, people will give their allegiance to each other based on the quality of the relationships that the network enables. Loyalty will also flow, not to monolithic organizations, but to architectures and channels that optimize opportunities for partnering. More and more in the E-conomy, people will identify as members of the network, not as units or nodes. As such, they will display an instinctive enthusiasm for maximizing the value of the network. In short order, the primary focus of companies in the E-conomy will shift from maximizing their own value to maximizing the value of the infrastructure as a whole. Nor are these companies naive. They understand that working toward the prosperity of the whole is their best strategy for enriching themselves. A company in the E-conomy is like the spider in its web. Unless the web is strong, every participant perishes.

Smart-size the Offer

Do not assume that the other fellow has intelligence to match yours. He may have more.

—TERRY-THOMAS, BRITISH HUMORIST

Smart offers come from organizations that learn by extracting information from every encounter with the customer. Make sure that no transaction is completed without at least some exchange of intelligence between seller and buyer.

It used to be that you could have any color Model T you wanted as long as it was black. The traditional economy says, "Take it or leave it." The E-conomy says, "Take it as you want it." Ford will soon never make the exact same car twice. That kind of customization requires information, and that information has to come from somewhere. All things being equal, the most accurate information comes from customers and buyers themselves. Getting that information may be tricky, but the point remains: your offer should be a factory of possibilities for extracting information from every exchange. Recognize also that it may not be feasible to extract information from every exchange, generally because the information may not have any value, it may be too costly to extract, or privacy issues may complicate the extraction.

Amazon.com does it well. Every time you express an interest in a book, Amazon.com will suggest another book that its software agents believe will also appeal to you. These agents are governed by the intelligence derived from tracking the browsing and book-buying habits of millions of customer encounters. Amazon.com gets smarter with each transaction.

Blockbuster Entertainment has the same idea but increases the stakes. Blockbuster's EntertainmentMinder provides subscribers with weekly personalized messages regarding new video, game, and CD releases plus video clips, reviews, special offers, and coupons. Users register at Blockbuster's Web site, where they fill out an online form and check off the categories of videos, games, or CDs they enjoy. They can download special software that places a white exclamation point in the bottom right corner of their monitor. The exclamation point flashes red when an update has been received and gives the user the ability to view a video clip. The revenue opportunities may justify the investment in the Web site, but it's the relationships that are built and the information extracted that will make the program a success.

Think Brand Equity and Channel Equity

Do not free a camel of the burden of his hump; you may be freeing him from being a camel.

—GILBERT KEITH CHESTERTON, BRITISH AUTHOR

Brand matters in the E-conomy. One of the most pervasive myths of the E-conomy is that the Web levels the playing field, negating the advantages of established brands and economies of scale. There's even a fancy word—disaggregation—for the separation of masses into their component parts. One myth of disaggregation is that the E-conomy operates as a great commercial equalizer in which any Johnny-come-lately can appear to be as qualified as the most established enterprises. In this age of narrowcasting, this particular myth goes, every consumer becomes a market-segment-of-one and brands become irrelevant.

Don't believe it. The reality is that with so many choices, customers will seek the comfort of what they know. Brand names suddenly take on stunning new importance in the E-conomy. A carefully cultivated brand name will become perhaps the most prized intangible value that an enterprise has to offer. Think Intel. Think Nike. Think Starbucks. Think Martha Stewart. These are brand names that drive value. Their owners consider the brands their most valuable asset. Why? Because a brand is something customers will pay extra for even if it's on a product or service that is identical to a competitor's.

Brand equity, then, is critical, but the E-conomy creates a new branding model: channel equity. In the E-conomy, brands will migrate from an image to a relationship to an experience based on value and services, which will be delivered to sophisticated buyers through the Net. The challenge will be to innovate, have a clear message of benefits, execute flawlessly, and create effective platforms for reaching out to and maintaining strong relationships with customers.

Channel equity represents the benefit that an organization has in its ability to deliver value. For example, 7-Eleven has amassed great channel equity by virtue of its 5,000 stores networked together. The company harnesses this channel equity not only to expand the notion of convenience beyond bread and milk, but also to create a whole array of financial services. Consumers trust 7-Eleven's channel equity when they buy money orders, make cash transfers, and engage in a growing number of financial services. There are no limits to how 7-Eleven can leverage this channel equity. In Japan, for example, 7-Eleven has partnered with a company that allows consumers to print books on demand at convenience stores. In E-conomy terms, both Yahoo! and America Online have established strong channel equities.

Competitors in the E-conomy acknowledge that brand management is one of their principal responsibilities. They understand that interconnectivity can be a two-edged sword when it comes to managing brands. On the down side, the Web has removed an element of control that companies once held over their brands. Brands can be destroyed or severely damaged, as Intel discovered a few years back when the Pentium chip went out with a bug in its floating-point arithmetic.

Planning Is Critical. Don't Do It.

The problem is never how to get new, innovative thoughts in your mind, but how to get the old ones out.
                                        —DEE HOCK, CREATOR OF THE VISA NETWORK

Our heading here is just a little facetious. Linear planning, the kind most of us have been trained for, is useless in the E-conomy. Net Readiness calls for speed and migration. Success requires holistic thinking of a kind that embraces the connectivity, simultaneity, and unpredictability of the E-conomy. Leading E-business storefronts must be able to identify opportunities and be agile enough to move quickly, partner quickly, and execute flawlessly. Net Ready enterprises will use many of the following principles to guide them.

- Prioritize correctly
- Execute ruthlessly
- New competitors emerge from unlikely corners of the E-conomy
- New entrants into the E-conomy frustrate long-range planning
- The expanded E-conomy requires a shift from hierarchical, linear thinking to a more holistic approach characterized by multidisciplinary rigor and dynamic planning
- Your portfolio is your plan (aggressively build and manage it)

- Discontinuous change, not orderly processes, is the order of the day
- E-conomy realities require simultaneous execution and nimbleness to permit real-time shifts in resources and direction

A Final Note to the Reader

If you are still reading—if you decided to risk a bit of your attention on the basis of whatever attracted you to pick up this book and get this far into it—chances are good that Net Readiness awaits you. Not that it's going to be easy. We know that the E-conomy is a harsh environment, as unforgiving as it is rewarding. Yes, it may enrich the innovative with competitive advantage and enormous wealth. But grudgingly. What the E-conomy giveth, it taketh away. Within months or even less, the competitive advantage evaporates and becomes merely the cost of doing business for everyone. Its mantra is, "What have you done for me today?" The E-conomy frustrates the merely creative. It destroys those who are faithful to the practices that once made them rich. And those who believe that they need not participate, the E-conomy renders irrelevant, the most humiliating discipline it can impose.

It's a journey that we cannot make without you, because the scenarios that we have described—scenarios for creating value in the E-conomy— are being rewritten by rule breakers like you. We have seen how the E-conomy turns the old order on its head. Buyers, not sellers, dictate terms. Readers, not authors, create the stories. Traditional boundaries? Irrelevant. Services become products and products are informatized until whatever demarcation gave them meaning is lost. Relationships between price and volume are out the window; one does not necessarily follow the other. In traditional environments, the name of the game is to raise prices at a rate faster than costs go up. In the E-conomy, we have seen, the game is to decrease costs faster than pricing falls, until everything seems to end up being free. We used to know the difference between structure and process, market share and market value, owning and using, employers and employees. Or we thought we did, and we took comfort in those certainties. Now no one knows. And we are comfortable in the certainty that no one knows.

In this book we have given you a road map for creating value in the E-conomy. We have provided metaphors that illuminate the heart of the E-conomy, much as a navigation beacon guides a pilot to a landing strip. The beacon is a reference point; it is essential, but it does not substitute for the skill of the pilot. The beacon just sets up the approach; it doesn't land the plane. That's still the pilot's job. So it is with this book. We hope that our metaphors will help navigate you through the risks and uncertainties of working in the E-conomy. Although the abundance of opportunities for you to explore may be considered a curse, Net Ready companies have the discipline to approach E-conomy investments in an intentional manner. Yes, there are always more opportunities than resources, and only you can choose among them. That's just the way it is in the E-conomy. This is new territory for everyone. All we can do is set up the approach. After that, you're on your own. We'd only slow you down, anyway.

A

Net Readiness E-Business Planning Audit

Existing organizations and start-ups alike recognize that tomorrow's opportunities can only be realized by full participation in the chaotic and high-risk worlds of the Internet, networked commerce, and the electronic marketplace. They know that it's not, and never again can be, business as usual. Instinctively, the entrepreneurs behind these companies understand that success is a function of a new set of competencies, principles, culture, and attitudes. To close *Net Ready,* we offer the ten-point Net Readiness E-Business Planning Audit.

The Net Readiness E-Business Planning Audit does not imply that you should be doing every E-business initiative mentioned here. No organization can do everything. Rather, this audit is best used to ensure that you don't overlook something important. The audit reviews all the issues we have discussed in this book. Your challenge is to choose from all the opportunities before you. You have to decide which opportunities present the highest business impacts for the lowest levels of risk and expenditure of resources. Use this checklist to help guide your E-business initiatives.

The Net Readiness E-Business Planning Audit has ten steps, each with several statements. For each statement, simply indicate whether the statement is true or not of your organization at the current time. If you are not sure, mark the "No" column. The ten steps are:

Step 1. Statement of Purpose

Step 2. Twelve-to-Eighteen Month Objectives

Step 3. Customers, Channels, Segments

Step 4. Competition

Step 5. Necessary Solution

Step 6. Plan for Implementation of Products and Services

Step 7. Financial Implications

Step 8. External Situations Affecting Objectives Attainment

Step 9. Problems Resulting from Interdependence

Step 10. Tactical Plan

	Yes	No
Step 1: Statement of Purpose		
Does our business have a well-articulated vision for its Internet initiatives?	☐	☐
Is our business' E-business vision widely communicated and understood?	☐	☐
Is senior management heavily involved in the development and support of E-business initiatives?	☐	☐
Is senior management attuned to the opportunities and threats enabled by the E-business initiatives?	☐	☐
Step 2: Twelve-to-Eighteen Month Objectives		
Does our business have an explicit and flexible metric system for measuring the success of our E-business initiatives?	☐	☐
Do our E-business initiatives support our business strategy?	☐	☐
Do we have the proper mechanisms in place to change directions with respect to E-business strategy should market conditions dictate?	☐	☐
Is the technology solution flexible enough to accommodate change over the plan period?	☐	☐
Does our business have the technological infrastructure and competencies to engage in E-business initiatives?	☐	☐
Step 3: Customers, Channels, Segments		
Are E-business–related technologies impacting customers?	☐	☐
Are E-business–related technologies impacting channels?	☐	☐
Are E-business–related technologies impacting segments?	☐	☐
Can the E-business sources of innovation be used to reduce dissatisfiers in terms of our products and services?	☐	☐

	Yes	No
Can the E-business sources of innovation be used to meet the changing required benefits?	☐	☐
Can the E-business be used to reconceive our product or service?	☐	☐
Can the E-business be used to redefine the value proposition?	☐	☐
Can the E-business be used to move our company up the food chain?	☐	☐
Can we use the E-business to separate our product's function from form?	☐	☐
Can the E-business be used to compress the buying process?	☐	☐
Does the profile of potential purchasers via the E-business fit with our existing customers?	☐	☐
Are channels utilizing E-business-related technologies? How might this usage change in the future?	☐	☐
Can new segments be attracted using E-business-related technologies?	☐	☐
Does the E-business pose any threats to existing products and services?	☐	☐

Step 4: Competition

	Yes	No
Does our portfolio of E-business initiatives compare favorably to that of our competition?	☐	☐
Can we (and our competitors) play any E-business models, given our competencies?	☐	☐
Does the E-business create risks for the emergence of new competitors?	☐	☐
Are our competitors implementing their E-business–related technologies?	☐	☐
Can we (or the competition) use the E-business to redefine the basis of competition?	☐	☐
Are our competitors using E-business–related technologies to enhance their products?	☐	☐
Can the E-business be used to attract customers from our competitors?	☐	☐
Can the E-business–related technologies change barriers to entry and/or switching costs in our industry?	☐	☐
Can the E-business be used to break our industry's unbreakable rules?	☐	☐
Can the E-business be used to redraw industry boundaries?	☐	☐
Will the E-business's ability to separate form from function impact the competitive landscape of our industry in the future?	☐	☐

	Yes	No

Step 5: Necessary Solution

Can E-business enhance or transform our value delivery system? ☐ ☐

Does the E-business's ability to separate function from form pose
a threat to our products or services? ☐ ☐

Can the E-business be used to enhance relationships with channel
partners? ☐ ☐

Can the E-business be used to reduce cost structures in order to meet
financial objectives? ☐ ☐

Step 6: Plan for Implementation of Products and Services

Can we undertake key business-to-business initiatives? ☐ ☐

Can we undertake business-to-end user customer initiatives? ☐ ☐

Can we undertake key intra-business initiatives? ☐ ☐

Is there synergy between our E-business initiatives? ☐ ☐

Are our E-business initiatives integrated with our business strategy? ☐ ☐

Do we have a clear definition as to who will drive strategy,
development, and implementation of our E-business initiatives? ☐ ☐

Are the roles, responsibility, and accountability for our E-business
initiatives clearly defined? ☐ ☐

Do we have change management plans in place for our E-business
initiatives? ☐ ☐

Is our business appropriately structured for E-business initiatives? ☐ ☐

Have we decided where the required skills and competencies
will be sourced from (internal or external) to accomplish
our E-business initiatives? ☐ ☐

Step 7: Financial Implications

Do we know how much money is specifically allocated to fund
our E-business initiatives? ☐ ☐

Have we understood and taken into account both the direct
and indirect E-business initiative costs? ☐ ☐

Do we know how the money will be generated? ☐ ☐

Do we have sufficient resources for ongoing maintenance, upgrades,
and enhancements? ☐ ☐

Does our E-business investment and cost structure compare with that
of the competition? ☐ ☐

	Yes	No

Are our financial projections based on the impact of future E-business technologies? ☐ ☐

Step 8: External Situations Affecting Objectives Attainment

Do we know in what areas are our E-business initiatives are most at risk? ☐ ☐

Do emerging technologies impact our business plan's risk equation? ☐ ☐

Do we know what will likely be the response from our competitors to the implementation of our E-business initiatives? ☐ ☐

Do we have a contingency plan? ☐ ☐

Step 9: Problems Resulting from Interdependence

Do we clearly understand the dependencies that exist between the entities involved? ☐ ☐

Do we know who owns the responsibility for managing these E-business relationships (e.g., relationship council)? ☐ ☐

Do we have a contingency plan? ☐ ☐

Step 10: Tactical Plan

Have we clearly identified and targeted manageable (three- to six-month) projects? ☐ ☐

Do we know what metrics will be used in the first year to track the success of our E-business initiatives? ☐ ☐

Do we understand the degree of dependency that our E-business initiatives have on other entities (e.g., IT)? ☐ ☐

Do we have the resources for the required infrastructure investment in the first year? ☐ ☐

Do we know how we will measure the impact of our E-business initiatives over time? ☐ ☐

Is there a plan to continually evaluate the metrics that are being used for E-business initiatives? ☐ ☐

Can our metrics for E-business initiatives be modified if needed? ☐ ☐

Are mechanisms in place to review and revise our strategy during the plan period? ☐ ☐

Have our assumptions about our E-business initiatives been clearly defined, and are they measurable? ☐ ☐

Have we established triggers to monitor with respect to our E-business initiatives? ☐ ☐

B

Comprehensive Net Readiness Scorecard

We asked you to complete an abbreviated version of this scorecard at the end of chapter 1. The scoring for this audit uses a weighted scoring algorithm, which makes it too cumbersome to score by hand. Please go the Net Readiness Web site (www.netreadiness.com) for a Web-enabled version of this audit. For readers who want to inspect the individual items that make up the audit, it is reproduced here.

Instructions:

For each statement, indicate to what extent you either agree or disagree that the statement is currently true of your organization. If you strongly disagree or disagree somewhat, circle 1 or 2, respectively. If you agree somewhat or agree strongly, circle 4 or 5, respectively. If you neither agree nor disagree, circle 3. If you are not sure, just leave the item blank and go on to the next one. Good luck.

Scoring Key:

1	2	3	4	5
disagree strongly	disagree somewhat	neutral	agree somewhat	agree strongly

The following statements concern your E-Business strategy. Do you agree or disagree?

Our business routinely evaluates competitors' E-business
initiatives.   1 2 3 4 5

The vast majority of our new application development is E-business oriented (Web-based versus client/server, mainframe, or ERP).	1	2	3	4	5
We have staffed our E-business projects with the proper resources to reach their goals.	1	2	3	4	5
We have created a twelve-to-eighteen-month road map, or journey, for success.	1	2	3	4	5
Our E-business efforts are mostly focused on strategic/value creation areas rather than on operational or marketing communications.	1	2	3	4	5
We have an established, standard IT infrastructure to be strictly followed by the corporation.	1	2	3	4	5
We exhibit ruthless execution when implementing E-business solutions (e.g., three months, three to six people).	1	2	3	4	5
Our business routinely evaluates competitors' Web sites.	1	2	3	4	5
We have a standard administrative process for developing a business case for E-initiatives.	1	2	3	4	5
We understand the security issues related to providing access to information over the Internet.	1	2	3	4	5
Our Internet solutions will be flexible enough to accommodate change (internal and external).	1	2	3	4	5
Our strategic plans include an E-business strategy.	1	2	3	4	5
Our current E-business activities are well-integrated with our business strategy.	1	2	3	4	5
We have established, measurable metrics for assessing the impact of our Internet initiatives.	1	2	3	4	5
We continually innovate our E-business product and service offerings through iterative projects adding to their functionality.	1	2	3	4	5
Our E-business solutions are customizable to both our needs and our customers.	1	2	3	4	5
Generating competitive advantage via E-business technologies is a top priority for senior management.	1	2	3	4	5
We have an established process for assessing and selecting alternative E-business strategies.	1	2	3	4	5
We have a strong, rapid development approach (three month-or-less project duration) for E-business applications.	1	2	3	4	5
We sufficiently invest in our Web site maintenance.	1	2	3	4	5

The following statements concern your business culture.

Our vision for E-business activities is widely communicated
and understood throughout our company.   1   2   3   4   5

IT is viewed as an E-business partner providing Internet
consulting services to the business unit.   1   2   3   4   5

The IT organization is well respected by business
management.   1   2   3   4   5

Our business can react quickly to changing market
conditions.   1   2   3   4   5

We have an E-business mind-set throughout all levels of
management.   1   2   3   4   5

We have developed an E-business culture within our
organization.   1   2   3   4   5

Senior management is heavily involved in the development
of E-business direction.   1   2   3   4   5

We have the agility to execute and move quickly.   1   2   3   4   5

The following questions concern your business resources.

We are providing the proper incentives for our people
to meet their E-business objectives.   1   2   3   4   5

My business unit has the proper funding to meet our
E-business initiative needs.   1   2   3   4   5

We have experience managing multiple relationships
(external and internal) simultaneously and effectively.   1   2   3   4   5

Our E-business efforts help recruit and retain the best
talent in our organization.   1   2   3   4   5

We understand the impact that E-business initiatives will
have on our employees (change management issues)   1   2   3   4   5

We are actively upgrading (e.g., cleansing data, migrating
legacy systems, etc.) our back-end systems to meet our
future Internet requirements.   1   2   3   4   5

Our business has strong IS/IT operations capabilities (e.g.,
capacity planning, networking strategy and operations,
contract negotiations, database administration, database
management, etc.).   1   2   3   4   5

Decision-making authority has been clearly assigned for all
E-business initiatives.   1   2   3   4   5

Business management has Internet knowledge, and IT has
business knowledge.   1   2   3   4   5

Roles, responsibilities, and accountability are clearly defined
within each E-business initiative team.   1   2   3   4   5

Our E-business applications are delivered on time and with
the needed functionality.   1   2   3   4   5

We have the technological infrastructure and competencies
to engage in E-business initiatives.   1   2   3   4   5

Total spending on E-business is high relative to other IT
spending (PCs, infrastructure, etc).   1   2   3   4   5

We have empowered our top personnel to manage the
Internet initiatives.   1   2   3   4   5

We have an established method for allocating business and IT
resources for Internet initiatives.   1   2   3   4   5

The ability of the organization to learn from E-business
projects is proven.   1   2   3   4   5

We have created clearly defined, E-business career paths
within our organization.   1   2   3   4   5

We have experience in selling services.   1   2   3   4   5

Business units have the flexibility to set their own E-business
application development investment levels.   1   2   3   4   5

The technical experience and skill set of the E-business team
is adequate to do the job.   1   2   3   4   5

The following statements concern your business relationships.

Our E-business applications are driven by customers' needs.   1   2   3   4   5

We have a strong set of partnerships with complementary
E-business players (e.g., Amazon.com and America Online).   1   2   3   4   5

We have, or are in the process of building, E-business–related
implementation expertise.   1   2   3   4   5

Our employees, customers, and partners have ubiquitous
access to business-critical information and processes.   1   2   3   4   5

Our business can quickly and effectively form and dissolve
relationships that are driven by clearly defined business
imperatives.   1   2   3   4   5

Our organization has processes in place to share E-business
learnings.   1   2   3   4   5

We have strong relationships with our extended enterprise
(e.g., suppliers, VARs, customers).   1   2   3   4   5

E-business activities are managed by a cross-functional team
that includes business and IT managers. **1 2 3 4 5**

The current organizational structure is well suited for
E-business initiatives. **1 2 3 4 5**

Each E-business project team member is measured on the
same metrics, which are clearly articulated **1 2 3 4 5**

Scoring

Complete the Web-Enabled Net Readiness Scorecard at www.netreadiness
.com

Index

About the Authors

AMIR HARTMAN serves as managing director of Cisco's Internet Business Solutions Group, working with customers and their E-business transformation. Hartman is also on the faculty at the Haas School of Business, UC-Berkeley, where he specializes in classes on E-business strategy. A well-known consultant and speaker, he is the coauthor of *The Search for Digital Excellence*.

JOHN SIFONIS is managing director at Cisco's Internet Business Solutions Group. A renowned information technology consultant and former senior partner in the Management Consulting Group of Ernst & Young, Sifonis is the coauthor of two other books: *Corporation on a Tightrope* and *Dynamic Planning*.